365

DAYS IN THE WORD

CALVIN BROWN

Trilogy Christian Publishers
A Wholly Owned Subsidiary of Trinity Broadcasting Network
2442 Michelle Drive
Tustin, CA 92780

For information, address Trilogy Christian Publishing
Rights Department, 2442 Michelle Drive, Tustin, Ca 92780.
Trilogy Christian Publishing/ TBN and colophon are trademarks of Trinity Broadcasting Network.

For information about special discounts for bulk purchases, please contact Trilogy Christian Publishing.

Manufactured in the United States of America

10 9 8 7 6 5 4 3 2 1

Library of Congress Cataloging-in-Publication Data is available.

ISBN 978-1-64773-070-3 (Print Book)
ISBN 978-1-64773-071-0 (ebook)

DEDICATION

This devotional is dedicated to the Almighty Father, Jesus Christ, and Holy Spirit and to all that do the will of the Almighty Father!

God is the strength, Jesus is the Way, heaven is the place, and the Bible is the truth.

FOREWORD

This devotional was written to help spread the Gospel of Jesus Christ with the overall intent to bring more glory to the Almighty Father. Of special importance is God so loved the world that He gave His only begotten Son for the sake of the kingdom, which includes us. We have to honor Him in spirit and truth. He has also provided His Holy Spirit as another gesture of love to help His children. We have to maximize every tool given to us for spiritual growth. The Almighty Father is constantly providing us iron to help sharpen our iron, and this devotional can assist any disciple of Jesus Christ through their days. It can also help others see the love of the Jesus Christ in their daily steps.

Jesus Christ gave us the minimum requirement, which is having faith the size of a mustard seed, but we must strive to have faith the size of a watermelon. Our faith is supernatural fuel!

Every day belongs to Jesus!

Acknowledgments

First, special thanks to the Almighty Father, Jesus Christ, and the Holy Spirit. Without them, there is no way I could've completed this devotional.

Secondly, I thank my loving, awesome, amazing, beautiful, and heaven-sent wife, Kenya Brown that has provided me the unconditional support that was very beneficial to me completing this devotional.

Thirdly, I thank those that have inspired me on my journey to be more effective for the kingdom of God such as the leaders of the Power of Prayer Ministry in Harrisburg, Pennsylvania; Third Baptist Church in Portsmouth, Virginia; Proceeding Word Church in Glen Allen, Virginia; Shechaniah Rivers Ministries in Carrolton, Virginia; the Spirit of Christ Ministry in Newport News, Virginia; The Mount Church, Chesapeake, Virginia; Mt. Gilead Full Gospel International Ministries, Richmond, Virginia; The 3 Angels Message Ministry, Powder Springs, Georgia; Mercies of Hope International Ministries in Kampala, Uganda; First Baptist Church in Norfolk, Virginia; Acts Fellowship in Bourne, Texas; the Now Faith and Family Worship Center in Jacksonville, North Carolina; and especially my spiritual parents Apostles Theadford Brinkley and Ernestine Brinkley in Rocky Mount, North Carolina of Deliverance Tabernacle of Praise Ministries. Also, my family members, friends to include my coworkers at Dahlgren, Virginia, and all those whom I served with in the U.S. Army for the encouragement and support too.

Lastly, I thank the Trinity Broadcast Network for the opportunity to publish this devotional.

JANUARY

Start the year in unity with the body of Christ! Staying aligned in the beginning will set you up to keep on winning! Please consider praying and fasting on the first day of year.
Happy New Year!

January 1

> In the beginning God created the heavens and the earth. (Genesis 1:1)

When children see the ice cream truck coming, they get excited because they know that there're treats on the truck. Since they have experienced receiving treats from the ice cream truck, they get excited with anticipation of receiving more treats. Adults' anticipation of the New Year is just like children's anticipation of the ice cream truck coming.

The New Year is here, and how can we receive the blessings within it? To receive the blessings within this New Year, we have to involve God in our plans for this New Year. Involving God in our planning helps us to align with Him, already knowing the plans that He has for us. You have to walk in agreement with God if you want to receive His blessings. God created the heavens and the earth, which means He is best equipped to help you start and enjoy the New Year. So what are your plans for this year? Have you included God in them? God is available. As He was before the beginning, He is also available now and beyond. He wants us to receive all the blessings that He has planned for us.

Start this year with getting closer to God. This happens through Jesus Christ. If you haven't already done so, please repent of your sins and accept Jesus Christ as Lord and Savior and receive the Holy Spirit. Please don't walk in unforgiveness this year. Doing these things and remaining obedient to God will help you receive so many blessings this New Year!

Amen.

January 2

> The earth was without form, and void; and darkness was on the face of the deep. And the Spirit of God was hovering over the face of the waters.
> (Genesis 1:2)

A farmer watches over his crops in anticipation of growth, provides the proper amount of water needed for the crops to grow, watches for and prevents insects and rodents from ruining the crops, and pays attention to the seasons that affect the crops too. Without a farmer, the crops wouldn't grow properly and would be susceptible to outside interference that would disrupt its effectiveness for usage.

This is similar to how and why God has given us the Holy Spirit.

In the beginning, the Holy Spirit was hovering over the faces of the waters, and today the Holy Spirit hovers over the faces of God's children, which includes you! He hovers in anticipation of future growth.

Please lean on the Holy Spirit more this year than you did last year. You will accomplish more this year through the help of the Holy Spirit. What is it that you need growth in this year? What seeds have you planted? You are the soil for your seeds. Jesus Christ is the living water and light for your seeds, and you need the Holy Spirit to help you remain good soil. This is your season! The Holy Spirit will help you be a greater farmer, and your harvest will be bountiful this year. Enjoy your day and ensure that you help others use the Holy Spirit to grow their seeds this year too.

Amen.

January 3

> Then God said, "Let there be light"; and there was light. (Genesis 1:3)

Parents use the light to help wake up their children in the morning for school. The light helps the children to wake up out of the darkness. If the children stay asleep in the darkness, they will miss the bus for school. The light is a sign to the children that they must get up and do what they need to do.

In the Bible, we see that there was light prior to the creation of humans! God ensured they saw light before they saw darkness! God's glory sets the tone for us every day!

God told Jesus Christ to let there be light to help with the growth of everything upon the earth, to include His children. Jesus Christ turned the light on, and since His Father gave Him all power and authority in heaven and on earth, that also means that only the Father or the Son can turn that light off. This light is God's glory that came before the sunlight in Genesis 1:14–18. God's glory was needed to help the growth of many things in the beginning, and it is available to help you today too! What is it that you wish to grow? What can God's glory shine upon for you today? Is it a relationship? Is it a new position? Is it communication with someone? Is it your finances? Whatever you need God's glory for, please call on Jesus Christ right now so He can let there be light in all that you ask for.

Let there be light in reflecting the image of our Creator! Let there be light in your household. Let there be light during interactions with your neighbors today. Let there be light on your job. Let there be light as you walk upon this earth acknowledging Jesus Christ as Lord and Savior over your life. Let there be light!

Amen.

January 4

Just as He chose us in Him before the foundation of the world, that we should be holy and without blame before Him in love. (Ephesians 1:4)

One of the reasons why we love newborn babies is because they are innocent. They haven't tasted the environments of the earth that taint humans. When they are in their mother's womb, they have no idea what's going on outside of the womb in preparation for them. Parents make plans such as where the babies are going to live, clothes they're going to wear, what food they're going to feed their babies, they will have rules in place for their babies to follow as they grow, and they will make education plans for their babies. Parents make these preparations because they know what they want for their babies. Those are the key thoughts for newborn babies.

Our thoughts for a newborn baby are similar to the thoughts that God has for us prior to our birth into the earth realm. He has plans for us that will ensure that we return to Him the way we were before we entered the earth realm. We will do this through Jesus Christ. Christ showed us how to be holy. He showed us how to be without blame. He showed us what love is and how to use love. He showed us that He is love. He showed us that seeking God brings forth treasures that surpass normal understanding. He is the One that will cleanse us in preparation for our return to the Father.

Please walk holy today! Please walk without blame today! Walk how you are going to walk in paradise! Walk with a purpose in your purpose! Walk and reflect the image of God! Walk in forgiveness! Walk in victory! Most importantly, please walk in love! The way you walk today has a major impact on how you are going to walk tomorrow. Christ could return today or tomorrow, and you have to be ready to go to paradise. Be holy because He is holy!

Amen.

January 5

> Who through faith are protected by God's power
> for the salvation that is ready to be revealed in the
> last time. (1 Peter 1:5)

We use extension cords to connect appliances and other devices to receive power. Most individuals have many appliances and devices connected to one extension cord, which is okay, but sometimes they have too many things connected to the extension cord. Think of your faith like we think about extension cords.

Our faith creates that instant connection to God's power. Our households and other believers benefit from our faith too. This is also why Jesus Christ spoke about our faith on numerous occasions. People were healed because of their own faith, and we see others that were healed because of other people's faith.

Your faith is essential to you and others. It paves the way to your salvation from God. It is that belief that it is already done before it's done! It's supernatural in that it connects you to the power that creates the supernatural. Please allow your faith to manifest today in that which you are seeking to accomplish or receive. The Word speaks "now faith," not later faith! Allow your faith to help you receive those things right now! Your faith can connect to God's power right now; if you desire it to do so, then He will make it so. Through your faith and God's power, "All is well" and "It is so."

Amen.

January 6

> And has made us kings and priests to His God
> and Father, to Him be glory and dominion for-
> ever and ever. Amen. (Revelation 1:6)

As we get older, sometimes we start forgetting things. We start forgetting where we placed our keys. We start forgetting where we placed our jewelry. We might forget about appointments and certain important dates. Those things are eventually remembered or found. This happens with age, but it doesn't necessary happen to everyone. One of the most important things we can't forget is who we are and where we come from!

Another great benefit in God sending His only begotten Son is that He reminded all of us of who we are. Jesus Christ walked in power and majesty. He walked according to His Father's ways. He walked as the High Priest He is to us. He reflected His Father's image of true royalty as we must to do too.

You are wonderfully made! You are an heir to supernatural greatness! You are a child of the King of kings! You are a child of the Lord of lords! You are endowed with the power of the Most High! Let this be a reminder of the blood that was given for you! Go throughout your day walking in royalty reflecting our High Priest Jesus Christ!

Amen.

January 7

> Behold, He is coming with clouds, and every eye
> will see Him, even they who pierced Him. And
> all the tribes of the earth will mourn because of
> Him. Even so, Amen. (Revelation 1:7)

In sports, great players are loved by the fans of the teams they play for, and they're hated by opposing teams that they constantly defeated. This is why there are mixed emotions when great players come to town. The opposition's fans that hate them know they can't stop the players' greatness, but they continue to hate them, and the other fans cheer with joy because they believe the great players are coming for another victory.

Ironically, this is how the return of Jesus Christ will be. The evil ones will tremble in fear, and the faithful ones will rejoice because of the return of the Risen King!

No one knows the hour, but we must assume that every day is that day. You should be filled with joy knowing that after you read these words, He could appear and you will be within the ultimate victory. Many will not be ready because they are attached to the world, thus glued to the evil one, but those that are faithful in truth shall light up and be lifted into the Light of Majesty. Remain tuned into His return, and ensure you do your best to inform others of His return. Please tell someone about Him today. You may be the light that they need to help them get closer to the Light! Amen.

January 8

> But you will receive power when the Holy Spirit comes on you; and you will be my witnesses in Jerusalem, and in all Judea and Samaria, and to the ends of the earth. (Acts 1:8)

Sometimes we get so busy that we forget to eat. Missing meals is a norm for many people, but missing too many meals in one day causes us to become weak as the day progresses on. Once we finally settle down for the day, we have to eat some food so our bodies can receive the proper nutrients. Our bodies can't survive without food for extended times.

The Word shows us that we need the Holy Spirit for the similar reasons food is needed for the body. There are many believers in Christ that do not know the power of the Holy Spirit. Ironically, the disciples walked with Jesus Christ, but they didn't receive the Holy Spirit until after the Resurrection. After they knew He was the Risen King, they were ready to receive the Holy Spirit.

Have you witnessed the power of the Holy Spirit? Have you told others about the Holy Spirit? The Holy Spirit empowers us to do exceedingly above normal people! If you are in need of a supernatural boost, please pray to the Holy Spirit right now. Please use the gift that the Lord has provided for you and the rest of us Christians.

Since you have the power, please use it today to bring God more glory.

Amen.

January 9

> Have I not commanded you? Be strong and of good courage; do not be afraid, nor be dismayed, for the LORD your God is with you wherever you go. (Joshua 1:9)

When our children play little league sports and participate in performances, they need us to attend their events. Performing in front of people is not an easy task, and our children need us there to encourage them. They can obviously perform without us, but our presence at their performances empowers them. This is also why we must pay attention to the children that do not have anyone attending their performances. Our presence will help them overcome their fears too.

God has always been with us! He sent His only begotten Son to help us too! He also provides His Holy Spirit for us too! He has provided enough for us to know that we are not alone in this world that tries to use fear against us. Sometimes fear tries to engulf us, but we have to remember that the presence of the Lord our God eliminates fear.

You have already won! You are in victory already, so whatever the obstacle is today, please remember that it is already finished in the sight of the Lord. He knows the plans for your life, which includes your next steps. You are not alone, and He knows what's best for you so be strong and of good courage today and beyond. Don't allow fear to win! You woke today in victory, and whatever you are about to do, please do it with a victorious mind-set!

Amen.

January 10

He was in the world, and the world was made through Him, and the world did not know Him. (John 1:10)

In the movie *Forrest Gump*, young Forrest didn't get on the bus until he and the bus driver exchanged names. After the exchange of names, it was considered that they knew one another. The exchange of names created a bond of trust and respect which was similar to a combination of salutes and a handshake. Shortly afterward, young Forrest felt secure enough to get on the bus. Similarly, accepting Jesus Christ as Lord and Savior is the first step in knowing Him. As you build your relationship with Him, you will salute and shake His hand every day.

Jesus Christ talked the talk and walked the walk in the spirit and earth realm. He also dominates both realms because has all power and authority in heaven and the earth.

Jesus Christ already knows your name, and you know His name. He wants you and other believers to spread His name so that those in the world can be saved too.

Do something greater today by informing as many people as possible about Christ Jesus. He loves when you introduce others to Him. Everyone has to know Him because there is coming a time when every knee will bow because of His name. Thanks in advance for helping others to know Him.

Amen.

January 11

Then a voice came from heaven, "You are My beloved Son, in whom I am well pleased." (Mark 1:11)

A shout-out is given to acknowledge someone, give them credit, and to show respect. People give shout-outs for good and bad reasons. When was the last time that you have received a shout-out?

The greatest shout-out ever given was the shout-out from God to His only begotten Son, "You are My beloved Son, in whom I am well pleased." God let everyone know how He feels about His Son!

To hear God say that He is well pleased with you would be the greatest thing you would ever hear. All of us must thrive to hear God say He is well pleased with us. What will it take to hear God say He is well pleased with you? This is possible if you maintain clean hands and a pure heart while keeping His commandments. Also, remain obedient while reflecting His image, and hopefully at some point you will receive that awesome shout-out from God.

Amen.

January 12

> Blessed is the man who endures temptation; for when he has been approved, he will receive the crown of life which the Lord has promised to those who love Him. (James 1:12)

Everyone has their favorite foods that they love to eat. Sometimes the desserts are more desired than regular foods, and they are some people's favorite foods. If you decide to focus on eating healthier or if you try to stick to a diet, the temptation of eating your favorite foods is hard to overcome. The temptation can seem overwhelming at times, but you can overcome it. There are many rewards from enduring the temptation of food such as positive weight loss, improved health, and the feeling of accomplishment. Overcoming these types of temptations prepares us to overcome sinful temptations. We can also lean on Christ Jesus to help us overcome those temptations.

Another great accomplishment of Christ Jesus coming back in the flesh is Him showing us how to endure temptation. Satan presented Christ Jesus with the greatest temptations, but Christ Jesus overcame them. Normal men would've lost that spiritual battle, but the Son of God that remains King of kings and Lord of lords couldn't lose that spiritual battle!

You have experienced many types of temptations in your life, and you might experience a huge one today. They are not easy to overcome. If you are currently trying to overcome certain temptations, please know that there is an awesome reward from God in your victories over those temptations. Satan wants you to lose those spiritual battles, but you can call on Christ Jesus to help you overcome them. Please don't try to overcome them alone. Remain victorious and receive the rewards that God has reserved for you. Amen.

January 13

Who were born, not of blood, nor of the will of the flesh, nor of the will of man, but of God. (John 1:13)

Men have no idea the experience of childbirth. They have to depend on the experience of a woman to explain the amazing experience of childbirth. Just like a woman has to tell a man the intricate feeling during childbirth, God would have to tell Christians the intricate experience of the spirit when we are born again. When we are spiritually reborn, only God can explain the total supernatural experience of how our sins are washed away and our new selves are birthed through Christ Jesus.

When we are reborn, it is not our flesh that's reborn but that which returns to the Almighty Father is reborn. Christ Jesus came back to save our souls because our souls impact our spirits, which must be reborn before they can return to the Almighty Father. We are born of God, and He wants us to reflect His image, not the image of man. Another reason why Christ Jesus gave us the Great Commission is because doing so will allow us to be part of the rebirth of another believer.

You are a born-again believer through a supernatural process that you can't see with your human eyes but you can feel it in your spirit. Christ Jesus assures your soul is cleansed and you have to do your part in remaining clean too. If you need to repent right now, please do so. Please remind others to repent too so as to be in position to always reflect the image of God. Being born of God is an honor, and you have to walk in His image today too. Amen.

January 14

> And the Word became flesh and dwelt among us,
> and we beheld His glory, the glory as of the only
> begotten of the Father, full of grace and truth.
> (John 1:14)

Many parents make sacrifices for their children because they love them. They don't have to, nor are they forced to do so, but the love that's within them empowers them to make the sacrifices. Even giving birth to a child places the woman in a position where she may not survive. That's an amazing sacrifice too!

When Christ became flesh, He placed Himself in spiritual harm's way. He sacrificed His time in paradise to help us. He was focused on saving our souls, and He came with His Father's blessings; thus He had no worries. He came because of His love for the kingdom of God, which includes us too. Let's respect His sacrifice with greater efforts for the kingdom, and if you have to make sacrifices for the kingdom of God, then do so in love. That's being Christlike!

What sacrifice can you make for the kingdom of God today or tomorrow? You can sacrifice your time to reflect the image of God, to pray for someone else, and to do other things so God can get more glory. Christ became flesh to help the flesh that His Father created, and the flesh that's reading this message must be respectful in honoring the ultimate sacrifice of the Son from the Father. Amen.

January 15

> John bore witness of Him and cried out, saying,
> "This was He of whom I said, 'He who comes
> after me is preferred before me, for He was before
> me.'" (John 1:15)

In most organizations, employees remain as quiet as possible when a VIP or top executive is speaking. No one talks nor make any sudden moments during that time because it would be deemed disrespectful. Although most won't say it, the VIP appreciates the respect that is given.

This is similar to what John did when Christ Jesus showed up. He let everyone know that it is Jesus who is the Christ. John did this in a very respectful way. He humbled himself too. This is also why God chose John to prep the stage for Christ Jesus. God knew that John was humble and respectful.

At your job or church, please ensure to pay the proper respect and be humble to those positioned or appointed over you. Even if you don't approve of them in position, please respect their position. It will also help to remind others to do the same thing so as to maintain good order and discipline. We have to remain accustomed to it now so it will continue to be first nature, not second nature, to us when we are in paradise.

Amen.

January 16

> For I am not ashamed of the gospel of Christ, for
> it is the power of God to salvation for everyone
> who believes, for the Jew first and also for the
> Greek. (Romans 1:16)

Today many Christians will say that they are not ashamed of the Gospel of Christ, but their actions are not lining up with their words. Society and Satan have convinced many Christians that it's not cool to be a Christian. Because of this sad trickery, there are some Christians that have chosen to associate more with unbelievers than other Christians. Some will not acknowledge their faith and belief in Christ Jesus among unbelievers because to them it is not a popular thing to do. That's called being ashamed of the Gospel of Christ too.

Under extreme circumstances, Christ Jesus never wavered in His representation of His Father, and we have to be the same in representing Christ Jesus. He wants us to "rattle the ground to disturb the snakes" via adhering to the Great Commission, but this can't happen if you are ashamed of the Gospel of Christ.

Does everyone know that you are a believer in Christ Jesus? It is understood that many locations do not allow Christianity or any type of religious beliefs to be discussed within their walls, and we have to respect those guidelines. However, we must take advantage of all other opportunities to express our love of the Father and Son. Today please consider saying "Hallelujah" or "Praise God" when you are out and about without feeling ashamed. Neither God nor Christ Jesus reside in a box, nor should your praise and actions for the kingdom of God!

Amen.

January 17

For in it the righteousness of God is revealed from faith to faith; as it is written, "The just shall live by faith." (Romans 1:17)

When you woke up this morning, you didn't float away. Why? When you took your first step of the day, you didn't float away. Why? This is because you depend on gravity to keep you grounded. You depend on gravity without thinking about it. This is because you expect those things to happen without worrying about them. That is the same way with faith.

You have no control over how it is going to happen, but you already know it's going to happen because you are trusting, believing, and knowing it's going to happen. That's faith.

There are things that you want and things that you need to happen to which your faith can help them become reality. Reflecting the image of God, ask God for those things today! Have faith in whatever you are asking God for, and it shall be because of your faith, Christ Jesus, and His Power that you shall receive those things. Your faith is the fuel that empowers your requests to God. Ask for them in Jesus's name! Amen.

January 18

No one has seen God at any time. The only begotten Son, who is in the bosom of the Father, He has declared Him. (John 1:18)

Challenge and password is a technique used by military forces in certain environments or while guarding resources. During challenge and password, a challenge is given after the person is recognized. The recognized person still can't enter without saying the correct password. Once the password is given, then the person is allowed to enter.

This is similar to how the door is opened for us to see God. We are born on the earth with life challenges and obstacles, but once we accept Christ Jesus as Lord and Savior, He becomes our Password to God. The Password will unlock mysteries, provide answers to the hardest questions of life, and unlock more blessings. Remember, Christ Jesus said, "No one comes to Father except through Me" and "I and my Father are One," which translates to once we have accepted Him as Lord and Savior, He and His Father become our Password to open many doors.

There may be specific doors that you need opened right now. You may have prayed and prayed for those doors to open, but they are still closed. You may have asked others to pray with you for those doors to be opened, but those doors are still closed. The challenge is your faith! The Lord mentioned on many occasions how powerful our faith is, and we have to use it according to its purpose. Use your faith continuously for the kingdom, and one day you shall see the Father. He is the Password to unlock your salvation and more blessings for your household. Give Him your hallelujah and worship every day because He is more than worthy. Declare Him, and He shall declare you now and forever.

Amen.

January 19

> So then, my beloved brethren, let every man be swift
> to hear, slow to speak, slow to wrath. (James 1:19)

Many of us would agree that it seems like there's not enough time in the day to do all the things that we want to do. However, every day we must remember that whatever was done yesterday can't be changed today. There is no way we can go back in time and change those things.

We can't go back in time, and we can't take back our words, nor our actions. God is the only one that can do that, and He won't do it. When Christ Jesus said, "But let your Yes be Yes and your No, No," He was also highlighting that what we do should be final because if we keep changing our decisions, then we would create confusion. We are to be precise and final like God and not create confusion like Satan. This is also why we must be slow to speak and slow to wrath because we can't go back and change either what we said or our actions from our wrath.

You have experienced many times in your life when you have said some things that you wish you could take back, but that's not possible. It's not always easy to bridle the tongue, but it will help in holding back your wrath too. Remember, you can't make people forget your actions, nor can you change what you have already done, so please seek Christ Jesus in helping you to bridle your tongue. There are many individuals, including yourself, that will benefit from Christ Jesus helping you with this matter! If the shoe fits, take it off! Amen.

January 20

> He confessed, and did not deny, but confessed, "I
> am not the Christ." (John 1:20)

You've heard, "The truth shall set you free." Many people are not free because they are set in their lies. This is why it is so refreshing when we encounter people that tell the truth. There is a lot gained from telling the truth, and most importantly, it helps to keep you clean.

We must continue to remind certain people that there is no truth in telling a white lie. Lies do not have colors. This is also why we don't indulge in lying, because the truth would become foreign to you. To tell the truth is to know the truth. In knowing the truth, you will have no trouble releasing it when you are supposed to. John was able to release the truth because he knew the Truth. He could've told a lie, but instead He confessed of what is within him.

Confess and do not deny the truth, and you will be blessed by the Truth! You may be in a situation that tempts you to lie, but please don't tell a lie. You must continue telling the truth like John and Christ Jesus did.

Live the truth, and it will be easy to speak it! Amen.

January 21

> Who through Him believe in God, who raised
> Him from the dead and gave Him glory, so that
> your faith and hope are in God. (1 Peter 1:21)

When you purchase new tires or when you have your tires rotated, you should strongly consider an alignment. An alignment will increase the life of your tires. Many people find out about the need of an alignment when their tires are worn down. It doesn't make sense to be reactive to a situation like this when being proactive will save more than just tires. Think about your last alignment and what would've happened if you didn't get that alignment.

Another great benefit of Christ Jesus coming back in the flesh was the realigning of faith and hope of God's children. Although God is omnipresent and always available for us, His children were not focused on Him as they should've been. God sent His Son, then raised Him from the dead, to which we believe in the faith and hope of His Son's sacrifice on the cross. Christ Jesus kept His faith and hope in His Father, which we have to do too. Faith and hope in the Father and Son are the keys to eternal victory!

Are you aligned with God? The things that you want and need the most will manifest if your faith and hope are aligned with the will of God. This type of alignment will allow you to receive eternal life. Stay proactive in your faith and hope in God before there is a crisis or need. Stay connected and never be neglected! Amen.

January 22

> And He put all things under His feet, and gave
> Him to be head over all things to the church.
> (Ephesians 1:22)

Mountains are mostly high in elevation with various weather conditions surrounding some of them. Those things make most mountains seem intimidating.

Many individuals have been hurt or have lost their lives trying to conquer particular mountains, and many of them have figured out that its best to try to conquer those mountains with assistance from others. To conquer a mountain is to reach its peak, which can also be termed as overcoming the mountain. If you are considering making an attempt to overcome a mountain, please call on Christ Jesus.

He is above everything to include mountains of evil, stress, depression, suicidal thoughts, loneliness, addictions, and hate! They are beneath His feet, and He maintains victory over all of them. A lot of time can be saved if we call on Christ Jesus when we first recognize the mountains instead of waiting until we are consumed by the mountains.

Are you consumed by one of those mountains? You may not be in those situations, but someone close to you might be in those situations, and they may need Christ Jesus right now. Most importantly, it doesn't make sense to call upon Him if you or someone else is holding on to the mountains. Give Him your mountains, and watch Him turn your plateau into a shadow, but only if you let go.

Amen.

January 23

> "Behold, the virgin shall be with child, and bear
> a Son, and they shall call His name Immanuel,"
> which is translated, "God with us." (Matthew 1:23)

In some organizations, when the director is not available, his deputy stands in for him. It's still business as usual because the deputy and the director are in sync. This brings so much comfort to the director and all the employees of the organization because in many other companies, it's chaos when the director isn't there to run daily operations.

This is similar to Christ Jesus being with us when He walked in the flesh. He reflected His Father well; hence, His Father said, "This is my beloved Son in whom I'm well pleased." This is also why He reminded everyone that He was doing His Father's business. He and His Father are one. When God sent His only begotten Son, He actually sent Himself. We have to go through the Son to get to the Father because once we are in the Son, we are also in the Father. "Greater is He, that's within you than he that's in the world." He is with you, and you must reflect Him!

Your words, actions, and mind-set reflect who your father is. Think about your recent actions. Do they reflect Christ Jesus? Your words and actions paint your portrait (soul). Your words and actions determine where your portrait will be hanging. Know that He is with you and reflect His image always! He sent His Son, and He is also sending you out every day to reflect Him. Other souls are in need of your reflection too! Mirror our Savior, and He will mirror His Father in blessing you! Amen.

January 24

> Now to Him who is able to keep you from stumbling, and to present you faultless before the presence of His glory with exceeding joy. (Jude 1:24)

Lifting weight in the gym can be therapeutic. Many do it to stay in shape, some do it to get stronger, some do it for competitions, and some do it for bragging rights. Essentially, all of them can be called weight lifters. Most heavy weight lifters will agree that it's a tall task trying to become the strongest person in the gym, but they keep pushing because they don't want to feel small in the gym. Essentially, no matter how strong someone becomes, their physical strength can't help them in spiritual battles.

It takes supernatural strength, not physical strength. You need supernatural strength to keep you upright in the spirit, especially during spiritual warfare. The enemy will try to push you down if he could, but instead of pushing you down, he uses other methods, hoping they will cause you to stumble into darkness. This is why you must call on Christ Jesus too! Christ Jesus is the light that darkness can't overcome! He has already defeated the enemy, and He is available to defeat anyone that's trying to cause you to stumble.

Christ Jesus is more than able to keep you from stumbling. Remain as strong as you can today, but please call on Christ Jesus right now if you are spiritually weak. He can help you avoid a lot of pain and suffering. The enemy wants you to go forward without the strength that you really need. Please allow Christ Jesus to help keep you clean and to win your spiritual battles while simultaneously keeping you clean enough to present you faultless before the Almighty Father. Amen.

January 25

> To God our Savior, Who alone is wise, be Glory and Majesty, Dominion and Power, both now and forever. Amen. (Jude 1:25)

God alone is so much more than we can imagine. Our personal relationships with Him help in describing who He is to us. In your lifetime you may have thought of excellent words to use to help describe God. You can use all of the available adjectives in all languages to describe how awesome God is to you, and they still won't be enough to completely describe Him. Even God didn't use many words to describe Himself as He told Moses, "Tell them I Am sent me to you." We don't know who He is outside of what we believe Him to be, which is why we can't depend on our words to quantify Him.

When you have time, please go through the alphabet and describe God like this or do better. He is awesome. He is the best. He is the Creator. He is the Deliverer. He is everlasting. He is the Father. He is the greatest. He is our Healer. He is always impressive. He is Jesus. He is the King. He is love. He is mighty. He is never-ending. He is omnipresent. He is our problem-solver. He is our qualifier. He is our Redeemer. He is our Savior. He is our Teacher. He is undeniable. He is the victory. He is our Waymaker. He is the X factor. He is Yahweh. He is Zion. That's still not enough adjectives.

There are simply not enough words to describe the Almighty Father. If you could use one word to describe God, please consider the word *love*. *Love* is one of the best words to use when trying to describe Him. This is why the first commandment starts with, "You shall love." God so loved the world that He gave His only begotten

Son. Love is an action, and God's actions are always fruitful and righteous. Show love today in all that you do, and you will be showing God. Show God, and He will show you love. Amen.

January 26

> Then God said, "Let Us make man in Our image, according to Our likeness; let them have dominion over the fish of the sea, over the birds of the air, and over the cattle, over all the earth and over every creeping thing that creeps on the earth." (Genesis 1:26)

One thing that we can't deny is our reflection in the mirror. Our reflections are images of ourselves that we can't touch, but we know they are us. Our images do not have power, but the image of God has power. We are the images of God, and He has given us power and authority in His Son Christ Jesus.

No matter your skin color, gender, height, or weight, it is with great honor to be made in the image and likeness of God. God wants us to reflect His image and imitate Him; thus, He gave us His only begotten Son to imitate. He could've chosen to make us in the image of anything else, but He chose Himself. This lets you know that He expects you and all His children to imitate Him.

You are wonderfully made for a reason! Reflecting the image of God will also keep the darkness away. Darkness doesn't like the light, which is why we have to reflect the light. Reflect His love, reflect obedience to Him, reflect obedience to His commandments, reflect His forgiveness, and reflect being strong and of good courage today and forevermore! In Jesus's name! Amen.

January 27

It is He who, coming after me, is preferred before me, whose sandal strap I am not worthy to loose. (John 1:27)

John the Baptist was an honorable man of God. He did more in one week than millions have done in a lifetime. He was favored by God, and Christ Jesus spoke highly of him. To know this about himself, he still didn't find himself worthy to loose Christ's sandal strap.

You may have done mighty works for God, and you may have been seen throughout all of heaven as a great believer, but you have to remain humble. John was humble, and so shall you be, if you hope to reside in paradise with Christ Jesus. If you encounter anyone that thinks they are worthy to loose Christ's sandal strap, please pray for them ASAP. Please keep a tight grip on humbleness, and let go of any self-righteousness.

There is someone watching you, and you should want them to see your humbleness. You should want them to see how respectful you are toward the Father and Son. Even Christ Jesus remained humble to His Father after He was given all power and authority of heaven and earth. This is why we must imitate Christ Jesus, because He showed us how a humble human being must conduct themselves. Amen.

January 28

Then God blessed them, and God said to them, "Be fruitful and multiply; fill the earth and subdue it; have dominion over the fish of the sea, over the birds of the air, and over every living thing that moves on the earth." (Genesis 1:28)

A teenager was home completing homework while her parents were at the grocery store. At some point the weather changed, and it began to thunder and lightning. Eventually, one of the lightning strikes caused the power to go out, so the teenager called her parents via her cell phone. She explained to her father that the power was off and she was sitting in the dark. Her parents rushed home, and her father went into the garage and flipped the circuit so the power could come on. If their daughter knew how to turn the power on, she wouldn't have had to sit in the dark!

Another great reason for Christ Jesus's presence was to show us that we have dominion. Many have forgotten that Christ Jesus is the Conqueror, the Savior, and the Undefeated Champion of Existence that flipped the switch to victory.

You must flip the switch today. Flip the switch of victory over all enemies—foreign, domestic, and of darkness—that forgot that God has given you power to trample upon all of them. Flip the switch by calling on Christ Jesus right now. Flip the switch, and watch your enemies flee. Flip the switch right now, and exercise dominion over everything that creeps upon this earth! Amen.

January 29

> The next day John saw Jesus coming toward him, and said, "Behold! The Lamb of God who takes away the sin of the world!" (John 1:29)

Most baseball players are successful because they have good hand-and-eye coordination. Without that ability, they will not have good recognition which allows them to make the proper connection with the baseball. They want to connect in a way to make the best impact upon the baseball. Other factors affect the process of hitting the baseball, but hand-and-eye coordination is most important. You can be the strongest or most athletic baseball player in the world, but without good hand-and-eye coordination, you will not be most effective.

John's hands were clean, and his spiritual eye was properly focused, so when Christ Jesus appeared before him, he immediately recognized him. He was able to connect to Christ Jesus in a way that all others couldn't.

You have to stay clean of distractions and darkness so that you can use your spiritual eye to focus on Christ Jesus too. What is keeping you from staying focused on Him? Will you be able to recognize Him if He was walking toward you? He is visible to those that are in His body; thus they can see Him in other bodies within His body. Remember this: "Greater is He that's within me than he that's within the world." Please reflect Him today more than you did yesterday, as this will help others to recognize Him if He came back today or tomorrow. Behold, He is coming back! Amen.

January 30

> But the angel said to her, "Do not be afraid, Mary; you have found favor with God. (Luke 1:30)

When you were young, at some point you had to go to a new school because you moved or because you were advancing to a higher grade. You didn't know what to expect because it was new to you, but there came a time when you got over being afraid of the unknown. How did this happen? You overcame! You are an overcomer!

Sometimes you can't overcome the unknown by yourself like Mary couldn't initially do by herself. The angel helped her, and today you may need Christ Jesus to help you overcome something which could help you find more favor with God.

God will send you an angel or someone to help you complete a task for the kingdom, so please know that you are not in it alone. The walk of a believer may seem lonely at times, but God will ensure there is someone available to help you when you are in need. Please try not to be afraid if an angel or believer sent from God approaches you. The Holy Spirit will help you in your discernment, which will also assist you in receiving favor. Your favor from God will help you give birth to victory today like Mary birthed victory called Jesus. Overcome and give birth! Amen.

January 31

So He came and took her by the hand and lifted her up, and immediately the fever left her. And she served them. (Mark 1:31)

Doctors are needed throughout the world. Due to their needed knowledge and skill sets, they are pillars within their communities. They are needed for the sick or injured individuals. I'm thankful that they exist to help others get better. I'm especially thankful for doctors because one of them properly diagnosed my brain injury, which led to emergency surgery that saved my life. Through surgery, my life and other lives were saved by doctors, but sometimes they can't save or heal an individual. This is an easy understanding because they are not God.

We need doctors, but most importantly, we need the Great Physician, our God, because He can do exceedingly abundantly above all that we ask for!

If you are a child of God, then you know that His healing action must translate into a reaction of you praising Him and giving Him more glory. He can heal you faster than any medicine can. Medicines can't cure everything, and doctors can't heal everyone, but I'm so glad that Christ Jesus has proven that He can cure and heal all things. Christ Jesus cures and heals in the supernatural, which is why the supernatural has to be introduced to all issues if you truly want them resolved. Please introduce Christ Jesus to your medical issues right now, and after your healing, please continue to remain obedient to Him while serving as one of His disciples. Be healed today in His Holy name! Give your testimony with joy! Amen.

FEBRUARY

Strengthening unions are a must, especially the union you have with Christ and then the union in your household. Those unions are your foundations!

February 1

> Thus the heavens and the earth, and all the host of them, were finished. (Genesis 2:1)

What have you started and have not completed? If you included God in the beginning, then you already know it's going to be a fantastic finish. If you didn't include Him in the beginning, then you should consider a pause in your efforts and invite Him into your task or mission. He is the Subject Matter Expert in creating a beginning and end, which means He can easily help you start and finish whatever you are trying to do. Please consider this ASAP!

No one should seek to waste time. Our efforts are centered on accomplishment. God has accomplished what no human can accomplish. He created the universe, and He knows everything that we are planning to do in it. Inviting Him into whatever you are planning guarantees the best outcome.

What if one of your children started building their house on your property without your permission? You have the land, but out of respect and courtesy, your children should still ask permission to build their house on your land. Once they asked you for permission, you will most likely assist them in accomplishing their task because it's still on your land and you love your children. That's also why we should consult God in all that we do, because we are living in His universe on His land! He knows the plans for everything in our lives, and He is the best Consultant available. Seek and ask Him then. Amen.

February 2

And on the seventh day God ended His work which He had done, and He rested on the seventh day from all His work which He had done. (Genesis 2:2)

Chefs are known for creating flawless meals, and those meals have their signatures on them. God has placed His signature on many things, and one of those things is the seventh day that God has blessed and sanctified. When you place your signature on anything, you are signifying completion and approval.

His signature must be respected!

Please do not allow another Sabbath to pass without resting on it and giving God all the praise and glory for it. Your obedience to the Sabbath paves the way for blessings on the other six days. We must make sure that we incorporate a day of rest in our work schedules. We are not machines. We were not created to work all our lives, and God provided the best blueprint to follow in the scripture above. Please remember that your mind, body, and soul are in need of rest, and since we were made in His likeness, we should rest on the same day He chose to rest on. Please take advantage of a blessed day to recharge and rest while simultaneously pleasing the Lord. Amen.

February 3

> And when they ran out of wine, the mother of Jesus
> said to Him, "They have no wine." (John 2:3)

Whenever you are hosting an event, you must ensure that you have everything that is needed. You have to also be diligent in planning, rehearsing, and accountability during the coordinating of events. Sometimes mishaps still happen even though there was great planning, rehearsing, and accountability. This is why you have to have as much help as possible. Christ Jesus is always available to assist you.

Please remember that Christ Jesus has been given all power and authority over heaven and earth! We will run out of the natural, but Christ never runs out of the supernatural!

He gives eternal life because He is eternal. His blood is eternal! When we accepted Him as Lord and Savior over our lives, we became eternal. The blood in our natural bodies will eventually dry out, but the blood of Christ will not. We host our natural life events to the best of our abilities, but we need the supernatural assistance of Christ Jesus to help enjoy most aspects of life. Please remain obedient to God, maintain your relationship with Him, repent today if need be, and imitate the walk of Christ Jesus, and you will never run out of the supernatural! Amen.

February 4

> But God, who is rich in mercy, because of His
> great love with which He loved us. (Ephesians 2:4)

We have witnessed many individuals show minimum compassion and sometimes no compassion to others. This is because they have moved forward to hurt or harm someone physically or spiritually instead of forgiving the person. Forgiving someone instead of punishing them is mercy. God showed us true mercy when He sent His only begotten Son! He also provides us mercy every day.

God could've allowed us to suffer because of collective disobedience, but He didn't. Instead, He sent Christ Jesus for the sake of the kingdom to help the human race.

God's mercy is available like oxygen, but you must be alive in Christ to inhale it! We must reflect God in showing mercy. We have no choice since we are children of God reflecting His image. You may be in a situation when you wouldn't consider showing mercy to specific people, but you have to. We can't be hypocrites and not forgive them. It's easier said and read than done, which is understood, but it will be done. God could've allowed us to remain in mental, physical, or spiritual prisons because of previous disobedience, but He showed us mercy, and today we are alive to return the mercy to someone else. Show mercy, and open a new door of blessings. Amen.

February 5

> Even when we were dead in trespasses, made us alive together with Christ (by grace you have been saved). (Ephesians 2:5)

Parents prepare meals for their families. Even the disobedient children are allowed to eat. The good children are sometimes confused and upset as the disobedient children get a chance to eat at the same table as them.

That's how many individuals may view you as God blesses you. Many will question your blessings; others will focus on your past, but God makes these special exceptions for your benefit based upon His will, your repentance, your obedience, your forgiveness, your clean hands, and your pure heart. You deserve your increase, no matter what others think!

This is also how it is referenced receiving our salvation. It's not because of our many efforts, but it's because of God's grace that we have an opportunity to receive salvation. His grace is sufficient, and we can't live without it. For this and many more reasons, we give God the highest praises and all the glory! Now and forever, we must remain dead to our trespasses to remain alive in Christ! God will forgive so you can live!

Amen.

February 6

> As you therefore have received Christ Jesus the
> Lord, so walk in Him. (Colossians 2:6)

Parents know exactly what their children want for Christmas. On the day of Christmas, the children open their gifts in excitement. Collectively, the younger children stay engaged with their gifts longer than older children because excitement seems to last longer in younger children.

God knew exactly what we needed in life; thus He gave us Christ Jesus. He knew that many believers would be excited at the fulfilling of prophecy and the opportunity to be in the kingdom of God. He knew that there would be many that would embrace the sacrifice that He and His Son made for us. He knew that many of us would remain excited about receiving victory and overcoming death.

Today many individuals complain that some believers are too excited or are overdoing it, referencing them expressing excitement of Christ Jesus. True love of the gift from God never decreases. The excitement leads to the continuous walk in Christ. Your walk in Christ is indicative of your excitement in Him! Walk in love! Walk in victory! Walk in your Savior! Amen.

February 7

> To those who by persistence in doing good seek
> glory, honor and immortality, he will give eternal
> life. (Romans 2:7)

If we are what we eat, then we should be partaking of Christ Jesus every day. When we partake of Him, we partake of the goodness of the Lord. His goodness will be seen in our efforts as we reflect the image of God. Reflecting the image of God is the least that we can do, and in doing so we are honoring Him. Those are some of the keys to receiving eternal life!

Those that are in paradise are on one accord. Here on earth we are strongly encouraged to be on one accord in Christ, and that includes doing good things. Do what you are!

Today be great at doing well even if someone is trying to ruin your day! The enemy will use his children against you because he doesn't want to see you do well. He doesn't want to see another child of God walking like Christ Jesus. The enemy doesn't want you to do well, but you must do so for the sake of imitating the Father and Son with a reward of eternal life. No matter the circumstance, continue to do good in faith and in love. Life can be a joyful action since you are purpose-driven for the eternal living!

Amen.

February 8

> Beware lest anyone cheat you through philosophy
> and empty deceit, according to the traditions of
> men, according to the basic principles of the world,
> and not according to Christ. (Colossians 2:8)

Adjusting to one another's cooking is sometimes critical to a happy marriage. It's rare if both spouses are great cooks, but it's possible. One of the things that you notice in marriages is sometimes one spouse compares the other spouse's cooking to his or her parents' cooking. Sometimes the parents' cooking is a good measuring stick, and sometimes the spouse cooking is better. Essentially, you would have to know what good cooking is before you could make such determinations.

God's Word is more than food for thought! It is the supernatural substance that empowers you to supernatural levels. As we stay immersed in the Word of God, we develop a foundation that helps us identify the deceptive distractions of the evil one. Let's walk in the ways and be led by the light of Christ so our lights can help others avoid the trickery of others.

This is why you must know the Word of God for yourself. Christ Jesus is the Word of God, and He is the standard. Please don't allow the worldly wisdom and trickery of man to mislead you. Just because it sounds good doesn't mean it is good. Please stay rooted in Christ so you can bear His good fruit. Call upon the Holy Spirit to help you discern the words and imagery presented by others. Please remember that even Satan can disguise himself as light, but he doesn't have the Holy Spirit; hence, test the spirits by the Spirit. Stay godly entrenched!

Amen!

February 9

> Therefore God also has highly exalted Him and given Him the Name which is above every name.
> (Philippians 2:9)

Name-dropping is when someone uses a name to impress another person or they use it to gain access. This happens every day for various reasons, and it will continue to happen because name-dropping seems to help a lot of people. In many instances, it doesn't work because the person that is name-dropping has no creditability.

We believe Jesus is the name that's above all names because we recognize Him as the only begotten Son of God that came in the flesh and laid down His life for the human race. Our faith in His name is critical in our usage of His name. The enemies can't touch the name, but they can touch the individuals that do not have clean hands and pure hearts. This is seen in Acts 19:15.

> And the evil spirit answered and said, "Jesus I
> know, and Paul I know; but who are you?

As you follow Jesus and imitate Him, your name becomes great too, but not greater than His name. Since you are a Christian, then your name is connected to His name, but you want the demons to respect your name like they respect the name of Jesus and the Apostle Paul's name. Believe in, trust in, and walk in the Name that's above all names, and your day will be much better than it was yesterday. Amen.

February 10

> For we are His workmanship, created in Christ
> Jesus for good works, which God prepared
> beforehand that we should walk in them.
> (Ephesians 2:10)

Normally, when kids are between the ages of three and five, they are constantly asking their parents, "Why?" They have questions about everything. They are quite curious of the unexplained, so they seek guidance from those who they believe have the answers to their questions. In the same manner, children of God want to know why God created us, so they seek the answers via prayer. Why?

God is good, and we were created with good intensions to do good works. Our good works help in many areas to include those that are burdened by the bad works of darkness. When we accept Jesus Christ as Lord and Savior, we are therefore new creations purposed for good works for the kingdom of God.

Today your good works are needed in your household, on your job, and in your community. You can't wait on someone else to do what God has equipped you to do. Bring Him more glory! Think about the people you are going to affect with your good works. Your good works are to bring more glory to God, to help build up other children of God, and to help those that are trapped in darkness. Someone will benefit from your good works today. Amen.

February 11

> And that every tongue should confess that Jesus Christ is Lord, to the glory of God the Father. (Philippians 2:11)

Cars are valued commodities that can be utilized for various means. Cars mainly provide transportation that we need for our jobs, leisure, sport, or family reasons. Cars are significant elements in our everyday life.

Our confession that Jesus Christ is Lord provides the much-needed supernatural transportation through all our situations that we experience in life. We need Him to take the wheel of our lives so that we won't crash into the dark places of the world.

When was the last time that you confessed Jesus Christ as Lord? Your answer is significant to other questions that you have reference certain events in your life. Your confession of our Advocate guarantees divine justice before the Ultimate Judge. Your confession of Jesus Christ as Lord also covers you and your household. If you haven't confessed Him as Lord in a long time, please consider doing it right now. Your sincere confession right now could open more doors of blessings and answers to your unanswered questions. Acknowledge Him and watch Him acknowledge you mightily. Amen.

February 12

> The LORD repay your work, and a full reward be given you by the LORD God of Israel, under whose wings you have come for refuge. (Ruth 2:12)

When people go to work, they are exchanging their time for money. They are expected to complete daily tasks associated to the work they are hired for. At the end of the pay period, the people expect a paycheck. In the same aspect, when we accept Jesus Christ as Lord and Savior, we are expected to spread the Gospel with the time that we have left on earth.

Jesus Christ said, "Greater works shall thy do." All of God's children shall do greater works to His glory. The Holy Spirit provides gifts so that we can do greater works. These greater works are the good works that are needed for the sake of the kingdom.

What have you done for the kingdom lately? What good works have you completed without expecting anything in return? We are to complete sincere sacrificing of our time in doing good works for the Lord. He already knows who is going to complete the good works, and He knows who is not going to do anything with the gifts they have received from the Holy Spirit. Seek the guidance of the Lord, and complete the good works that you are capable of doing to His glory. He sees your good works and will protect you so you can continue doing good works for Him. Amen.

February 13

For it is God who works in you both to will and
to do for His good pleasure. (Philippians 2:13)

Remote control cars, planes, and boats are fun to have because you can direct them according to your desires. Those remote control items were created for specific purposes, and their owners are extremely happy when they are using them. We are not robots or remotely controlled devices, but God can utilize us in such a way if we allow Him too since He is in us and we are in Him.

We can do all things through Christ who strengthens us because greater is He that's within us than he that's within the world. The Apostle Paul mentions that he is in chains for Christ because he has submitted to Christ, as shall all those that have accepted Jesus Christ as Lord and Savior.

We heard the phrase, "Let Jesus take the wheel." You have to allow Him to complete the works within you to reflect His Father's image. When you stand down in your temples, you allow the Lord God to maximize your gifts for the good of the kingdom. God knows the plans that He has for you, and He works within you to help you complete those plans. Please don't fight against the will of God but allow Him to fulfill His purpose for you and the kingdom today. Amen.

February 14

> But the natural man does not receive the things of the Spirit of God, for they are foolishness to him; nor can he know them, because they are spiritually discerned. (1 Corinthians 2:14)

It can be frustrating listening to someone speaking a language that you don't understand while they are trying to get you to do something for or with them. You would need an interpreter, or you would have to learn the language. Learning the language would better benefit you and anyone else that knows that language. Knowing the things of the Spirit of God is similar to knowing a different language.

The indwelling of the Holy Spirit is the supernatural key to receiving the things of the Spirit of God. The Holy Spirit will help you maximize the things that you receive from God. The natural man can't understand the things of the supernatural because it's like not knowing a foreign language.

Have you received the Holy Spirit, or have you asked the Holy Spirit to reveal Himself in you? If you haven't done so, please repent of your sins and forgive whom you need to forgive, then ask Jesus Christ into your heart to be Lord and Savior over your life or recommit to Him and ask for the gift of the Holy Spirit. You shall receive power, and you shall receive understanding of the things of the Spirit of God. Please do so right now, and please ensure that you introduce Jesus Christ and the Holy Spirit to as many people as possible so many others can receive the things of the Spirit of God. Amen.

February 15

> Be diligent to present yourself approved to God, a worker who does not need to be ashamed, rightly dividing the word of truth. (2 Timothy 2:15)

Military recruiters have to go to many places to recruit individuals for the military. People avoid them and speak badly about them, but they remain diligent in their efforts to reach their recruiting goals. No matter what the public said about them, they still went out every day doing their best to reach their goals.

Believers are similar, but we don't actively recruit individuals. We spread the Gospel while allowing the Word of God and our testimonies to touch the hearts of others. We can't be ashamed of the Gospel of Jesus Christ. So essentially, we are sometimes seen as recruiters for the Creator helping others attain the Greatest Opportunity.

The Greatest Opportunity provides eternal benefits with heavenly protection. Let's be diligent in helping others not miss the chance of a lifetime. You've broken speed limits and sometimes incurred parking violations for the sake of your job because you are diligent in your efforts to get paid. Without breaking any laws, please have the same dedication in helping others receive the Greatest Opportunity. Amen.

February 16

> If one of you says to them, "Go in peace; keep warm and well fed," but does nothing about their physical needs, what good is it? (James 2:16)

Talk is cheap because most of time the person doing the talking benefits more from the words than the people hearing the words. Our help should be directed to the physical and spiritual needs of people rather than just their ears.

God has always done great things for us, and we must repay Him by loving our neighbors as He loves us. When He gave His only begotten Son, we greatly benefitted physically and spiritually.

When was the last time you did something meaningful for someone in need? Hopefully, it hasn't been that long of a time, but please consider doing a good deed today. Please do so without sounding an alarm or looking for anything in return. Your good deed will help someone feel greater. The Lord can see your intentions. Reflect the image of God, and love your neighbor as you ought to. It's within your reasonable service! Amen.

February 17

Thus also faith by itself, if it does not have works, is dead. (James 2:17)

The human body can't survive without blood. It also can't survive without oxygen. Therefore, having blood and oxygen are essential to our existence on earth. Both are different but play vital roles in the functionality of our bodies. Without either one, our bodies are dead.

We were created in the image of God, and He ensured that we had everything that we needed to function on this earth. A combination of the mind, body, and soul produces faith and works if we will ourselves to do so. God wants us to maximize our faith and works so that we can be more effective for His kingdom and others on earth. Christ Jesus knows our capabilities too, which is why He said, "Greater works shall thy do." The works are greater through faith.

Faith alone is powerful, and with works they create supernatural fruit. Combine your faith and works to help someone else or your household today. Let your faith be the hammer and your works be the nail as this analogy can be interchangeable. So today go forth and maximize your faith and works to reflect the investment that Jesus Christ made for you. Amen.

February 18

> And the LORD God said, "It is not good that man should be alone; I will make him a helper comparable to him." (Genesis 2:18)

A peanut butter and jelly (PB&J) sandwich is a very good sandwich. Peanut butter and jelly are the main layers of that sandwich, and you can't call it a PB&J sandwich with one of those layers missing. They are comparable layers in their placement within the sandwich but different in their purpose within the sandwich. This is similar to the comparison of husband and wife in a relationship (Jesus is the Bread).

God knows the hearts and minds of His children. He knows that collectively, we long for companionship. Companionship helps in so many ways, especially reference Jesus Christ. Christ once said, "Where two or three are gathered in my name, there I will be in the midst." Two believers of Christ Jesus can do amazing things. The enemy doesn't want this to happen; thus, he pushes to destroy relationships. Your companionship is strongest in Christ (the Bread).

God didn't create us to be alone. If you are single, please remember that God knows the plans that He has for you. You have to trust Him in connecting you to that comparable mate. Many of us have made too many wrong choices, but now allow God to deliver your mate in His time. If you have a mate, please remember that you are comparable, and your mate is not less than. Take your union to God and ask Him to bless and protect it. Remember, it makes no sense to eat PB&J without bread, so it also makes no sense to be in a relationship without Jesus Christ. Amen.

February 19

> Jesus answered them, "Destroy this temple, and I
> will raise it again in three days." (John 2:19)

We've heard the quote, "Don't be so heavenly minded that you are no earthly good," but how about "Don't be so earthly minded that you are no heavenly good"? Some people's eyes are wide open, but they are still blind. Wherever your eyes are fixated is where your mind is planted.

Christ Jesus was always teaching on the level of His audience. He was telling the audience that if His human body is destroyed, He can supernaturally resurrect it in three days. The audience was focused on the temple building being destroyed; thus, their reply was referenced a building. We have been blessed to understand the verse today, but we must apply this verse in our lives today reference our temples.

God created us in His image according to His likeness, and we must remember that we live forever in Jesus Christ. If you are threatened with physical harm, please remember that vengeance is the Lord's and He can restore you from physical harm and death. He can restore anything of yours that the enemy destroys. So today if you encounter threats to harm, please remember that Jesus Christ is your shield and has the power to restore you. He can resurrect anyone and anything if you have faith. Amen.

February 20

> I have been crucified with Christ and I no longer
> live, but Christ lives in me. The life I now live in
> the body, I live by faith in the Son of God, who
> loved me and gave himself for me. (Galatians 2:20)

Pronouns take the place of nouns, and personal pronouns are mostly utilized to take the place of people. When you accepted Christ

Jesus as Lord and Savior over your life, you allowed Him to become the Personal Pronoun of your life.

Your old self passes away, and now He orders your steps. The indwelling of Christ requires you to maintain clean hands and a pure heart. The Bible says that David once asked God not to take His Holy Spirit away from him. David said this because he had done some things not pleasing to God. Do not let your actions push the Holy Spirit away from you too.

As you go about your day, please allow Christ Jesus to guide you. Allowing Him to have the wheel of your life will bring forth great fruit while bringing more glory to God.

Please let Him be your Personal Pronoun today and forevermore. Also, introduce Him to someone else today if the Spirit leads you to do so.

Amen.

February 21

> And it shall come to pass that whoever calls on
> the Name of the Lord will be saved. (Acts 2:21)

Are you saved? Have you called on Christ Jesus to save your soul? It would be an internal crime to miss out on a free, supernatural, and eternal opportunity. Please don't be like certain individuals waiting for the opportunistic time to call on the name of the Lord to be saved. Tomorrow may be too late to call on the name of the Lord, especially if it's the Day of the Lord!

The opportunity to be saved is not like a job opportunity. Job opportunities come a dime a dozen, but we must treat the opportunity to be saved like it is a once-in-a-lifetime opportunity. This is an opportunity too that can't be placed on a shelf. When pondering the opportunity to take advantage of a job, you can negotiate your salary, but when it comes to living forever in the kingdom, you can't negotiate your salvation.

Call on the name of the Lord right now so that you can be saved if you haven't already done so. Confess with your mouth that you are a sinner; confess that you believe that Jesus died on the cross for our sins and rose on the third day; and ask Him to come into your heart to be your Lord and Savior after He has cleansed you of your sins. If you have strayed away from Him and need to recommit to Him, please do so right now. Also, please be sure to ask others if they have called on the name of the Lord to be saved too. Amen.

February 22

Flee also youthful lusts; but pursue righteousness,
faith, love, peace with those who call on the Lord
out of a pure heart. (2 Timothy 2:22)

The Apostle Paul once said, "When I was a child, I spoke as a child, I understood as a child, I thought as a child; but when I became a man, I put away childish things." Part of his message to us is to move on to greater things in life that enrich our purpose in life.

Think about the sales representatives that knock on your door. They are persistent at promoting products that they hope you will buy. Similarly, you have to be persistent in promoting and buying into the new you. The old you have passed away, and you should've moved forward as a mature soul in Christ.

The new you have to pursue those things that Christ Jesus pursued and displayed. In doing so, your renewed mind, clean hands, and pure heart will propel you closer to the Father. Your old self pursued those things for the flesh that will remain on earth, but the new you should pursue those things (righteousness, faith, love, and peace) that are for the spirit that will follow you into paradise. Pursue that which will keep you renewed! Amen.

February 23

> And the Scripture was fulfilled which says,
> "Abraham believed God, and it was accounted
> to him for righteousness." And he was called the
> friend of God. (James 2:23)

Abraham's actions to sacrifice his son were the first to imitate what God was going to do, referencing the sacrifice of His Son. Abraham was sincere in his trusting and believing in God, from which he received more favor and blessings. Abraham chose to be more than an acquaintance or associate to God; he chose to be a friend of God.

Your intentions show if you are an associate, acquaintance, or friend to God. You can talk all day, but it's your actions in obedience, giving, and loving to God that show if you are really His friend.

Think of a person that you know as an associate to you, think of another one that is an acquaintance to you, and then think about the one that is a friend to you. The one that is a friend to you should be the one that make sacrifices for you, loves you, is always there for you, and doesn't complain about helping you. Hopefully, you have identified Jesus as that Friend, and hopefully, you have a few Christians that fit that description too. Be another one of God's best friends forever. Amen.

February 24

> Who Himself bore our sins in His own body
> on the tree, that we, having died to sins, might
> live for righteousness by whose stripes you were
> healed. (1 Peter 2:24)

Just like zebras can't physically change their stripes, the devil can't change the stripes that Christ Jesus received for us so that we can be healed.

Some zebras' stripes change if they move to certain climates, but the stripes of Christ Jesus will never change no matter the climate, situation, or era. Today many individuals believe the Bible should change with the era, but that is an error fueled by the evil one that committed the first error in the first era. Please recognize and respect the sacrifice.

Christ Jesus took upon Himself to help the human race, knowing that there would be ungrateful souls that wouldn't appreciate His sacrifice. He also knows that there is a remnant that loves Him and respects His sacrifice for us. This is why we have to live for Him, imitate Him, and reflect the image of His Father. The body of Christ keeps healing others, and the only individuals that are healed are the ones that are in Him. Please respect the sacrifice and all that He endured for us. He is more than awesome! He is Lord! Amen.

February 25

> And they were both naked, the man and his wife,
> and were not ashamed. (Genesis 2:25)

Today as you walk amongst people, you'll see that they are carefree walking about with their clothes on, but those same people would be embarrassed to walk around naked. Today anyone walking around naked would be considered crazy.

As Adam and Eve walked without shame, they had no worries because they were focused on the glory that God had provided them. After they partook of the forbidden tree, their eyes were opened. Their disobedience contributed to the constant war between flesh and spirit over the soul. They shamed themselves and dishonored God in the processed; thus, they tried to hide themselves from His omnipresence.

Today many believers are disobedient, shame themselves, and most of them dive into other sources (trees) for knowledge instead of trusting and depending on God. Please don't imitate them as they shame themselves and dishonor God. Stay naked (spiritually inclined) before God, not covered with sin and disobedience. Stay loyal to the one from whom and where all your help comes. Staying naked before God will allow Him to clothe you with favor and an abundance of His blessings. Claim it, frame it, and hang it in your heart! Amen.

February 26

> And that they may come to their senses and escape the snare of the devil, having been taken captive by him to do his will. (2 Timothy 2:26)

Many of our children are caught up in the ways of the world. It's hard to pry them away from the world because the world has been presented as the place to be. They are actually caught in a web of deception created by the evil one, and parents have to help them out of the deception. The deception keeps them in spiritual prisons.

Many churches have church ministries focused on inmates in physical prisons, but they also have individuals within their church walls that are trapped in spiritual prisons. Those prisons are within the snare of the devil, and he uses those individuals as instruments against believers within churches.

God's children must stay consumed in Him so as to avoid spiritual prisons ran by Satan. As long as you stay obedient to God, He will keep His hand on you, and the devil will not be able to touch nor imprison you! Pray for someone that you know is trapped in a spiritual prison, and if you need prayer reference avoiding spiritual prisons, please call on Christ Jesus right now. The only thing you should be seeking to be locked into is the Word of God. Amen.

February 27

> But the anointing which you have received from Him abides in you, and you do not need that

anyone teach you; but as the same anointing
teaches you concerning all things, and is true,
and is not a lie, and just as it has taught you, you
will abide in Him. (1 John 2:27)

Some students eventually become teachers. Then they imple-
ment curricula in the teaching of their students. It's a process that is
needed and has been proven successful. The Lord sent us His Holy
Spirit to ensure we had the perfect Teacher to guide us in our learning of His Word.

The Holy Spirit is our Guide and Teacher lest we fall victim to
the agendas of the world. He will ensure we don't fall victim to those
that are attempting to bend the simplicity of the Gospel.

As you continue to walk with God and show yourself approved
before Him, according to His will, He can bless you with this anointing. It is a combination of spiritual wisdom and a supernatural
empowerment. The Bible contains the curriculum from God that
you must utilize to help make disciples of His Word, utilizing this
anointing. If you have this anointing, please help prepare others to
receive it. If you are a Christian and you want this anointing, please
maintain clean hands and a pure heart, then ask God for this anointing. Ask and you shall receive! Someone is about to be blessed from
your anointing. Amen.

February 28

And it shall come to pass afterward that I will
pour out My Spirit on all flesh; Your sons and
your daughters shall prophesy, your old men shall
dream dreams, your young men shall see visions.
(Joel 2:28)

Boxed cereals are great. There are so many types of boxed cereals
that some people eat as snacks, but boxed cereals were created with
the intent of being eaten with milk. Some people use chocolate milk

to eat them, but they were created to be eaten with white milk. If you eat boxed cereals, what's your favorite one?

When milk is poured upon the cereal, the cereal becomes what they were created for. They integrate properly with the milk to bring satisfaction to the one that's partaking of it. This is similar to what will happen on the Day of the Lord when God pours out His Spirit.

Have you witnessed miracles, signs, and wonders? If not, this day will be the most significant day of the future. His children are the ones that will receive this pouring out. Please ensure your household, children, grandchildren, friends, and family members are positioned to receive this pouring out. You already know that you will be blessed if this experience happened tomorrow, and you have to ensure others are positioned for that day. Thanks in advance for helping others prepare for the Day of the Lord. Amen.

MARCH

This is a good time of the year to ensure things are being completed and not building up, which would add stress later in the year! Having personal things in order will free up more time for you to spend studying the Word of God.

March 1

> Now the serpent was more cunning than any
> beast of the field which the LORD God had made.
> And he said to the woman, "Has God indeed
> said, 'You shall not eat of every tree of the gar-
> den'?" (Genesis 3:1)

In school, it would be inappropriate for a student to try to teach a class. Teachers are certified to be in position to teach, and students can't afford to be taught by individuals that are not certified to teach. Our Creator is the only One that certifies chosen ones to teach His creations. We are made in His likeness to receive His teachings, and the teachings must come from Him.

The devil was the first false teacher, and he has many false teachers working for him today. This is why we must study to show ourselves approved before God so that we can stand firm against the devil or his false teachers trying to mislead us.

You have encountered false teachers in your life, and you will encounter many more. Please don't allow them to cause you to do something that will affect the generations after you. You were wonderfully made to be a great student of God, so please listen to Him so that you can pass all your tests. Whatever test you are about to take, ask Jesus to protect your mind during your test. Amen.

March 2

> Many are saying of me, "God will not deliver him." (Psalm 3:2)

When you are going through some tough situations in life, there will be many opinions referencing how you got in those situations. Many will judge you and try to doubt a positive outcome for you. Many will say that you deserve to be in the situation that you are in. When this happens, please remember to trust God.

Job, King David, and Christ Jesus experienced this. Their faith in the Almighty Father helped them overcome the obstacles of darkness, and so shall you.

You are in Christ, He is in you, He is in the Father, and the Father is in Him. You are connected through faith, and God will deliver you out of whatever it is today or whatever obstacle that comes before you. Remain strong and of good courage while trusting and believing that God will deliver you out of any circumstance. All your help comes from the Lord! Amen.

March 3

> But You, O LORD, are a shield for me, My glory and the One who lifts up my head. (Psalm 3:3)

His shield of love, peace, and joy helps us deal with life. We need God's hand to keep the extra spiritual weight off of us. The world and darkness will pound us if we allow them to, but I'm so glad that there is a God in heaven and He is here on earth too. Call on Him today to help you lift your head.

King David needed help throughout his reign, and God is the only one that could provide the help that was needed. God is a present help available for all of His children. He is helping you right now. He is helping you in a way that will elevate you even though you can't see Him working in the background.

Life events and betrayal will cause your head to sink into sorrow, depression, or hurt, *but God* is always willing and able to lift your head up above it all. Christ Jesus is the Way to the Father, and you have to trust, believe, and have faith in the Way that God has provided to lift your head. He will reenergize you and help you get through the days that weigh heavy on your heart. It is so! Trust and believe! Amen.

March 4

That the LORD called Samuel. And he answered,
"Here I am!" (1 Samuel 3:4)

Some of the reasons you don't answer your phone when specific people call is because either you don't trust them, know of their trickery, or you know they want to impact you in a negative way. But when the Lord calls you, please know that you can trust Him and He will use you to help the kingdom in a righteous way.

Samuel thought it was Eli that had called him, which was why he went to Eli three times. Eli eventually realized that the Lord was calling Samuel, and Eli provided Samuel the proper guidance. Today many Christian leaders help followers of Christ Jesus recognize when the Lord is calling them. This is one of the reasons why all children of God must be entrenched into His Word.

Please ensure that you are in a relationship with God so that you will be prepared for a call from Him. If the Lord called you right now, would you answer the call? In some instances, you may need someone to help you interpret the Lord's voice. Today, please consider saying, "Here I am, Lord." Say it in sincerity for preparation of

Him calling you. Put your seat belt on and be prepared for His reply. Put your seat belt on! Amen.

March 5

> Trust in the LORD with all your heart, and lean
> not on your own understanding. (Proverbs 3:5)

Think about your life and analyze how far your way of doing things have helped you. Many individuals believe they have it all figured out, and they are okay with where they are in life. This is a collective mind-set of many individuals that need to change ASAP. We are limited in our understanding; thus, we limit ourselves if we don't trust that God's knowledge surpasses all understanding.

Following God's good understanding is one of the keys to continuous favor. One of the reasons why it is hard for many to stop leaning on their understanding is because they are used to having control. They have collectively allowed their carnal understanding to become a comforter; thus, they don't want to function without that type of comfort.

Please go about your day trusting in God, keeping Him first, knowing that He will redeem you, knowing that victory is already written in this day too, and have faith in whatever direction God takes you. Stand firm in God, and He shall help you in all understandings that will free you, help you, elevate you, prepare you, and teach you while bringing Him more glory. Amen.

March 6

> I the Lord do not change. So you, the descen-
> dants of Jacob, are not destroyed. (Malachi 3:6)

You have encountered many individuals in your life that have changed toward you and will not help you. Please be encouraged because they will keep changing, and you can't stop them from changing, but we serve an awesome God that will never change.

God spoke through Malachi to His children of Israel, letting them know that He doesn't change. Their doubt and disobedience didn't change who God is, but He let it be known that His favor to them can be changed. Today we must remind the world and others that God stands on His promises, and He doesn't change, but His favor can change.

You might have had a setback, and all seemed lost, but God is available for you today as He was yesterday and is tomorrow. God will not change who He is, but He can change how He is to you if you don't keep Him first. Repent if need be, and allow the Lord our God to help you and reboot your life. Amen.

March 7

> Do not marvel that I said to you, "You must be
> born again." (John 3:7)

If you ask a sprinter to start the race again because someone else made a mistake, they will be upset and sometimes confused because it was not their fault. The sprinter will have to line up again to try to win the race. In a similar manner, Adam made a mistake, and now we must take advantage of the opportunity to be born of the Spirit (again) so we can win the race.

In the beginning, we see that the tree of the knowledge of good and evil was forbidden as it fed the flesh, and the tree of life was available for consumption to feed the spirit. Adam's actions spearheaded the use of the knowledge of good and evil, which could lead one to being consumed by the second death (Revelation 21:8) while Christ Jesus's sacrifice leads to the tree of life allowing us to overcome the second death living eternally (John 3:16).

The blood of Jesus cleanses us so that we can be filled with the Holy Spirit and equipped to help others be born again. Please help someone be born again, and if need be, please recommit yourself so as to stay within the presence of God. Amen.

March 8

> I know thy works: behold, I have set before thee
> an open door, and no man can shut it: for thou
> hast a little strength, and hast kept my word, and
> hast not denied my name. (Revelation 3:8)

In the midst of our walk in life, we encounter so many situations that wear us down, but through it all we must continue to keep the Lord first. Because of His omnipresence, He is an on-time God, which is why the phrase "He might not come when you want Him but he'll be there right on time" is so popular.

Christ spoke Revelation 3:8 to the angel of the church in Philadelphia. Today we have to examine ourselves to ensure we have been keeping His Word and not denying His name.

Look back on your recent setbacks and stressful moments. Did you still praise Him in the midst of your troubles? Did you keep His name on your tongue and heart when all seemed lost? Your answers are between you and Him. Remember that He knows everything that you do and think, so please ensure you remain clean enough to come through the door that He has opened for you. When you reflect His image, it is similar to you saying, "Knock, knock." Amen.

March 9

> Then the LORD God called to Adam and said to
> him, "Where are you?" (Genesis 3:9)

With today's technology, parents can track their teenagers' location. They can track them via their teenagers' cell phones or via the vehicles that their teenagers are driving. While already knowing their location and trying to gauge their teenagers' truthfulness and focus, parents will call their teenagers and ask them for their location. Will your teenagers be ashamed to acknowledge their location because of their actions and disobedience to you? You should already know the answer to that question as God already knew Adam's location.

God knows where we are at all times. He wants us to know where we are. He knows everywhere that you are going today, and He knows what you are going to be doing. Would you be ashamed if He interrupted you and spoke to you at any part of your day? Would you be ashamed of your actions during that time? Your answers are between you and Him.

Go about your day knowing that God loves when we reflect His image. He is watching you right now waiting for your hallelujah's to Him and your continued obedience to His commands. As you remain in Christ Jesus and reflect His image, God will be pleased with your location. Those things will influence you to say, "Here I am, Lord," whenever He calls to you. Amen.

March 10

> He who would love life and see good days, let
> him refrain his tongue from evil, and his lips
> from speaking deceit. (1 Peter 3:10)

The earth will eat away untreated wood, and you will lose money, so when you are building a deck or any wood structure that has to remain connected to the earth, the wood has to be pressure treated first. You have to ensure that you strengthen the wood to withstand all the elements of the earth. In the same manner, we must strengthen our minds to help us enhance the image that we are projecting.

Our minds spearhead the words that come out of our mouths. Those words are like additional paintbrushes used to paint our portraits.

Many events can cause you to speak out of your normal character, and it is understood, but you must repent and work on that area through help from the Lord. His help will greatly keep you as holy as possible. You must be holy because God is also holy; thus, your thoughts which guide your speech will be holy too. Let's keep clean hands and pure hearts to maintain such thoughts. Amen.

March 11

My son, do not despise the chastening of the Lord, nor detest His correction. (Proverbs 3:11)

We have to show our children that for every action, there is a reaction. If they do something negative, we have to help them understand that their actions are not fruitful. If we don't do anything to correct them, then we do not truly love them.

On numerous occasions, God let the children of Israel know that their actions were not acceptable. They received correction that was warranted of their offenses.

None of us are perfect, and even though we pray, repent, and ask for forgiveness, the Lord may want to usher in His correction to help us. Have you done something that you know will bring forth consequences from the Lord? The Lord our God may be completing some correction in your life right now, and you may not like it, but let it be so. Our Creator is the best one to mold us, and we have to trust and believe that His way of correction is needed. We will definitely benefit from His reaction to our actions. His corrections are a form of mercy. Let Him mold you when others would scold you. Amen.

March 12

Therefore, as the elect of God, holy and beloved, put on tender mercies, kindness, humility, meekness, longsuffering. (Colossians 3:12)

When we watch our favorite athletes, entertainers, and others do great things, they make being great look easy at times. They do it over and over again as if being great is a routine. Most likely, their greatness comes from having conditioned hearts and minds to focus on the things that make them great. Are your heart and mind conditioned to be great? The best example to follow in being great is Christ Jesus because He is the elect of God.

Christ Jesus is the greatest to ever walk upon the earth. He walked upon the earth with tender mercies, kindness, humility, meekness, and definitely long-suffering in obedience to His Father. We have to follow His lead because He gets it from the One that He said is the greatest of them all.

Your day might have many ups and downs, but keep this scripture on your heart and mind as you encounter whatever comes your way today. Remember, whatever you put on helps others to put it on too. Put on the things of the Lord so you can reflect His image upon others to help them experience spiritual growth, freedom, and peace. Help them to become great too! Amen.

March 13

> Bearing with one another, and forgiving one another, if anyone has a complaint against another; even as Christ forgave you, so you also must do. (Colossians 3:13)

The mind is the cornerstone of our temples. It is constantly under attack from our flesh, the enemy, mind-sets, and particular principalities. If it is not properly conditioned, it will be used against us because the condition of our minds impacts our decisions.

The condition of the mind plays a vital role in forgiving one another too. Many individuals have been hurt very badly, and it is harder forgiving those that are closest to us. This is why we must look upon the Messiah and see what He has done reference forgiving. He once said, "Father, forgive them because they know not what they do." In the midst of His suffering, He still forgave them. You can do the same thing.

You can read scripture and receive an excellent motivational speech about forgiveness, but sometimes it's not easy to forgive. It's not easy due to different experiences and mind-sets. This is why we have to keep our minds conditioned with the Word of God while yearning to walk as Christ. In all of our imperfections, we were forgiven and were allowed to continue with life, so please dig deeper within yourself to forgive others too. Forgiving opens doors of blessings while unforgiveness closes door of need. Keep those doors open for you and your household. Amen.

March 14

> But above all these things put on love, which is
> the bond of perfection. (Colossians 3:14)

You have heard the phrase "Put a bow on it." It is used to refer to something being finished in victory. Put love on it. Some situations can get better much faster if you put love on it. God did it!

God so loved the world that He sent His only begotten Son. The prophecies had to be fulfilled, so God put the Messiah on it! God's Word doesn't return void, but it does fill all voids. Christ Jesus filled the void of perfection needed for the hearts of God's children.

What is it that you need victory over? Is God going to get all the glory for putting a bow on it for you? God already knows the answers to those questions, and you do too. You have done a lot of things to imitate the Lord, but now put love on all that you do and ask for, then you shall receive more than you are expecting from the Lord. Love is one of the reasons why God can and will do exceedingly abundantly above all you can ask for. Put love on all the things you are giving to help your brothers and sister in Christ. If you don't put love on, then there is no way you can put on the full armor of God. Put love on today, and go about your day allowing love to deflect anything that's not love. In Jesus's name! Amen.

March 15

> And let the peace of God rule in your hearts, to
> which also you were called in one body; and be
> thankful. (Colossians 3:15)

The Almighty Father is most powerful, and nothing alters His ways. He is the author of many things, and one of them is peace. His peace is similar to His knowledge as it surpasses all understanding, and it can't be broken.

The peace of God in your heart prepares you to receive something great. Look at it as a waymaker from the Waymaker. It sets the tone for a rhythm of blessings coming your way through the Lord. It can also be seen as the caboose to the train of favor from God you are about to receive. In receiving these things from the Creator of the Universe, be thankful.

Your day needs the peace of God in it, so please invite it in. The peace of God in you will take up all the space in your mind that you will not have room for negative distractions. Please allow the peace of God to help you help someone receive peace today. This year has to be a year of peace for you. Make it one! Amen

March 16

> For God so loved the world that He gave His only
> begotten Son, that whoever believes in Him should
> not perish but have everlasting life. (John 3:16)

When children receive gifts, they are extremely happy. They know their parents gave them the gifts, and after receiving the gifts, they focus on the gifts. They don't think about the efforts that helped them receive the gifts because they are focused on enjoying the gifts.

We have received Christ Jesus, and we are overjoyed to have Him as Lord and Savior. He is the center of our lives, and we are thankful to receive such an awesome gift from the Almighty Father.

Let's not lose sight of God providing the sacrifice. This was an ultimate gesture of love for us, and we can't take the sacrifice for granted. We have received the gift of eternal life through the sacrifice of the unblemished Lamb.

God didn't have to send His Son, nor did His Son have to come, but the ultimate love task was completed in love. Today please make sure that you give Him more praise, glory, honor, respect, and love. He is more than deserving, and He is watching you show Him love. Please do this today and provide Him another spiritual hug of love. Please don't go to sleep without giving Him a hallelujah. Amen.

March 17

> And suddenly a voice came from heaven, saying, "This is My beloved Son, in whom I am well pleased." (Matthew 3:17)

In the military at shooting ranges, soldiers receive assistance while trying to hit their targets because it is impossible for someone to become an expert without experience and training. Since most enlistees arrive to training with zero experience in shooting, the training is needed to produce experts. Expert shooters are needed in the military because they can help save lives.

Jesus Christ is the only One that has walked this earth as an expert without having any previous human experience and training. He came onto the scene shooting down the works of Satan following the guidance and experience from His Father. He encountered many distractions but maintained being an expert, which ultimately pleased His Father.

God wants you to be an expert, and the only way to do it is reflecting His image walking as Jesus Christ walked the earth. Jesus Christ has provided the experience, and the Holy Spirit is available to help train you to reflect His image. Reflecting His image will please the Almighty Father. Please go about your day reflecting His image, and remember that the weapons of your warfare are not carnal but mighty in God. Do these things, and He will be well pleased with you too. Amen.

March 18

> My little children, let us not love in word or in
> tongue, but indeed and in truth. (1 John 3:18)

Talk is always cheap unless you have a job that involves mostly talking. Our talk has to be meaningful, but it will never be more significance than of our efforts. This is also why many individuals say actions speak louder than words. That is why when we love, we have to love with actions and truth, not solely with words.

Many times in the Bible, we see God talking and expressing Himself through works and truth. His greatest expression is when He sent His only begotten Son to be the sacrificial Lamb for us. God and Christ Jesus showed us the ultimate love indeed and in truth.

You have spoken the words of love throughout your life, but today seek to show love with action and truth. Seek to imitate the love that Christ Jesus expressed as He walked upon the earth. Let your actions of love and truth ignite something special in someone today. We've heard "The truth hurts," but with love it feels awesome. Amen.

March 19

> Repent therefore and be converted, that your sins
> may be blotted out, so that times of refreshing may
> come from the presence of the Lord. (Acts 3:19)

When sprinters line up to race, they start to focus on the finish line. Their demeanor and focus have changed with the intent on winning the race. This is what we have to do in life too after our conversion into Christianity.

The first step in winning the race of life is to ensure that you are equipped to do so. Confess that you are a sinner, repent of your sins, confess that you believe Jesus died on the cross for our sins and that He is the Christ, ask Him Jesus Christ to come into your heart and cleanse you, ask Him to be Lord and Savior over your life, and receive the Holy Spirit. Now that your sins are blotted out, the new race starts.

You will fight the good fight and win the race. Jesus Christ will be with you now and forevermore. You are victory. You are a winner. Maintaining clean hands and a pure heart with Jesus as your Lord will allow you to experience the times of refreshing from His presence. Don't allow distractions to lure you out of the presence of the Lord. Rebuke all things that try to pull you out of His presence. If your obedience to Him is not neglected then you will stay connected! Amen.

March 20

> Now to Him who is able to do exceedingly abundantly above all that we ask or think, according to the power that works in us. (Ephesians 3:20)

There are countless things we can do if we put our minds to them. This is also why we are able to accomplish many things with our natural abilities. If we believe, have faith, and stay persistent in our efforts, then we are almost unstoppable. There are many things that we can't do no matter how we try to do it.

This is why we have to call on the name that's above all names. There is power in the name of Jesus! When we accept Him as Lord and Savior and ask Him to come into our lives, we invite the power into our lives too.

That power is working within you too if you have asked Him to come into your heart. That power that works in you will allow the Father to do things amazing with you and for you. We are limited in our own power, but the power of God can't be capped. Unleash more blessings by remaining obedient to and worshipping only one Master. Allow that power to flow through you and help somebody else today. When you ask in Jesus's name, it's like turning the light switch on, allowing the power to flow and complete the circuit. Complete the circuit every day, in Jesus's name. Amen.

March 21

> But he who does the truth comes to the light,
> that his deeds may be clearly seen, that they have
> been done in God. (John 3:21)

When we were very young and able to go about our days, some of us would go and pick fruit from some trees. We were innocent in our doing, which is why we never got in trouble eating from those trees. Our innocence drew us to do more innocence and to stay innocent.

Just as we were drawn to the fruit trees in our youth, we should be drawn to the Lord. He is our tree of life and our light. He will illuminate our paths, ensuring that we can see more blessings. All we have to do is be obedient, maintain the faith, and be workers of the truth.

Today let your light shine brighter through doing the truth. There is someone that needs to see you walking in the truth imitating the light. Someone is going through some major issues in life, and as they see the God in you, it will help them get through the situation. Your help may be through a phone call, text, visit, or to a random person you never knew. You will be able to help this person overcome their situation by allowing the light to use you. God will be pleased today as you reflect His image helping that one soul that you are supposed to help today. Thanks in advance for what you are about to do. Amen.

March 22

> And whatever we ask we receive from Him,
> because we keep His commandments and do
> those things that are pleasing in His sight.
> (1 John 3:22)

Spoiled children are seen as bad children because most of them express themselves in negative manners when they can't have their way. There are other spoiled children that don't express themselves in negative manners. Those children don't express themselves in negative manners because their parents have instilled some form of self-control within them.

Some Christians act like spoiled children because God keeps blessing them. He will give us the desires of our hearts if we keep Him first and remain obedient to Him; thus, we become spoiled but in a good way. He has always kept His Word! He is known to bless those that are pleasing to His sight, and He is known for taking His hand off of those whom are disobedient to Him.

What is it that you want from God? What is it that you want Him to bless you with? He is always a willing God, and He is willing to bless you right now if you would simply ask Him for it. This is only applicable to Christians with clean hands and pure hearts. Ask Him for something that will bless you and His kingdom! Ask for it in Jesus's name. Amen.

March 23

> For all have sinned and fall short of the glory of
> God. (Romans 3:23)

Many people believe that since they are not murderers, thieves, and adulterous, then they are clean enough to enter the kingdom of God. This is a belief within many but not true according to the Word of God. A sin is a sin, no matter the severity of the sin. No human being is perfect! Although none of us are perfect, God can still use us.

The Bible is filled with many individuals that have fallen short of His glory, and He still used them to be fruitful for the kingdom. We may not be perfect, but that won't stop us from getting better while staying in position so He can use us.

Do you remember the last time you sinned? Did you repent? Did you forgive yourself? Did you forgive the person or persons that needed your forgiveness? Repent and forgive if need be so you can remain clean, and try to help others from continuously falling short of the glory of God. We can't keep falling short of His glory, which is why we need to repent and forgive ASAP. Get and keep sin off of you so you can be in the presence of God. Amen.

March 24

> When you lie down, you will not be afraid; Yes,
> you will lie down and your sleep will be sweet.
> (Proverbs 3:24)

Joy comes in the morning and will stay with you if you keep other things away. Joy has a twin named Peace. Joy and Peace will keep your heart and mind at peace if you allow them to. This joy and peace comes when you remain obedient to the Lord.

God wants us to follow the plans that He has prepared for us. Some individuals have allowed others to influence them into not following God's plan, but we can't fall into that category. Essentially, we are responsible for our own actions, and the aim should always be to produce a positive reaction. Obedience to God will help provide calmness within you and allow you to rest easier than you would if you were disobedient to Him.

Allow your obedience to bring forth that sense of security and comfort that can't be duplicated. Keeping His commandments and reflecting His image is not hard to do if you truly love Him. Make the adjustments that are needed in your life today. Pray and fast for the answers that you are seeking, and ask Him to point out those people and things that are in the way of you maintaining your obedience to Him. He wants you to have no worries, either when you are asleep or when you are awake. He loves you more than you know. Amen.

March 25

> The LORD is good to those who wait for Him,
> To the soul who seeks Him. (Lamentations 3:25)

The Bible teaches us that we can do all things through Christ that strengthens us. We can't use that strengthening to rush into something without the Lord. Sometimes we can get a little antsy, but we must wait on the Lord to ensure the proper outcome.

We can't rush God. His will be done also means it will be done in His time. He is an on-time God because He created time. This is also why He is the only One that can step in and out of time while still being on time.

You may want that blessing to be here today, but God may want to deliver it tomorrow or next week. Please trust in Him to be God. He knows the end before the beginning, which means He knows when to bless you too. Your blessing is coming. Stay ready in anticipation. Claim it, frame it, and hang it in your heart! Amen.

March 26

> For the LORD will be your confidence, And will
> keep your foot from being caught. (Proverbs 3:26)

Trouble seems to come at times when we are already inconvenienced. It shows up out of nowhere and adds negative energy in our lives. We can't allow trouble to hang around us because it will try to steal our joy. Trouble is like a noun; it can be a person, place, or thing.

Meshach, Shadrach, and Abednego allowed God to be their confidence when they were thrown into the fiery furnace. While they were in the furnace, the Lord showed up and protected them as they walked out of the furnace unharmed.

If you are going through anything right now or know someone that is going through something right now, please call on the name of Jesus right now. He is the only One that can rescue anyone from any situation. Let Him be your confidence today and tomorrow. He can help keep your foot out of the snare too. Let the Bible keep you spiritually fed to help you avoid being misled. Let the Lord our God lead you! Amen.

March 27

> Do not withhold good from those to whom it is
> due, When it is in the power of your hand to do
> so. (Proverbs 3:27)

One of the biggest struggles for some people is giving money to the beggars. Many individuals believe that all beggars are scam artist, but that is not true. Once you release your gift to them, it is up to them to use it for good.

God knows that there are many individuals that will remain disobedient or allow the evil one to rule over them. Knowing these things and more, God still gave His only begotten Son to be the sacrifice. God deemed it good to send His Son.

Today or soon you may encounter a moment to give or not to give, but know that once it leaves your hands, the receiver has to do well with it. Let's not allow our flesh and mind to withhold a blessing from someone that is due a blessing. Your giving is more powerful than you know. Remember, God doesn't change His promises, so when you give, He will bless you accordingly. Be mindful in your giving and release according to your heart. Let the goodness of your heart help to open doors for others too. God is the greatest giver and we must imitate His giving nature. Amen.

March 28

> There is neither Jew nor Greek, there is neither
> slave nor free, there is neither male nor female; for
> you are all one in Christ Jesus. (Galatians 3:28)

When we were little children, we love to color things within our coloring books. We used different types of crayons to complete our coloring efforts. Those crayons came from a box of crayons that were provided by our teacher. Each crayon was used to help create pictures and other designs.

Believers in Christ Jesus are of many different backgrounds but in one body, just like all those crayons in one box. God has allowed us to leave our mark upon the earth just like the crayons leave a mark upon paper. The main point is whom we allow to use us to make marks upon the earth.

Please allow God to use you today to make fruitful marks upon the earth. Please don't allow the devil to use you. As you are presented with different philosophies and beliefs, please remember that the Word of God is the only one that stands now and forever. You are in the body of Christ to make a difference for good, and there are others that will benefit from your mark upon this earth through Christ Jesus. Thank you for allowing God to use you today. Amen.

March 29

> And if you are Christ's, then you are Abraham's
> seed, and heirs according to the promise.
> (Galatians 3:29)

Some children that are adopted don't know that they are adopted because the parents don't want to tell them the truth. This happens a lot, but I'm so glad that when we became children of God through Christ Jesus, we came back to our original Father.

Our human parents are actually our adopted parents because our spirits come from God, and when we return to our Father, our spirits live in His mansions forever. It's kind of hard for most to grasp that truth, but that's how we should approach our parents and our Parent.

As a child of God, you will enjoy the benefits of being an heir according to the promise. God can't lie as you will enjoy more mercy and grace today through His love. You are wonderfully made to receive more than you have received, so please expect more from the Father, especially if you know you are making a positive difference in the lives of many saints. You are within the body, and He takes excellent care of His children. Go about your day expecting to receive everything according to your inheritance through God! You are an expecting heir to supernatural and natural blessings. Claim it, frame it, and hang it in your heart! Amen.

March 30

He must increase, but I must decrease. (John 3:30)

Expressing respect to another person is one of the most humbling gestures to do. It's not easy for everyone to do, but it is an awesome gesture to witness. When was the last time that you expressed respect for another individual? Think about it. Would it be hard for you to exalt someone up while you take a seat? Your answers help paint your portrait.

John the Baptist humbled himself to express respect for Christ Jesus. He was popular among the people and his disciples, but he chose to be popular to the kingdom of God by honoring the Son of God. John the Baptist knew his place, and it was to decrease as the Lord increases.

No matter how high you are elevated on this earth, please decrease when it comes to the Lord. No human being is above Christ Jesus. You might be popular, but your popularity can't save your own soul. Humble yourself always, and keep Christ Jesus elevated above you. This type of respect will reflect upon many others and will allow you to remain in the good graces of the Almighty Father. When you decrease for Jesus, you increase in humbleness and faith. Amen.

March 31

> He who comes from above is above all; he who is
> of the earth is earthly and speaks of the earth. He
> who comes from heaven is above all. (John 3:31)

Many military members have debates over which branch of the service is the best. All of them are significant, but the Air Force is said to be the best because they fly above the other branches of service, and they can keep the enemy at the greatest distance away from us than any other branch can. The Air Force flies high like Jesus and can come down to the other branches whenever they want to.

God sent His only begotten Son from heaven. Jesus came from above to help those that were grounded to the earth. He created multiple branches and continues to create branches. He makes Christians a superpower that will always be undefeated.

Please give thanks to the Lord for coming down from above to help us. He is also above your current situation and will raise you above it in due time. As sure as He defeated the enemy, He will defeat that circumstance that's trying to rise above you. Give it to Him right now! He has all power and authority to defeat anything that rises up against you today. Once you release it to Him, consider it another victory in Jesus's name. Be sure to give God the glory He deserves too. Amen.

APRIL

———————

The first quarter of the year is nearing complete. Finish this quarter with a review of your beginning efforts. Make the necessary adjustments to stay aligned with Christ, which will help you in maintaining the stability in your household.

April 1

> Hear me when I call, O God of my righteousness! You have relieved me in my distress; Have mercy on me, and hear my prayer. (Psalm 4:1)

When our kids get in trouble, we have to be there for them because we know they are not perfect. We were once their age, and we know that it is easy to mistakes or get caught in snares. Our approach to helping them is essential to how they move past the situation and not repeat it. One of the most important aspects of helping our children is them knowing that it is our love that's fueling us to help them, just like the love of Jesus helps us when we need Him.

The Almighty Father knew that King David was not perfect, but He still listened to David's prayer and helped him. The Almighty Father was there for David, and Jesus will be there for you even in your imperfections. Your sincere repentance takes the cover off the keyhole, and now the key can be utilized to help you.

Jesus Christ is the key and the door to the Almighty Father. The Almighty Father hears those that abide in His Son because He abides in His Son. He hears His children when they call out or pray to Him, and He hears you too! Call on Him right now if need be, and do not hold back in prayer. Let those tears flow, and He will dry them with blessings. Forgive who you need to forgive, and repent if need be. Others are believing in your breakthrough too, in Jesus's name. Claim it, frame it, and hang it in your heart! Amen.

April 2

> With all lowliness and gentleness, with long-suffering, bearing with one another in love. (Ephesians 4:2)

Life is not easy, but we have to believe that it gets better. There are many individuals that don't believe life is going to get better because they have been in a bad situation for such a long time. This is why we need to be connected with fellow believers in Jesus Christ. Everyone is not living a stress-free life, and sometimes another Christian helps you to get through your worst moments. Satan and his children want you to stay to yourself and keep your worries to yourself. If you isolate yourself, you will be helping darkness try to overcome your light.

God knew that we needed Jesus Christ, so He sent Him to help us. There is no way we can survive in this darkness on earth. Jesus Christ is the Light, your strong tower, and the present help that was sent to help ease any and all suffering. He showed us that since He overcame it all, so can we through allowing Him to comfort us. We have to imitate Him by being there for our fellow Christians.

There are things we can do by ourselves, but some things require brotherly support in the Spirit. The Comforter can help you help someone endure the circumstances of life. We need us more than we have ever needed us. If you do not have someone that can help you endure your circumstance, please pray to the Comforter, and surely He will usher in the support you need. After overcoming those things that eclipsed your joy for a moment, please help others in similar circumstances that you have overcome. Helped people help people. Amen.

April 3

> But know that the LORD has set apart for Himself
> him who is godly; The LORD will hear when I call
> to Him. (Psalm 4:3)

In many countries throughout the earth, most people have either house phones or cell phones. Due to the increase is technology, almost all the phones have caller ID. Caller ID allows you to see who is calling, which can be very beneficial due to prank calls, telemarketers, and other people that you don't want to talk to. This is similar to God not wanting to talk to the ungodly.

If the ungodly calls out to God, He will not answer them unless it's within His will. The ungodly have to convert into being godly if the person or persons want God to hear them. There are also many individuals that present themselves as godly but are doing ungodly things; thus, God won't answer their prayers. Please don't be in that group of people.

To be godly is to reflect the image of God. This you know in your own heart if you are reflecting His image. If you have clean hands and a pure heart for the Lord, to include the absence of unforgiveness, and have repented necessarily, it is then that He will hear you too. Call out to Him right now if need be, and have faith that He hears you. Please be prepared to provide your testimony too so that He can get more glory. In Jesus's name! Amen.

April 4

> You are of God, little children, and have over-
> come them, because He who is in you is greater
> than he who is in the world. (1 John 4:4)

Bullies take advantage of the weak. Most of the bullies will soon meet their match or be overcome by another bully. Most people believe that all bullies are bad, but there has been one good bully. Jesus came and bullied the strongman. Thank You, Jesus!

He wants us to be bullies over Satan's children instead of allowing them to continuously bully us. When Jesus gave us power to trample upon scorpions and serpents, He was also informing us that the powers of darkness can't bully us anymore. We are in Jesus Christ, and since He has all power and authority in heaven and earth, then His children are greater than the demons that roam the earth. You have the Captain of our salvation in you.

You are what's inside of you! If you have accepted Jesus Christ as Lord and Savior, then you are greater than. God is greater than, and Satan is less than. Jesus Christ said, "My Father is greater than them all." We are of the greatest, and we shall remain victorious because we are in the kingdom, and kingdom towers over the world. The prince of darkness is powerless against the King, and the King is within us. You are empowered with greatness, and Satan hates it. He can't touch the power we have. Hallelujah! Enjoy your great day, and everywhere you go, let your greatness flow. Greater are you! Amen.

April 5

One Lord, one faith, one baptism. (Ephesians 4:5)

A normal car or truck only needs one key, one engine, and one body style. There are other components that are needed too, but the key, engine, and body style are the main elements of your vehicle. It is awesome to have your own vehicle too. You can drive it alone or use it to help other people that are trying to go somewhere. Most importantly, you can only drive one car at a time. Now meditate on Jesus Christ as your personal Lord and Savior. You can only have one Lord!

If someone other than Jesus wants to lord over you, then you must call on Jesus ASAP. There are many individuals that aggressively pursue being lords over people, and their overconfidence plays a role in their tainted mind-sets. Be thankful that Jesus is Lord and no one can compare to Him, so when the little lords try to manipulate you, please introduce them to the only Lord of your life.

Our Lord has made it possible for us to partake in the kingdom as heirs. Thank You, Jesus! There are many philosophies and many false teachers, but one truth requires your obedience to the Word that will keep you. You have already encountered feeble words that can distract you from your calling, but please stay focused on the Lord's treasures. You have been called to do mighty works, and the other ones want to hamper you in your purpose, but not so. Not today. Fight on in your measure of faith to bring God more glory through believing in one Lord, one faith, and one baptism. In Jesus's name! Amen.

April 6

> Be anxious for nothing, but in everything by prayer and supplication, with thanksgiving, let your requests be made known to God. (Philippians 4:6)

If you approach a vending machine and it is out of order, then you have to seek out another vending machine to get the item or items you are looking for. In many instances, there are multiple vending machines in the same area. Once you find a working vending machine and you see what you want, you insert your money or credit card to receive what you want.

We serve only one God, and only one God can deliver everything that we are requesting. It feels great knowing that our God is always in order, and when He receives our currency (faith, reflection of His image, and obedience to His commandments), we will receive what we are asking for.

It's about your approach! Think for a moment on how you have approached God in the past. Consecrate yourself, humble yourself, and come to Him in love with the intent that He is going to get glory for answering your request. After you have given it to God, let it go and let God have His way. Let Him work His precision in your decision. Also, ask expecting and in faith! Send a preceding hallelujah and shout glory to the risen King because your answer is already manifesting. Amen.

April 7

> Therefore submit to God. Resist the devil and he
> will flee from you. (James 4:7)

Many individuals don't go outside because they don't want to deal with the bugs. Because of their dislike of the irritating bugs, they use bug repellent to keep the bugs away. In our Christian walk, we have to keep the devil away, and he stays away if we reflect the image of God. Reflecting the image of God also invites Him in our presence, and as long as He is in our presence, we don't have to worry about the devil trying to stay in our presence.

The devil will come, but it is your obedience to God that will impact how long the devil stays in your presence. The devil doesn't want to see another reflection of God, which is why you must repent and forgive too. Those things help to keep openings and cracks closed, which help to keep the devil and his children away. They stay away most of the time because they know that at anytime, God will show up and deal with them.

God is the best repellent! His presence repels that which is not of the light. Light cancels out darkness easier than you can read this sentence. You are of the light, and as your faith increases, so does your light. The devil can't stand in the light, nor does he want you to reflect the light. Be a greater reflector of the light today because someone else needs your light to help repel darkness away. Amen.

April 8

> Finally, brethren, whatever things are true, what-
> ever things are noble, whatever things are just,
> whatever things are pure, whatever things are
> lovely, whatever things are of good report, if there
> is any virtue and if there is anything praisewor-
> thy—meditate on these things. (Philippians 4:8)

Whenever someone leads the way in doing something great, they set the tone for others that will follow them. This is why leaders that have walked the walked while providing great results set the tone for all that follow them. Tone-setting helps others that have little faith in themselves, lack motivation, or want to see some form of evidence to help push them to accomplish things.

Jesus Christ is the greatest leader to walk the earth because He set the tone that was needed to inspire humankind. He is the greatest tone-setter, and we have to follow His lead. He was able to set the tone because of His mind-set.

The state of your mind sets the tone for your day. The proper mind-set greatly assists you in meditating on godly things. If your day has started off or is ending in a negative manner, please regain your focus so you can use your godly mind-set to bring God more glory. A godly mind-set greatly influences your alignment, direction, and worship. It helps in receiving guidance from the Holy Spirit too. It helps you produce good fruit and help more people. That mind-set will help you meditate on those things and enjoy the rest of this day. It's a mind-set that you won't regret. Amen.

April 9

> The things which you learned and received and
> heard and saw in me, these do, and the God of
> peace will be with you. (Philippians 4:9)

Mirrors are fascinating objects. They are used to reflect images and light. If you stand in front of a mirror, then leave its presence, the next person that stands in front of it will bring forth another reflection. God stays the same, and He has millions of His children trying to reflect His image daily.

Are you reflecting His image?

He wants you to reflect His image so as to bring Him more glory and to join others in reflecting His image. No matter the distractions of today, please reflect His image. The enemy wants you to reflect him in any way possible, but you must reflect only one Master.

The Almighty Father is our Master. He gave His only begotten Son for many reasons, and one of them was to show us the image we must reflect. The world has so many images within it that many are trying to reflect, but the only image to reflect is the image of God since we were created in it. Satan will try to convince you that since you were created in this world, then you should reflect it, but the Word of God says that we were created in His image according to His likeness. It's hard to become something you don't truly know, and now that we know the true standard of reflecting the image, we are equipped to please the Almighty Father. Bring Him more glory today via reflecting His image. Amen.

April 10

> Jesus answered and said to her, "If you knew the
> gift of God, and who it is who says to you, 'Give
> Me a drink,' you would have asked Him, and He
> would have given you living water." (John 4:10)

When you were studying for the test to receive your driver's license, you had to study the signs too. You studied the signs because you have to know the meanings of them since they help you during your driving. In the same manner, you have to study Jesus Christ because He is the greatest sign of God that helps you while you are navigating through life.

One of the reasons why our Lord and Savior want us to adhere to the Great Commission is because we have to enlighten millions more about Him. Making disciple includes developing a clear understanding of Jesus. You have to know Him before you can effectively teach others about Him.

Knowing Jesus will help you when He encounters you. When He encounters you, you will know it is Him mostly because He doesn't present Himself just for show. He encounters you to help you counter your unbelief and to counter the obstacles in your life. Jesus wants to encounter you now with living water, and if you already have His living water, then please offer Him to an unbeliever today. Someone needs to know and receive Him today so that they can receive living water too. Thanks in advance for helping someone else receive Jesus. Amen.

April 11

> And He Himself gave some to be apostles, some prophets, some evangelists, and some pastors and teachers. (Ephesians 4:11)

Do you own a company, or do want to own a company? The strength of a great company is not in the amount of money but in the personnel positioned in the core of the company. The chief operating officer (CEO), chief information officer (CIO), chief marketing officer (CMO), chief operating officer (COO), and chief financial officer (CFO) working together on one accord are the strength of a great company. Not one person!

The apostolic gifts working together on one accord are the strength of a church. The apostle is the CEO, the prophet is the CIO, the evangelist is the CMO, the pastor is the COO, and the teacher is the CFO. You can have a huge church, but without the strength of the church, it will not be maximized. This era of Christians debate about the apostolic gifts because of interpretations and particular teachings. These gifts are needed today more than they have ever been needed.

Do you have or desire an apostolic gift? He needs more warriors for the kingdom. He needs more leaders to help lead efforts that adhere to the Great Commission. He needs you! You will do greater works for God once you accept the calling. You are meant to do more for the kingdom, and an apostolic gift will definitely empower you to do more. The Lord gives these gifts, not man. Please go forth if you have been sent and help others go forth too. In Jesus's name! Amen.

April 12

> Nor is there salvation in any other, for there is no other name under heaven given among men by which we must be saved. (Acts 4:12)

When football season starts, fans are anxious to see who made it onto the roster. There are a lot of veterans and rookies fighting for roster spots. The general manager is responsible for making the final decision on the rosters. In some situations, the coach or owner plays the role of finalizing the final roster.

Jesus Christ is the Owner, General Manager, and Coach that makes the final decision of who is saved on the roster of salvation. Are you correctly practicing what He preached? Are you helping others make the roster too? Are you respectful to Jesus Christ?

The Name that's above all names saves all day every day and forever. The earth contains many powerful men and women, but they can't save your soul. They can save natural things, not supernatural things. The name of Jesus is a supernatural force that can't be contained nor destroyed. It has proven itself, and there is no denying it. It is the reason why you are able to read this. Jesus! Call on His name early in the morning and throughout your day not to bring attention to yourself but to give God the glory. Claim it, frame it, and hang it in your heart!

Amen.

April 13

> I can do all things through Christ who strength-
> ens me. (Philippians 4:13)

Some people take all their clothes to the cleaners for various reasons, and some people iron all their clothes. Ironing clothes is a simple process, especially if you have a good iron. No matter the iron, they have to be plugged up to receive the power needed to press the clothes. You are an iron, and the Lord needs you to press on!

Jesus Christ pressed on during His walk upon this earth knowing the pain and suffering that awaited Him. He endured long-suffering and more for the kingdom. He showed us how to press on. He knew that He could do whatever needed to be done because He trusted His Father. He wants us to imitate Him in this manner too by believing that we can do all things through Him.

You may have some issues in your life right now that need to be resolved ASAP. The best way to resolve those issues is to be plugged into Jesus Christ. He supplies the power needed to help you press through those issues. Are you plugged into Him now (is He your Lord and Savior)? Please don't allow a lack of unrepentance and unforgiveness to prevent the power from flowing to you. Ask for His help, and you will be blessed according to the will of His Father. Stay plugged in! Amen.

April 14

> Do not enter the path of the wicked, and do not
> walk in the way of evil. (Proverbs 4:14)

Sometimes while driving on the roads, you see the signs that inform you that if you take the wrong turn, you will be headed in the wrong direction. Going in the wrong direction can cause accidents and place you in areas you don't need to be in. Would you knowingly drive straight into darkness on a sunny day?

I don't believe so!

One of the reasons Jesus came back is to be the greatest light for us. He showed us how we are to stay illuminated and how to overcome that which wants us to walk the path of unrighteousness. Wickedness wants you to walk like its father, Satan, but you are too precious of a gift to allow him or his children to guide you in the wrong direction with the intent to capitalize on your imperfections.

As you read the Bible, Jesus is the way that will help keep you in godly places. As seen in Genesis 19, the wicked places can be destroyed by God if He chooses to do so, which is why you must stay clear of wicked paths and locations. Every time you find yourself pondering paths and locations, please consider Sodom and Gomorrah as God was proceeding with His wrath no matter what. Go where He is glorified, and you will be in a safe place. Amen.

April 15

> For we do not have a High Priest who cannot sympathize with our weaknesses, but was in all points tempted as we are, yet without sin. (Hebrews 4:15)

In the military, most of the officers that were once enlisted seem to receive more respect from enlisted personnel than officers. This is because the enlisted personnel know that that those type of officers have experience in being in the trenches. They understand that those officers can relate to practically anything that they may be experiencing in their lives as soldiers.

Jesus Christ came back and set the greatest example of a leader. He walked the walk! His attitude reflected His leadership, and our attitude reflects His leadership. He is the Captain of our salvation that knows our weaknesses and our sensitive areas. He knows what we need to help us overcome temptation and trickery.

You may be tempted beyond measure today or almost fell into temptation last night. Temptation comes like the wind, but you don't have to take it in! Most temptations are temporary fixes that satisfy the flesh, and sometimes it takes a more help to help you overcome temptations. Please consider praying and fasting more than you've ever done in your life. It will help with self-control too. Call out to Jesus and ask Him to help you fight temptation whenever it shows up. Don't let temptation knock you out! Press on, child of God! Amen.

April 16

> Therefore we do not lose heart. Even though our
> outward man is perishing, yet the inward man is
> being renewed day by day. (2 Corinthians 4:16)

When a caterpillar is in a cocoon, we can't see the process. A cocoon is the outer shell that ages, but after a particular amount of time, the caterpillar transforms into a butterfly. Once fully developed, it's ready to take flight to help the environment.

Once you become a child of God, He molds you on the inside mostly via the Holy Spirit. The indwelling of the Holy Spirit helps to perfect your inward man (your spirit) that the flesh can't perfect. The perfecting requires the supernatural power of God since the spirit will return to God, which will seem like a new environment to you.

Your spirit needs daily renewing, especially since you may be in a position where others need to be renewed by your spirit. Your renewed spirit makes a difference everywhere you go, which is why Satan wants to distract you from being an awesome light in the darkness of the world. Your renewed spirit is a powerful tool for the kingdom, so please go about your day helping others to have renewed spirits too. God is going to use you to help renew another Christian. In Jesus's name! Amen.

April 17

> For our light affliction, which is but for a
> moment, is working for us a far more exceeding
> and eternal weight of glory. (2 Corinthians 4:17)

Have you had your wisdom teeth removed? When they start piercing the gums, they can be very painful. The onslaught of pain can be unbearable, which is why most seek surgery as soon as possible. When they are finally removed, there will be exceeding joy once all the pain is gone.

Jesus Christ laid down His life for His people, and although it was extremely painful, His pain was for our gain. He withstood a heavy affliction so we would only have to withstand light afflictions. His heavy affliction brought the Almighty Father more glory.

You may be going through something right now and can't see the good that it will produce, but know this: that God is working it out for your victory. You have been through many things in your life, and once again you have the Lord to help you as you press on. Call on Jesus Christ, and believe in another victory. Your light affliction is manifesting into a mega blessing. Keep the faith, and watch your situation bring God more glory. Press on, child of God. Amen.

April 18

> While we do not look at the things which are
> seen, but at the things which are not seen. For
> the things which are seen are temporary, but
> the things which are not seen are eternal. (2
> Corinthians 4:18)

Someone was asked to describe love, and they described the physical aspects of love while another individual was asked to describe love and described some unseen aspects of love. That individual said that you can't taste, touch, nor smell love, and it is also powerful and eternal. The unseen aspects of love are almost identical to that of spiritual sight. Both of them can be utilized to help, connect, empower, and uplift a brother or sister in Christ.

When Jesus Christ walked the earth, many individuals were focused on His natural body, not His spiritual body. Their minds were trained on natural things, which made it difficult for them to initially receive Him as the Christ. Before and after His resurrection, He opened the spiritual eyes of His disciples. Today we must use our spiritual eyes too so that we can receive more from the Lord.

Not everyone attempts to use their spiritual eye, which allows you to see in the unseen. Your spiritual eye is a supernatural element that will help you see through certain situations and people that don't have your best interest. The indwelling of the Holy Spirit provides the spiritual sight that God wants you to have while Satan forges efforts to spiritually hack your natural eyes and your spiritual eye. Ask Jesus to help you focus your spiritual eye so you can see the snares of Satan. Satan's snares are temporary, just like things seen with natural eyes, but you can't afford to stay in either one of his snares for any period of time. Look more at the unseen and enjoy eternal visions of help, restoration, and love. Amen.

April 19

> And my God shall supply all your need according to
> His riches in glory by Christ Jesus. (Philippians 4:19)

Remember the people that promised to help you or those that you believe can help you. Where are they now? Most of them will ignore your calls and messages because they can't deliver on what they promised or what you believed they could do. This is why we have to lean on God for our needs. What are you in need of? You need two key elements to receive your need. Those elements are your faith and Jesus Christ; you have both, and both are of God.

Your faith and Jesus Christ provide the key elements of those things that you need to manifest. Man can supply some of your needs, but the Almighty Father supplies all your needs. Your needs are tied to heaven and earth, over which Jesus Christ has all power and authority. Not man! God's resources are endless with no excuses. Reflect His image and likeness, and your needs will always be met.

Your needs will be met if you are reflecting the image of God. It is then that you will be able to say to Jesus, "Let." Keep God first and continue to give Him the highest praise and all the glory too. You can choose to be limited or be limitless. Choose limitless! God is limitless, and all your needs shall be met in Jesus's name! Claim it, frame it, and hang it in your heart! Amen.

April 20

> But these are the ones sown on good ground, those who hear the word, accept it, and bear fruit: some thirtyfold, some sixty, and some a hundred. (Mark 4:20)

A tree bearing fruit will keep others fed. For a tree to bear fruit, it needs a seed, the sun, water, proper environment, and the ground. If all these are aligned, then fruit will come forth. There is no way anyone should throw seeds on concrete and expect a harvest. Even so, you yourself must be planted on good ground because you too are a seed.

You are the seed of the Seed. Jesus Christ is the Son and Living Water, while the environment is your renewed mind, and the good ground is a pure heart. If this describes you, then you should be experiencing or the experiences are manifesting right now for you to bear an abundance of fruit. There will be inward and outward growth.

Are you growing where you are? Are there fruit multiplying from where you are? Remember, if you keep God in it, you will win it! Let everything that you sow be sown on good ground in Jesus's name. Believe and receive! Amen.

April 21

> And being fully convinced that what He had prom-
> ised He was also able to perform. (Romans 4:21)

Have you ever made a promise you couldn't keep? Some individuals have made promises they couldn't keep, and those that didn't
receive the promises will most likely not believe in any promises from
that individual. It's an awesome feeling knowing that Jesus Christ
keeps His promises and will perform them accordingly.

Having Jesus Christ as Lord and Savior, reflecting the Father's
image, and your faith are the keys to witnessing Jesus Christ perform
His promises.

Your faith can place you in position if it's the size of a mustard
seed. No one can stop Jesus Christ from performing His promises,
and no one can stop your faith but you. Your faith is invaluable! Jesus
Christ is about to perform a promise in your life because you have
agreed to align your faith with His promises. Complete your alignment so you can complete your assignment! In Jesus's name! Amen.

April 22

> For there is nothing hidden which will not be
> revealed, nor has anything been kept secret but
> that it should come to light. (Mark 4:22)

Has someone done something to you but you can't say anything
or you don't want to say anything because you want to protect a job,
family member, or your name? You don't have to expose that person
to the public, but you can give that situation to the Lord. As seen in
Ezekiel 10:12 and Revelation 4:8, the four creatures had many eyes,
and those eyes symbolize God seeing everywhere and everything. He
can see those things, and He can see the things within you that need
to come out too!

Jesus Christ has all power and authority in heaven and earth; thus, He can see as the Father sees since they are One. He can see your talents and gifts because He gave them to you, but you must not keep them hidden away.

Please don't allow fear to trick you into hiding your talents and gifts. Satan loves when children of God keep their talents and gifts hidden, but you will not please Satan. You must allow your light to shine bright before man so as to bring God more glory. In Jesus's name, your talents and gifts shall illuminate areas according to God's will, and you shall be blessed accordingly. Amen.

April 23

> But the hour is coming, and now is, when the true worshipers will worship the Father in spirit and truth; for the Father is seeking such to worship Him. (John 4:23)

Some of the top athletes are not always the most athletic ones. They are the ones that can perform better under pressure than those that have the same, if not more than, talent as them. They are more driven and focused during critical times of games, and the coach can depend on them at the end of games.

Many people don't want to hear it, but the end-time is coming. If you are driven and focused now, then God can depend on you to help others prepare for that hour. Being driven and focused impacts your praise and worship of the Father, and you should be worshipping Him in Spirit and Truth.

God wants you to worship Him in the Spirit (Holy Spirit) and Truth (Jesus Christ). When you are worshipping Him, please remember that it's all about Him and not you asking Him for anything. Worship Him in love and sincerity too. He is more than worthy. Now think about how and when you are going to worship Him today and tomorrow. Consecrate yourself, and enjoy worshipping Him today. He is waiting! Amen.

April 24

> Then He said to them, "Take heed what you hear. With the same measure you use, it will be measured to you; and to you who hear, more will be given. (Mark 4:24)

A chef is a true chef only if he has proven to be practically flawless in preparing above-average meals. Those meals are prepared with the proper measures, and those measures create a chef's signature.

Your measuring is like a signature. This is why we must have the mind of Christ and the indwelling of the Holy Spirit. The Helper will help you measure what to say and do. The proper measure greatly assists in how far you will go and how much you will receive. Let the Holy Spirit mold your signature.

It would be better that He helps you apply the proper measure than for you to continue spilling your measure. Remember, just like you should be able to lift your own body weight, you should be able to lift your own measure. In the same manner, you must look at our measure. If your measure is spiritually fit, when reversed, you'll be able to handle it. Measure your measure! Amen.

April 25

> Therefore, putting away lying, "Let each one of you speak truth with his neighbor," for we are members of one another. (Ephesians 4:25)

In military boot camp, you are trained on many things, and one of the most important things you learn is teamwork. That introduction to teamwork also assists in developing a brotherhood or sisterhood (battle buddies), and that bond carries forward as you progress as a service member. The overall intent is to develop a teamwork mind-set, and that will be beneficial during combat.

Teamwork is built on many things to include trust. Speaking the truth builds trust, and that trust helps to win battles. Jesus Christ is the truth that wins our spiritual battles, and we have to team up with Him every day to ensure we remain victorious. We have to be in Him to defeat them! We can't win spiritual battles without Him.

Enjoy your day with the truth. Rebuke all lies, and strengthen your relationships with your brothers and sisters in Christ. They need you more than ever. Lies are of Satan, and he wants to drive wedges between brothers and sisters in Christ, but not today or tomorrow. He is not going to stop your momentum of truth. Speak the truth today and tomorrow as it will help your brothers and sisters in Christ. Lies can't coexist with the truth, which is why Satan can't live in paradise. Speak the truth to your neighbor as it is like loving neighbor as you love yourself. Amen.

April 26

> Jesus said to her, "I who speak to you am He."
> (John 4:26)

Can you hear me now? That is what Jesus has said to many believers, but not everyone is listening. Has He been speaking to you? He speaks in different ways, and if you are seeking Him, you will find Him and hear Him. He will let you know that it is He that is speaking to you. Earnestly desire to hear His voice and to be in His presence. He is most likely watching you read this sentence. Let your desire be like a springboard, and use it to spring-deep into His Word. This will help you get closer to Him and recognize Him when He speaks to you.

What would you do if Jesus Christ appeared to you and spoke to you right now? I guarantee you will be amazed and overjoyed. We don't know when He is going to show up to speak to us, which is why we must live as if He is going to show up right now. Most importantly, how will we know it's Him?

One of the main reasons Jesus gave us the Great Commission is because we have to introduce others to Him. Making disciples includes teaching others about who Jesus is and how He is the true love of our lives. He is the Son of the Almighty Father, and they are One. He is the centerpiece of our joy and the lifeline of eternity. He is the Captain of our salvation and Owner of our souls. He empowers power and provides light to the sun. He is eternally undefeated and will keep defeating enemies for eternity. He is our King. He is Jesus. Amen.

April 27

> Do not turn to the right or the left; Remove your
> foot from evil. (Proverbs 4:27)

This famous quote has physical and spiritual meaning, "If you don't stand for something, you will fall for anything." The placement of your feet impacts your standing or falling. You must stand for Jesus as He stood for us. He didn't have to come, nor did the Father have to send Him, but He came to stand in the gap for us. He is standing at the right hand of God and loves the feet that are not planted in evil but in His body.

Please don't allow stress, pressure, and the influence of others to guide your feet to evil. The enemy would love for you to drift off the path of righteousness, but God wants you to stay focused on the light that will keep you out of darkness. This is why you must have your feet shod with the preparation of the Gospel of Jesus Christ. If your feet are not in the Gospel, then you stand a strong chance of having them planted in darkness.

There are many distractions that can influence the placement of your feet, but you must stand firm in the Lord and follow His way. Follow His way to a greater today and tomorrow. Give way to the things that will keep your feet from darkness, and watch more doors open for you from the Lord. Have your feet shod with the preparation of the Gospel, and dust them off when needed. Hopefully, you won't have to dust your feet off in the places that you frequent the most. Amen.

April 28

> Now we, brethren, as Isaac was, are children of
> promise. (Galatians 4:28)

You can't depend on the ziplock seal of man because when things get hot in your life, the seal of man will melt away. Similarly, the welding of iron can't seal you stronger than the promise of God. You are supernaturally sealed if you are a child of God. There is no flame hot enough to melt you away from the promise of God.

The promise of God seals and delivers you away from the immediate snares of Satan. Satan convinced a third of angels to follow him, and today he uses trickery and lies to convince others to walk with him. His intent is centered in his hate that you are in the promise of God.

Knowing you are a child of promise too, please reflect the image of God. Satan hates to see the many promises of God walking the earth. Be a greater reflection of His image today as it is better to live in a promise than in a lie. Help others in their walk today. Remind them that they are children of the promise too. In Jesus's name! Amen.

April 29

> But from there you will seek the LORD your God,
> and you will find Him if you seek Him with all your
> heart and with all your soul. (Deuteronomy 4:29)

A magnet's invisible magnetic field (love) either attracts or repels. Magnets attract when a north pole (God) is introduced to a south pole (Christians), which is a holy form of spiritual magnetism.

This highlights that it's the internal properties within an individual that determine if he/she can find God.

God has made himself available through His only begotten Son. Jesus Christ purifies us to be able to be in the presence of the Father. We have to walk as He did so we can find the Father. Jesus Christ provides His Word to also teach us how to remain clean enough in preparation of us finding God.

The Lord wants to be found, and if you have clean hands and a pure heart, you will be able to find Him. Even if you had a flare-up, road rage incident, or have spoken words you shouldn't have spoken, please know that it's not too late to be clean again. Repent if needed, and forgive the ones that you need to forgive. It's the absence of repentance and forgiveness that could keep God's presence from you too. Seek Him with the intent to bring Him more glory. Consecrate yourself today, and enjoy His presence. In Jesus's name! Amen.

April 30

> And do not grieve the Holy Spirit of God, by whom you were sealed for the day of redemption. (Ephesians 4:30)

It is not easy for a child to understand why their parents are extremely upset when they do negative things. Most parents are upset because they spent valuable time training their child up, and to witness them conduct themselves contrary to the training can be quite frustrating.

Jesus Christ provided precise guidance, and He walked the walk, referencing how we are to conduct ourselves. He ensured we received every nugget to help us properly reflect the image of God. We have no excuses! We must walk like Jesus Christ so the Holy Spirit can work within us. The Holy Spirit can't work in a dirty house, so please keep yours clean.

Evaluate your attitude before you go about the rest of your day because your attitude drives your actions. Those things influence you, in pleasing or grieving the Holy Spirit. All Christians' daily aim should be to please the Almighty Father while steering clear of those things that will grieve Him. Grieving is a manifestation of certain thoughts not pleasing to God. God provided the Holy Spirit as a seal of His spiritual purity and not of obscurity; thus, we must consistently conduct ourselves in a manner of respect of that which is within us. You are a glory carrier, and within that glory is the Holy Spirit who is absent of grieving. Claim it, frame it, and hang it in your heart! Amen.

MAY

May God's grace, goodness, and favor continue to cover your household. He provides the best coverage with the best benefits!

May 1

> Therefore, having been justified by faith, we have peace with God through our Lord Jesus Christ. (Romans 5:1)

In the military, special forces go places were normal soldiers don't go. They are specially trained and equipped to handle all situations. They pave the way for others to follow. They are elite and have faith that they are the best at what they do. Their belief and faith fuel their training and missions.

Jesus Christ is our Special Force! He went where no other force wanted to go! He went to the cross for His people. He was specifically equipped with faith the size of the universe.

He conquered and paved the way for us.

When that time comes today for you to lean on your faith, please remember that you are paving the way for others to follow. You may have to be that special force for someone today. Don't look for approvals or pats on your back as your rewards will be greater than those. Believe that you are making a difference even when most don't believe so. As long as the Lord can see your sacrifice, that's the greatest reward to receive. His eyes are on you!

Claim it, frame it, and hang it in your heart! In Jesus's name! Amen.

May 2

> Give heed to the voice of my cry, my King and
> my God, for to You I will pray. (Psalm 5:2)

When you were a kid, do you remember whose name you called when you got hurt? Have you noticed that when children get hurt, they know to call for "mommy" or "daddy." Even if the parents didn't teach them to call them when they get hurt, the children automatically do it. That's because of the relationships they have with their parents.

Your strong relationship with Jesus Christ will keep His name at the front of your thoughts. When you get hurt or are in need of assistance, you will automatically call His name because of your relationship with Him. No other name should come out of your mouth before His name. He will answer you with precision and help you make the best decision.

Cry out to Him as soon as possible. Please don't let your day get started without releasing what could weigh you down all day. You can call this person or that person, but the ear of the Lord is the best place to rest your cares. He will answer the prayers of those that reflect His image. If you are reflecting His image, then expect an immediate answer. Trust and believe! He is waiting! Pray in Jesus's name! Amen.

May 3

> Blessed are the poor in spirit, For theirs is the
> kingdom of heaven. (Matthew 5:3)

If you use the proper ingredients, you increase the probability of preparing a great meal. Some chefs mix in different ingredients to add to the dishes that they are preparing with the intent to create great results. In many instances, chefs have figured out that there are some ingredients that will never work with particular dishes.

Pride, greed, an inflated ego; love of money; and other distracting ingredients will never mix with grace. Those ingredients block the humble pie from rising. Jesus Christ is the ultimate humble pie, and He wants all of God's children to come taste and see that He is good.

The only way to taste Jesus is to be poor in spirit. Satan wants to manipulate most to believe that they don't need Jesus nor more of Him. Satan is not poor in spirit, and he wants others to follow his lead. He was not humbled in who he was in the kingdom. His lack of humbleness led to his eviction.

Remain humble in spirit, and keep thirsting after God. Keep pursing more of Him. Keep wanting Him to use you more and more. The humbled will be utilized to greater degrees for the Lord. Stay humble, my friend! The reason why the proud don't eat humble pie is because the ingredients contain grace! Amen.

May 4

> Blessed are those who mourn, for they shall be comforted. (Matthew 5:4)

The Hoover Dam, levies, and other structures prevent water from flowing down into particular areas. If the water is allowed to flow, it will saturate the lands and cause flooding. Sometimes the water needs to flow because particular lands need the water to help the environment prosper.

The Almighty Father wants your tears to flow. He doesn't want you to hold them back, especially when you are mourning. Just like the water needs to flow to particular lands to help the environment prosper, your mourning helps in receiving the comfort for your heart and mind.

When someone mourns, they are projecting a sincere expression of their heart. Jesus expressed a sincere expression of His heart when He was mourning for Lazarus. He let His mourning flow. If you know someone that's mourning or if you are mourning, please know that it can help resurrect the heart and mind of others too. Please let your mourning flow, and the Almighty Father will provide the comfort needed for you and others. Your mourning adds to the pillow of comfort the Lord wants to provide for you. Mourn and receive the pillow of comfort needed to bring the peace to your heart and mind. Amen.

May 5

> Blessed are the meek, for they shall inherit the earth. (Matthew 5:5)

Parents institute allowances for their children with conditions. Guidelines are set, and if they are met, then the children will receive the allowance. Most allowances are given in the form of money and some in other ways. Hopefully, you received all your allowances if you were promised them.

The Bible provides conditions that we must meet so that we can receive blessings and favor. Look at it as a quid pro quo system instituted by the Lord. It's a system that is divine and will never be broken. Do you want to receive more blessings and favor from God? If yes, please meet His conditions.

Be patient, not easily angered, and selfless throughout your day. These things will allow you to maintain the control that's needed to overcome the pressures of the day. Some days can be more overwhelming than others, and the meekness you exude today will be beneficial to so many others. Amen.

May 6

> Blessed are those who hunger and thirst for righteousness, for they shall be filled. (Matthew 5:6)

When we see movies about astronauts in space, we see them wearing helmets. Those helmets are connected to oxygen since there is no oxygen in space. No human can survive in space without oxygen. Similarly, no one can live in heaven without righteousness.

Righteousness is received from the Lord our God since He is the King of Righteousness. He will provide it to those who desire it as they reflect His image. This is also why the Word teaches us that none (no humans) are righteous, but know that He that resides in us is righteous. We must hunger and thirst for righteousness because it also keeps us in the presence of the Lord. Do you want righteousness?

Your day will be blessed today because you are thirsting for that which helped to create today. Righteousness is a building block of the Lord's image, so desire it throughout your day. Desire it as it will help you counsel and console someone. Let the Lord fill you up with it, and let it overflow into those that He places in your path. Receive righteousness in Jesus's name. Amen.

May 7

Blessed are the merciful, for they shall obtain mercy. (Matthew 5:7)

Have you ever thrown a boomerang? It will come back to you. It doesn't seem as if it will come back to you after you throw it, but as you watch it take flight, it will return to you.

This is how mercy works too. If you give mercy, you shall receive it. The Almighty Father didn't have to create us, sustain us, nor send His only begotten Son, but He did. Mercy is factored into those things, and mercy is available for us every day if we give it as the Lord has given it to us.

You have to give mercy to many individuals that you don't like, especially those that have hurt you. Mercy and forgiveness are an awesome team, and when you give them, they help you win. Keep winning today! Let mercy flow like the air you are breathing. Let it be effortlessly given, and you shall receive it likewise from our Savior. Amen.

May 8

> Blessed are the pure in heart, for they shall see
> God. (Matthew 5:8)

Have you ever been to the Luray Caverns? It is a beautiful place to visit. The caverns are a joy to view, but the viewing of Crystal Lake caps an awesome tour. The water is pure and still, which provides a mirror reflection of the structure above it. If the water wasn't pure and still, it wouldn't be as wonderful to view.

Only the ones with clean hands and a pure heart can ascend to the hill of the Lord. The pure heart allows the blood of Jesus to flow throughout the bodies of those that believe in Him. It's His blood that allows us to be in the presence of His Father.

Your pure heart helps you in reflecting the image of God. We were created in His image, and a pure heart is one of the main components of reflecting His image. There are things that arise throughout our days that will allow us to showcase the spiritual status of our hearts. Showcase the purity of your heart as Jesus did. Do it under all circumstances, and you will benefit according to the promises of our Lord. Amen.

May 9

> Blessed are the peacemakers, for they shall be
> called sons of God. (Matthew 5:9)

Referees play major roles in sporting events. They are instituted to ensure the participants follow the rules and guidelines. In many instances during sporting events, we can see the need of them as they help to enforce discipline too. In other instances, some individuals do not like them because they help to stop cheaters, rule-breakers, and other selfish individuals that impact the good order and discipline of the sporting events.

Jesus is the Prince of Peace. He has provided His Word to help His children finish the race. His children must imitate Him through enforcing the rules and guidelines too while becoming children of peace, which also makes us peacemakers. Everyone doesn't like us peacemakers, but we must press on imitating the Prince of Peace.

You may be thrust into a situation to be a peacemaker, and the individuals involved may not like your intervention, but it must be done. You can't turn a blind eye to a situation that needs peace. Relationships, arguments, fights, and other situations need your prayers and sometimes your physical attention. Please seek the Lord before you proceed. Amen.

May 10

> Blessed are those who are persecuted for righteousness' sake, for theirs is the kingdom of heaven. (Matthew 5:10)

How many years have you been working? In those years, you have worked thousands of hours and were paid for those hours. You've also worked and received overtime pay, and there were times when you were not paid for the extra work. Your mind is conditioned for the work for pay system, thus preparing you for working and getting paid for kingdom work.

We are to be living sacrifices for the kingdom of God, and He will pay us according to His will. As followers of Jesus Christ, many have been and many more will be persecuted for His sake, and He has promised to reward us. We need not worry about the persecution because vengeance is the Lord's. Our persecutors will receive the wrath of God, and we shall receive His blessings and favor.

Please do not let the changing world impact your work for the kingdom. Fear not, for the Lord is with you! When reflecting the image of God, you have to stand firm in His commandments, knowing that your actions make a difference for Him. The ones that persecute you have to answer to a wrath that they can't recover from, so press on for the Lord our God. Amen.

May 11

> Therefore comfort each other and edify one another,
> just as you also are doing. (1 Thessalonians 5:11)

In building team cohesion, the military has confidence courses. As you maneuver through the courses, there are some obstacles that require teamwork. You have to help your teammate overcome the obstacle, or your team can't advance. Families should consider engaging obstacle courses as the courses can be great teaching tools too. That's if the whole family is physically able to do so.

Jesus Christ overcame the greatest obstacles for us, His family. The Almighty Father comforted and lifted Him up, setting the example for us to follow. We have to love our neighbors as we love ourselves in comforting and edifying one another.

Comforting and edifying someone doesn't require physical interaction. Your prayers, words, and presence are enough. This is true if you are reflecting the image of God. There are many individuals that are in need of comfort and edifying so they can overcome some obstacles that most can't see. They are hurting internally, and your efforts may help to save a life or lives. You may be in need of comfort too, and no one knows it, but comfort is on the way. Give it, and watch it return to you. The greatest things you can do today is to comfort and edify someone, especially if they are not expecting it from you. Do it in love! Do it while not seeking anything in return. Do it knowing that someone will be blessed. Do it in Jesus's name. Amen.

May 12

> For You, O LORD, will bless the righteous; with
> favor You will surround him as with a shield.
> (Psalm 5:12)

It is said that during battles, kings were protected as they maneuvered through the battlefield. They were surrounded by skilled men most of the time, which helped them to survive during battles. The righteous has to be protected!

God's favor will protect the righteous ones too. You are royalty since you are a child of God. He is within you, so righteousness is within you. He provides favor to those that reflect His image. Keep reflecting His image, and witness His favor flowing in your life.

Every day you go into battle, so go about your day knowing that the Lord has surrounded you with favor. Don't worry about the battles you lost in the past when you didn't have God's favor upon you. Today is a new day. You are a child of the Righteous One. He ensures His obedient children receive more than expected. Expect His favor as He blocks anything spoken against you. Expect His favor to comfort you, and provide the peace you need for today. Expect His favor to win your spiritual battles too. Claim it, frame it, and hang it in your heart. Amen.

May 13

> For you, brethren, have been called to liberty; only do not use liberty as an opportunity for the flesh, but through love serve one another. (Galatians 5:13)

Prisoners are set free when they have served their time. They are expected to be better citizens within the communities. It is expected that they have learned from past mistakes and will live a clean life now that they are free. Are you maximizing your freedom from your past life?

The Almighty Father wants all of His children to be free on earth as they will be free in paradise. Jesus Christ paid the ransom for us to be free. He has also ensured that neither Satan nor death locks us away from freedom. We are free to walk in love and uplift one another in the way of Jesus Christ.

You are free to do many things with your life, and since the Son has set you free, please use your freedom to love your neighbor.

Everyone that you encounter today may not have experienced brotherly love but you can bless someone today. When the opportunity presents itself, please take advantage of it; you will be bringing God more glory by uplifting another child of God. Thanks in advance for spreading the love of God today. In Jesus's name! Amen.

May 14

> You are the light of the world. A city that is set on
> a hill cannot be hidden. (Matthew 5:14)

One of the purposes of a light bulb is to provide light to dark areas. There are different types of light bulbs, but essentially all of them provide light. They help to stop people from stumbling in darkness, and they enlighten areas to expose hidden things.

Jesus Christ came and is the light that all needed to see. We had to see what right looks like, so God sent His only begotten Son to show us how to properly shine our lights. Reflecting the image of God allows His light to shine through us too. Darkness can't stand in the presence of the light, so please keep reflecting His image.

You have to stand out. You have to be the light that God wants you to be. There are many individuals watching you but are not telling you that they are watching you. You are inspiring them, and they feed off of your light. Know that your walk is unique as it doesn't require you to be in everyone's presence to have an impact on them. Your light is impacting many individuals, and they will let you know in due time if not already. Thanks for reflecting the light from the light, which helps those trapped in darkness. Amen.

May 15

> And if we know that He hears us, whatever we
> ask, we know that we have the petitions that we
> have asked of Him. (1 John 5:15)

God is the only resource that can provide every resource that we need. He is not capped! He is not limited! He is always willing and able to provide for His children. He can do exceeding abundantly above all we ask, so let's ensure we maintain clean hands and pure hearts. We have to repent if need be and forgive too. We must keep ourselves in position to receive what we are asking for.

In the beginning, the Bible says that the Almighty Father spoke to Jesus and Jesus let those things manifest. This is an awesome teaching element for all believers because we must reflect the image of God if we want Jesus to allow our requests to manifest. Are you reflecting the image of God?

If you are reflecting the image of God, your request is guaranteed to be heard by the Father. He tunes into those that walk like Him. We are not on this earth to live from paycheck to paycheck. He wants us to live in freedom, in abundance, and in joy. He is Almighty and will grant us mighty things, so please don't hesitate to ask Him for anything as long as it is to bring Him glory. Ask in Jesus's name today, and receive according to His will. Amen.

May 16

> Confess your trespasses to one another, and pray for one another, that you may be healed. The effective, fervent prayer of a righteous man avails much. (James 5:16)

There are many medicines that we can take to help us heal. Health professionals also provide guidance, referencing procedures to help us heal. Even today you might need healing, and there are medicines or procedures that can help you, but please consider calling on the name of Jesus first.

Jesus Christ stands in the gap for us. The Almighty Father sent Him because He was ready. He was ready to trample upon all enemies in His Father's name. He is available to heal you too. By His stripes you are healed! We must imitate Jesus in being ready for kingdom work too.

Some of the healing that's needed is more spiritual than natural. If someone calls you today in need of you standing in the gap for them, are you prepared for spiritual battle? The best way to be prepared is having clean hands and a pure heart while being in praying and fasting mode. There are some individuals that need your assistance today with them winning spiritual battles. Are you ready? You may be the difference in expediting victory for a neighbor. Thanks in advance for helping someone win another spiritual battle. Your prayers are an element of victory! Trust and believe! Amen.

May 17

> Therefore, if anyone is in Christ, he is a new creation; old things have passed away; behold, all things have become new. (2 Corinthians 5:17)

In the military, it is an honor to advance to the next rank. One of the hardest transitions is going from E-4 to E-5. The promotion requires you to be stronger, a leader, a trainer, more courageous, and much better than you used to be. It's not easy for everyone to transition into the new role, but it must be done. Similarly, you must transition into the new creation in Christ so that you can be more effective for the kingdom.

Jesus Christ showed us how we must walk as new creations. He showed us that we must do next-level work for the kingdom. He showed us that we can do greater works. He showed us that the power of God will assist us in our efforts for the Father. The power of God will help you do greater works for the kingdom as a new creation.

You know that you are in Christ as a new creation when the old things are truly gone. This is why the fire is also needed to burn away the things that prevent the indwelling of the Holy Spirit. Go about your day being an awesome new creation, knowing that you are making a difference for the kingdom. You are needed more than you know. You have become a new creation to do greater works, and those greater works help others do greater works. Thanks in advance for being another awesome new creation in Christ. Amen.

May 18

> In everything give thanks; for this is the will of God
> in Christ Jesus for you. (1 Thessalonians 5:18)

When a movie is made, you can watch it over and over again. If someone hasn't seen it before, you can narrate the movie for them. This is similar to the will of God. The movie of life is already done in the will of God, so be thankful in every episode of it.

God has declared the ending before the beginning, which means He has already prepared your blessings. Even when it doesn't look good, it will be good. This is also why we have to count it all joy. So give thanks in everything, because as long as you are flowing in the will of God, all things will be for your good.

The mercy of God allows you to be here today. No matter the good or the bad that you experience today, please give thanks to be able to go through it. Many individuals live life taking God for granted because they forgot He is Almighty or don't know He is Almighty. In Jesus Christ's name, please walk in Him and give thanks in everything because even in giving thanks for what you see is a bad situation can help expedite the revelation of the good in it. Amen.

May 19

> We know that we are of God, and the whole
> world lies under the sway of the wicked one.
> (1 John 5:19)

In particular buildings, the superintendent is responsible for maintenance and in some situations the rent too. It's all dependent upon the direction of the owner of the building. Some superinten-dents can be extremely abusive, which is why some owners make frequent visits to their properties.

Satan was cast down to earth and is called the prince of the power of the air. He operates similar to an abusive superintendent. He hasn't stopped being a spiritual bully, so let's forge offensive efforts against him and his children. We can't always be on the defensive, so let's be on the offensive and inform the wicked one that his sway has no play with us. The Holy Spirit will highlight the sway for you and help you stay away from the snares of the wicked one.

This is why you must have the indwelling of the Holy Spirit! He helps you in dealing with and overcoming the wicked one. Please remember that Jesus Christ has all power and authority in heaven and earth. He is the way, the truth, and the life! The wicked one has a sway, but you have the way! The way overcomes the sway with ease, so please stay within the way. There are some individuals that you know have been influenced by the sway to stay away from church, but please help them break away from the snare they are in. Please pray and fast about this, then go forth helping someone else being more than a conqueror. In Jesus's name! Amen.

May 20

> When He saw their faith, He said to him, "Man,
> your sins are forgiven you." (Luke 5:20)

It's best to be able to follow a good example. Following a good example can save time and prevent unnecessary mistakes. Have you followed a good example? Have you set a good example for others? Has your example helped others? Jesus Christ is the greatest example to follow!

Jesus Christ set an awesome example for all of us to follow. His faith saves over a trillion souls. His faith paved the way for our faith. His faith can't be matched. His faith is the foundation that is the fountain of faith. Our faith must flow in His faith so we can help others too. He is always looking for those will faith the size of mustard seed or greater.

He can see your faith. Your faith can help others in need too. Use your faith to intercede for a friend today. There are so many individuals that need your faith to help them. Your faith can also be utilized like a bridge to help others receive supernatural help. Please pray about whom you can help today. In Jesus's name! Amen.

May 21

> For the ways of man are before the eyes of the LORD,
> And He ponders all his paths. (Proverbs 5:21)

The latest home security systems provide the capability for homeowners to view the majority of their home. Parents use the systems to check on their children and babysitters too. The omnipresence of the Lord is a supernatural security system that protects His obedient children. As you stay in His presence, He identifies the intruders and deals with them accordingly.

God is all-seeing! He sees and knows everything about you. He knows who is trying to plot against you, and He knows how to defeat them. Let Him order your steps so you can stay on the paths that He has blessed for you.

The Lord saw what you did yesterday. He will see what you do today too. He has already tuned into your channel before you started reading this. He requires your obedience so He can bless your comings and goings. Know that He is watching you, so walk in love and in the Spirit. Please God in all your ways today. Amen.

May 22

> But the fruit of the Spirit is love, joy, peace, longsuffering, kindness, goodness, faithfulness. (Galatians 5:22)

Some inspectors or auditors have checklists. The checklists assist them when they are completing inspections, audits, or evaluations. If you have ever utilized a checklist, you know that they are tools that can be utilized to gauge, examine, and account for things. Similarly, God has provided you a checklist to gauge yourself and others.

The fruit of the Spirit is a checklist. It helps to keep us on track for the Lord. The fruit of the Spirit provides a healthy spiritual diet that's needed to help the body of Christ. The fruit of the Spirit can also be utilized to gauge growth, maturity, and the understanding of a believer.

Utilize the fruit of the Spirit to complete your personal evaluation. Doing this will assist you in knowing what type of tree you are and what tree you are partaking of. It will help you get back on track and help you identify others that walk in the Spirit. The fruit will keep you ready to be utilized by our Lord. Let the fruit help you win every day. Let the fruit help you win today in Jesus's name. Amen.

May 23

> And begged Him earnestly, saying, "My little daughter lies at the point of death. Come and lay Your hands on her, that she may be healed, and she will live." (Mark 5:23)

There are different types of automotive repair businesses. Some businesses do all types of car repair, and some specialize in particular areas of vehicle repair. Jesus is like the repair shop that can repair all vehicle issues. Jesus is the one-stop shop!

Jesus showed His supernatural healing power many times throughout the Bible. He is available today to perform more miracles. He is willing if we are willing to maintain clean hands and pure hearts. Are you in need of healing? Are you in need of a miracle? Do you know someone else that is in need of healing from Jesus? Jesus can do it!

If you want to see a miracle, look in the mirror. You are a walking miracle. You can help others be miracles too. Continue to make yourself available for praying and fasting with and for others. Sometimes, another's faith can help someone else be healed (see Luke 5:20). Stay as clean as possible so you can help someone experience being a miracle. This is your reasonable service. Amen.

May 24

> Most assuredly, I say to you, he who hears My word and believes in Him who sent Me has everlasting life, and shall not come into judgment, but has passed from death into life. (John 5:24)

Have you ever cosigned for a car? Did the other person default on the loan? Did you have to pay the loan off, or was the car reposed? It is a bad situation to be in, especially if the other person makes no efforts in the agreement. A situation like this is similar to a Christian not doing their part after they accept Jesus Christ as Lord and Savior.

The Almighty Father gave His only begotten Son, and His Son is the only one that can cosign for us. He paid the debt to free us and to keep us. We are His investments, and we must keep improving so He can receive great returns on His investments. He cosigned for us knowing who would please Him and who would disappoint Him. Are you pleasing Him?

You can't cosign for anyone to get into paradise. None of us can give salvation, but many believe they save people. Jesus Christ is the only one that can save souls, and we have to be aligned with Him so He can use us to assist Him in saving souls. He has paid the debt for those that want to enter into paradise, and your obedience helps to reach others that He has invested in. Thanks in advance for helping Jesus receive greater returns on His investments. Amen.

May 25

> If we live in the Spirit, let us also walk in the
> Spirit. (Galatians 5:25)

The mirror can't lie. It provides the exact reflection of whom or what is standing in front of it. Seeing your reflection also helps rearrange your image to your liking, and it helps you to verify that you are ready to walk out in the public among others. Ensure your image is appropriate before you start walking among others.

Jesus Christ reflected His Father's image best. The Almighty Father let it be known that He was pleased with His Son. When the Spirit came upon Jesus, it rested within Him. He showed us how to walk in the Spirit. He remained clean, and we have to reflect the image of God so we can walk in the Spirit too.

Are you reflecting the image of God? You don't have to answer the question for yourself. Others can answer the question for you. There are many in the earth realm and the spirit realm that can answer the question. Ensure you are walking in the Spirit because those in the spirit realm look for those without the indwelling of the Holy Spirit. Walk in love because the Spirit is love, and if you find yourself not walking in love, then you are not walking in the Spirit. Repent if need be. Forgive if need be. You have to be clean to walk in the Spirit. Your walk is not only about you but is also about helping others. Please walk in the Spirit and let Him use you to help others walk in Him too. Helped people help people! Amen.

May 26

> Assuredly, I say to you, you will by no means
> get out of there till you have paid the last penny.
> (Matthew 5:26)

You are free when you have no debts and can travel when, where, and however long you chose with zero restraints. Until you have addressed your debtors, you are not as free as you need to be. Being in debt keeps you restricted, and you must do your part to be free as soon as possible.

Jesus Christ paid the debt for us to be free. He has set us free, and we must not enslave ourselves to anything or anyone. We are chained to the Gospel of Jesus Christ and must help others be freed from spiritual prisons of darkness.

You are a child of God, which means you are free indeed. You are free because you have accepted Jesus Christ as Lord and Savior, and He has cleansed you. You know you must repent of your sins to help you get back into the presence of the Lord. Those that refuse to stop sinning and reject Jesus are in a prison; you can't congregate with them. However, please be ready to help them come out of the spiritual prisons of darkness that they are in. You are a difference-maker equipped with the light that overcomes darkness. Reflect the light for others and yourself so as to avoid those prisons. Amen.

May 27

> When she heard about Jesus, she came behind
> Him in the crowd and touched His garment.
> (Mark 5:27)

When we are new to an area and are in need of a primary-care physician, we have to use reviews to help narrow down our choice of doctors. The reviews help in making a decision but not necessarily the best decision. The reason we seek a doctor is because there are questions that we do not have an answer for.

Our Great Physician has proven to be our answer. He can heal a whole country with one word. There is neither disease nor illness that He can't cure. Where it would take hours and days for man to come up with a possible cure, the Lord can cure anything in a moment. He is willing to heal, right now!

You might be in need of healing right now. It might be something that you don't know about, but Jesus can heal it right now.

You may have been told that it can't be healed, but the Lord can do exceedingly abundantly above all we can ask. Asking for healing must be done in faith. Your faith is part of the equation of healing. Jesus is available to heal us if only we touch His spiritual garment with our faith. Your faith can go to places that your physical body can't go. It can connect to the supernatural, helping to bring forth miracles, signs, and wonders. Ask for healing right now in Jesus's name! Claim it, frame it, and hang it in your heart. Amen.

May 28

> But I say to you that whoever looks at a woman
> to lust for her has already committed adultery
> with her in his heart. (Matthew 5:28)

We've always heard that you are innocent until proven guilty. In the court of law, evidence has to be presented before the court to prove guilt or someone can admit to being guilty as charged. Until evidence it confirmed or until a confession is provided, a person is innocent. Are you innocent or guilty of not pleasing God?

God knows our hearts and our minds like we know how many fingers and toes we have. He can look into the areas that we can't see. He knows your heart right now. He knows if you need to repent, forgive, or confess. Please know that it takes a pure heart to approach the Lord.

Your heart contains the evidence that convicts you. Your words can deny the evidence but can't change the evidence in your heart. Your heart has to remain clean so you won't be prevented from approaching the Lord. If you find yourself drifting in an area that doesn't please God, then please repent ASAP. Not repenting is similar to keeping a wall between you and the Lord. Let your innocent heart be lacking evidence to convict you of things that displease the Lord. Amen.

May 29

> But Peter and the other apostles answered and
> said: "We ought to obey God rather than men."
> (Acts 5:29)

A doctor has proven that he or she is capable of functioning in areas of their expertise. If you go to see one of them and they are not in the office for that day, there is no way you are going to allow a receptionist to examine you.

Jesus Christ said that His Father is greater than them all. There is none greater than God, and therefore there is no word greater than His Word. His Word contains guidance and more that requires your obedience.

You have seen in your lifetime that it is best to follow what has been proven than to follow the unproven. Many have made promises and can't keep them, but God is most faithful to see all His promises through for you. He wants you to first obey His commandments and statues so that you can prosper. He wants to be in your presence more and more, but this requires obedience on your part. Obey the proven God! Obey Him without seeking anything in return. Obey Him in love. Obey Him in truth. Obey Him like Jesus obeyed Him! Amen.

May 30

> I can of Myself do nothing. As I hear, I judge;
> and My judgment is righteous, because I do not
> seek My own will but the will of the Father who
> sent Me. (John 5:30)

Wisdom is an awesome teacher! Elders have experiences that younger individuals or novice can benefit from. Unfortunately, most young people and novice believe they have it all figured out. Just like a puzzle can't put itself together, neither can you! Let God!

God declared the end from the beginning, knowing all that will happen in between the two points. Between those two points is everything that He has already blessed for you. All you have to do is surrender to Him and allow Him to guide you to the treasures that He wants to release to you.

Surrender to God instead of going against what He has laid out for you. You have proven how far you can take yourself, so let God show you how far He can take you. Submitting yourself to the will of the Father opens unseen doors with countless blessings. Let Him lead you! Let God! Claim it, frame it, and hang it in your heart! Amen.

May 31

> For this reason a man shall leave his father and mother and be joined to his wife, and the two shall become one flesh. (Ephesians 5:31)

If you place two seeds together, they won't grow. If you place soil with soil, they won't grow. This is why seed must be placed with soil. A true gardener knows this basic concept and continues the process so as to keep producing. A seed can live by itself but is most relevant when it is sown in good ground.

God pulled soil from the earth and joined it with a seed of His to produce man, then later He formed woman from the man. God used Adam and Eve to set the proper tone in matrimony. They didn't become one spiritual body, but they became one flesh through the love of God. God sent His only begotten Son who is the seed. The seed was sent to earth and became one with His bride.

Your union must imitate how Christ loves the church. Christ and the church live for eternity because of love. It is love that strengthens and keeps your relationship together as it keeps Christ and the church together. Christ came to become one with the church, and no one can separate them as no one can separate your marriage if it is of God. Marriage is becoming one loving flesh as the church has become one with the Author of love. Amen.

JUNE

You are at the midway point of the year, and you have to remain focused. Things can become mundane, but you have to do things that add a spark to your household. Break up the routines to add awesome memories.

June 1

> Take heed that you do not do your charitable
> deeds before men, to be seen by them. Otherwise
> you have no reward from your Father in heaven.
> (Matthew 6:1)

There are many factors that help to define a great meal. One of the most important factors is the food being cooked properly, especially baked meat. If you take it out too soon, it will make the overall meal bad. Most of the time this happens if the baker is anxious or a novice in cooking. In life, you can't be anxious to tell man things to please them, or the end results may not be pleasing.

Jesus came in the name of His Father, completing the work for the kingdom. Many individuals misunderstood His purpose and were convinced He was on assignment to please them, but He stayed the course to please His Father. If your focus is to please God, then man will receive fewer notifications of your efforts.

Christian work is through Christ to please the Father, not man. Be anxious for nothing, especially not to please man in your works, to include charitable deeds. Its ok to complete your charitable deeds without displaying them on social media and group text messages so as to please man. God's eye on your charitable deeds is enough. He will allow the worthy to witness your charitable deeds according to His will. Be content in pleasing God alone and receive rewards beyond measure. Amen.

June 2

> Have mercy on me, O LORD, for I am weak;
> O LORD, heal me, for my bones are troubled.
> (Psalm 6:2)

Normally, when someone is stranded and they can make a sign either on the ground or via usage of material, they create an SOS. The SOS is a sign of distress, and the maker of the sign is in need of rescue or help. Do you need the Lord right now? Send your SOS to Him now! Send it via prayer!

Throughout the Bible, we see God healing His children. He is the Great Physician. He is equipped to heal anything. Call on Him for the healing that you need, knowing that He has never been and will never be associated to malpractice. He is the only one that can heal simultaneously in the earth and spiritual realms. Ask Him for healing with the intent of Him getting more glory.

Please examine yourself; repent if need be, and ensure that you are not walking in unforgiveness. You want to make sure there is nothing preventing you from being healed by the Lord. Please pray and send your request to Him now. If you are not in need of healing, please pray for someone else to be healed. Trust and believe the Lord's healing is on the way. Claim it, frame it, and hang it in your heart! In Jesus's name! Amen.

June 3

> So do this, my son, and deliver yourself; For
> you have come into the hand of your friend: Go
> and humble yourself; Plead with your friend.
> (Proverbs 6:3)

When we get loans for our cars and our homes, the financial institutions follow the guidelines within the loan agreements to recoup their money. Very seldom do they have mercy on the borrowers. It would be great if they would have mercy on us when we humble ourselves and ask them for mercy. This is why we must to be lenders instead of borrowers.

Jesus humbled Himself to complete the Father's business, and He did it at the highest degree. We have to humble ourselves too. We don't have everything figured out, and humbling ourselves to another helps to usher in grace. Pride gets in the way of being humble. Keep pride away as it is similar to a wall.

Your Christian friends have received mercy and grace from Jesus Christ, and they are most likely to give both to you too. When you are living the truth and walking in the Spirit, it is easier for you to humble yourself. Know that humbling yourself is better than crumbling yourself! Humbling yourself is a form of inner strength instead of a sign of weakness. It takes a strong person to humble themselves when they are used to being independent and strong. Your real friends will bless you! Amen.

June 4

> And you, fathers, do not provoke your children
> to wrath, but bring them up in the training and
> admonition of the Lord. (Ephesians 6:4)

For every action, there's a reaction. Some parents have told their children that if someone hits them, then they need to hit them back.

That teaching if carried through to adult stage would have an impact on how you raise your children. If every time your children lash out at you and then you lash out back at them, it sets them up for failure because you are not displaying the restraint they need to learn. Have patience with them, and be slow to wrath, lest you train them to wrath.

The Almighty Father has had next-level patience watching some of His children in their disobedience. He could've wiped humanity out of the universe, but because of His mercy and grace, we are still here. He has shown all of us how we must deal with our children. He has always been firm with love during the correcting or reprimanding of His children. He set the best examples in raising children.

A father has to remember that for every action, there is a reaction. A child's mind is still developing, and they haven't developed the restraint as many adults have. As hard as it is sometimes, please show them the mercy that will help develop them in becoming mercy carriers too. They are sponges to firm correction if it is delivered in love. Let love lead you during the reprimanding of your children as it helps to bring forth the best results. Amen.

June 5

> And when you pray, you shall not be like the hypocrites. For they love to pray standing in the synagogues and on the corners of the streets, that they may be seen by men. Assuredly, I say to you, they have their reward. (Matthew 6:5)

There are numerous famous entertainers in Hollywood, music, and sports. Most people know more entertainers than the producers behind the scenes. The producers get some attention, but not at the level of the entertainers. They get less attention while making a huge impact. That's how we must be in praying. Let's pray behind the scenes to make a greater impact through the Lord.

Every time Jesus prayed, He didn't make Himself a spectacle, nor did He pray for it to be a form of entertainment. Praying to God is sacred and should be conducted as such. The only eyes and ears that need to be on your prayers are the ones that created your eyes and ears.

Your prayer time should be protected. It should be uninterrupted. It is your special time with the Almighty Father, and you have to make every moment count. Remember to be silent for a moment to see if He is going to speak to you. The Lord may not want to answer you in the presence of others, so please consider praying in secret more. Praying to be seen could render you unseen in the eyes of the Lord. Let the hypocrites receive their attention from man and lose blessings while you pray in secret and avoid a painful lesson. Amen.

June 6

> I am weary with my groaning; All night I make
> my bed swim; I drench my couch with my tears.
> (Psalm 6:6)

If you blow a balloon up with the air from your lungs, the balloon won't take flight, but if helium is blown into the balloon, then it will take flight. Just like helium is needed to help balloons take flight, tears are like helium as they inflate your request to the Lord to bring forth blessings.

God hears the sincere cries of His children. Many individuals have cried in the Bible, but none more important than Christ. Jesus wept for Lazarus, and shortly afterward, we see the supernatural work to create a miracle. Weep like the Lord!

Cry out to God. Crying out to a brother or sister in Christ is okay, but they can't answer your tears the way God can. Let your tears flow so He can take them in and comfort you. Your tears are keys to supernatural doors and fuel for blessings. Let the Father see them roll off of your face into His reservoir of favor. In Jesus's name your tears will be answered. Claim it, frame it, and hang it in your heart! Amen.

June 7

> Do not be deceived, God is not mocked; for
> whatever a man sows, that he will also reap.
> (Galatians 6:7)

When driving around some mountains, there are signs that warn you of falling rocks. Some of the rocks that fall are huge. Once those rocks start falling, their momentum won't stop until they have reached a stopping point. This is similar to God's wrath. Once His wrath is in motion, there is nothing that can stop it. He is the only one that can stop His wrath. Please stay out of the path of His wrath.

The Almighty Father's wrath doesn't discriminate. He is most powerful, and it doesn't make sense to place yourself in position to receive His wrath. Reflecting His image keeps you away from His wrath. He loves to be pleased and will reward you accordingly, and He hates to be mocked; hence, He provides His wrath accordingly.

Please ensure that you are walking in His Word and not against it. There are many individuals that are providing trickery, sorcery, and other acts in mockery of God. Please stay away from them because as He releases His wrath like He did upon Sodom and Gomorrah, everyone in the vicinity was in jeopardy of destruction. Please the Lord and avoid His wrath too! Amen.

June 8

> Also I heard the voice of the Lord, saying:
> "Whom shall I send, And who will go for Us?"
> Then I said, "Here am I! Send me." (Isaiah 6:8)

After basic training and other specific training are complete, soldiers have to report for duty. As they report for duty, they have to complete missions for the command. They forge great efforts in completing the missions because that's what they signed up for. When you became a Christian, you signed up to be a soldier for the

Lord, and He wants you to report for duty. Don't be absent without leave (AWOL) from the Lord!

The Lord is always waiting for those that are called by His name! He is looking for them to stand up within themselves and have the fortitude it takes to go forth for Him. He knows there are many individuals within the earth realm that are capable. Are you ready? Greater is He that's within you, so step up and step out for the Lord.

Have you told the Lord, "Here I am"? It is your reasonable service. Not too many Christians have presented themselves to the Lord for kingdom work, but you can do it and do more. You have watched others hide and some be lukewarm, but you can be fire for the Lord and help others. Trust in Him, and let Him use you. Greater works shall you do. In Jesus's name! Amen.

June 9

> And let us not grow weary while doing good,
> for in due season we shall reap if we do not lose
> heart. (Galatians 6:9)

Have you every participated in a marathon? There are many individuals that compete in them to win and some that participate for other reasons. No matter the reason, the objective is to finish the marathon. Life is like a marathon, and God wants His children to press on doing good works, knowing the race is already won.

When the Almighty Father sent His only begotten Son, He knew His Son was going to press on doing good works for the kingdom. He knew His Son was not going to give up. He knew His Son was going to endure until He could no longer endure. He knew these things because Jesus walked in His Father's image in love.

If your heart and mind are properly set, you will be able to press on for the Lord. As you are walking in the image of God, He is expecting you to trust Him. Your efforts are empowered with enough love, so keep doing good, and the Lord is going to open the windows of heaven for you when you least expect it. Do good not to receive anything, but do good knowing that everything you need is already on the way. In Jesus's name! Claim it, frame it, and hang it in your heart! Amen.

June 10

> Finally, my brethren, be strong in the Lord and in
> the power of His might. (Ephesians 6:10)

When a train is moving at full speed, it is extremely powerful. Everything within that moving train is caught within its power too. That's how it is for us when we are moving in the power of His might.

Jesus Christ said that the Almighty Father is greater than them all. He was letting us know that no one is more powerful than His Father. The Word also reminded us that "Greater is He that's within me than he that's within the world." We have to be strong in the greatness within us.

Knowing that you are a child of God and He is most powerful, please do not go forth today in fear. There are many forces at work to deter your thinking and believing. You are on the right track within the most powerful train in the universe. This train, will never derail! Be confident in your efforts knowing that His power sustains you and will uplift you when you are weakened. Believe this in Jesus's name. Amen.

June 11

> Put on the whole armor of God, that you may
> be able to stand against the wiles of the devil.
> (Ephesians 6:11)

When trains were first created, Indians found out that their weapons couldn't harm those within the train. The Indians would try to attack the people within the train, but their efforts were not fruitful. Similarly, when you have the whole armor of God on, you are able to withstand the works of the enemy.

Notice Satan could only approach Jesus but could never overtake Him. Satan couldn't advance against Jesus Christ because the Lord kept on the whole armor of God. He can't win against victory. When Satan approaches you, you must ensure he receives the same results as he received when he encountered Christ.

As you go about your day, know that you are protected against all enemies foreign and domestic. Know that no one can overpower the Lord our God, and since you are within Him, then no one can overpower you. Walk throughout your day with the whole armor of God on. The wicked situations that arise won't stop you from pressing on for the kingdom and other aspects of your life. The enemy knows his works have no power against those that put on the whole armor of God. Keep the whole armor of God on, knowing that today is another day in victory. Amen.

June 12

> For we do not wrestle against flesh and blood, but against principalities, against powers, against the rulers of the darkness of this age, against spiritual hosts of wickedness in the heavenly places. (Ephesians 6:12)

Most boxers shadowbox in preparation for boxing matches. They are not hitting anything, but they are getting mentally prepared for battle. We can't shadowbox in real life as we go into daily spiritual battles. Focusing on flesh and blood instead of the root is just like shadowboxing as you are not hitting the target that needs to go down. Don't allow the enemy to blind you from the root.

Notice that Jesus Christ attacked the root. He knows how to cut down the trees of darkness that's rooted in the works against His children. He won battle after battle, and He is available to win your spiritual battles for you too. He is the Champion of the universe because He is undefeated in both the earth and spiritual realms.

Naturally, our focus is on the enemies we see in the earth realm, but most of the time, our fight is against those things that move like shadows. Please don't stay locked into the fleshly being that you see before you, but seek the Holy Spirit to help you see the darkness that's working against you. Then you will know what to pray for. After the enemy or enemies are identified, pray to God and let Him reach out and touch them for you. The power of God shall overpower them right now if you let Him. Let God in so you can win. Amen.

June 13

> Therefore take up the whole armor of God, that
> you may be able to withstand in the evil day, and
> having done all, to stand. (Ephesians 6:13)

As seen in the past, warriors tried to cover their whole body to help them fight during warfare. If they left an area unprotected, they placed themselves in jeopardy. The enemy is always looking for an opening.

Jesus Christ walked the earth not worried about the attacks of the wicked ones. He was always covered in the armor of His Father. He knew He was setting the example for us to follow. Walking in the armor of God with confidence is bad news for the opposition.

When you leave your house, you have to put on the whole armor of God. You don't know where the spiritual attacks are going to come from. The enemy is crafty and will not always attack you from known angles. As long as you have the whole armor of God on, you are ready for spiritual warfare. Spiritual warfare is not fair, so please beware of the curveballs that come too. Stay vigilant and ready throughout your day. The enemy doesn't take a day off from attacking God's children, which means we must not go a day without the armor of God on. Be ye always ready! Amen.

June 14

> Stand therefore, having girded your waist with truth, having put on the breastplate of righteousness. (Ephesians 6:14)

In boxing, you have a better chance at defeating your opponent through completing successful body blows. The body blows are within the waist and chest area. If those areas are pounded correctly, it makes it harder for the body to stand up. If you have the truth and righteousness within you, you will be able to overcome the lies of Satan and his other attacks.

As Jesus Christ was completing His Father's work, Satan influenced many to lie, and he tried to attack the Lord's heart through the death of Lazarus and attacks on others. The truth defeated the lies, and the miracles withstood the attacks on His heart.

Satan fights with lies and against your heart. He is going to try to hit you in the gut and heart to break you down. He will try to use individuals that are close to you too. His works can't overcome the truth and righteousness! His works compared to the truth and righteousness of the Lord is like comparing a bubble trying to survive in a hurricane. Use the truth and righteousness as you encounter spiritual warfare. As the lies and other works of the enemy come your way, stand firm and watch those arrows of darkness fall in the spirit realm. In Jesus's name! Amen.

June 15

> And having shod your feet with the preparation of the gospel of peace. (Ephesians 6:15)

There was an avalanche, and a group of mountain climbers were trapped. One of the men started climbing out of the snow, and as he was climbing, he noticed it was extremely hard for him to climb, but he kept on climbing upward because he believed he would soon be out of the snow. As he broke through the snow and reached solid ground again, he noticed a rope tied to him. He had been pulling two other climbers with him. They lived and thanked him for pushing through the snow. That's how we must be in spreading the Gospel of Jesus Christ.

Satan wants us to think that our efforts to spread the Gospel of Jesus Christ are not fruitful. The Lord has deposited the readiness and motivation within His children to go forth to complete the work for His kingdom. Jesus Christ showed us the readiness and motivation to press on, and we must do the same thing in spreading the Good News. Others that came before us did their part in spreading the Gospel, and now we must do our part in spreading the Gospel today. We are equipped with the readiness and motivation to get it done. We are the evidence for Christ!

Trust and believe that you are making an impact for the kingdom of God. Your efforts are needed, and there are many individuals that will let you know how your efforts positively impact them, and the Lord knows your works too. It is best that you don't see all that have an impact on you as much as you want to see whom you impact through spreading the Gospel. Jesus Christ is pleased that you are spreading His Gospel. Keep pressing on with adhering to the Great Commission as there is coming a time when you see the fruits of your labor for Christ. Thanks in advance for spreading the Gospel of Jesus Christ. Amen.

June 16

> Above all, taking the shield of faith with which
> you will be able to quench all the fiery darts of
> the wicked one. (Ephesians 6:16)

As elephants maneuver through the jungle, they are not moved by annoying gnats. Gnats can bite, but they can't penetrate the skin of an elephant. Since they are ineffective against the elephant, the elephant will keep pressing on with its day. We have to be like elephants treating demons like annoying gnats, knowing they can't penetrate our faith.

Jesus wasn't worried about demons while He walked on the earth because His faith is unmatched. His faith is one of the reasons He pleased the Father. Once, while speaking to the disciples, He told them that having faith the size of a mustard seed would suffice for some things, but we must seek to have faith the size of a watermelon.

You have to walk in the power of God with unwavering faith. Your faith must be like elephant's skin against gnats. Your faith has to be able to stand between a boulder and an egg. Your faith has to be able to strengthen another lion when it is weak. Your faith has to be a foundation of power when all seems lost. Your faith is a supernatural weapon that Satan hopes you can't and won't master. Maximize your faith, especially during spiritual warfare. In Jesus's name! Amen.

June 17

And take the helmet of salvation, and the sword of the Spirit, which is the word of God. (Ephesians 6:17)

When it is cold outside, parents must ensure they place hats on their children's head before they leave the house. The hats help to prevent them from getting head colds and other sicknesses. In some instances, kids in the neighborhood would convince your children that the hats don't help, but you must enforce your standard. In a similar manner, the enemy wants to convince you that there is no salvation. The devil is a liar!

Satan doesn't stop his works to deter us from the truth. He wants us to be lost in his confusion without hope. We have Jesus Christ, which means we have hope and more. He has set us free indeed.

The enemy will try to make you doubt God, Jesus, and your salvation. He will try to use any negative moment in your life to influence you to doubt God's saving grace. You have been delivered from the things (sin, sickness, and death) that try to keep you captive. Satan wants you to believe there is no hope from those things but the unblemished Lamb made it possible for salvation to cover us.

Allow your faith in salvation received from Christ to thwart the wiles Satan now and forevermore. Amen.

June 18

> Praying always with all prayer and supplication
> in the Spirit, being watchful to this end with all
> perseverance and supplication for all the saints.
> (Ephesians 6:18)

Every day we encounter many situations, and every situation requires different responses. In some instances, you will find yourself dealing with multiple situations which you have to prioritize dealing with. Tag a prayer to each one of them, especially the spiritual situations for fellow Christians.

We see in the Bible how Jesus Christ prays for various reasons. He could've completed a prayer to cover everything, but some situations are unique and require specific prayer. We also see Him praying for His disciples too. He is the greatest Intercessor. We must imitate Him in being intercessors too.

As you go about your day, pray about everything. You want to ensure you are applying the proper measure to everything, and the best way to do this is via the Helper. For the spiritual results, we must pray in the Spirit. Please maintain clean hands and a clean heart to help facilitate your advantage during spiritual warfare. Praying in the Spirit for other Christians intercedes and provides advantages for them too, which Satan and his children hate. Thanks in advance for helping others in spiritual warfare too. Amen.

June 19

> And for me, that utterance may be given to me,
> that I may open my mouth boldly to make known
> the mystery of the gospel. (Ephesians 6:19)

Some people utilize home security systems with the capability that allows you to enter your home via a key or via keyless entry. This type of system gives you an advantage instead of isolating you to one way to unlock the doors to your house. We need these types of advantages because they help with having a peace of mind. In spiritual warfare, we need all advantages to help us win. We have to ask God to release them to us now.

The Holy Spirit provides the utterance that you need to unlock particular doors. Many forsake utterance because they do not have it or are not aware of what's in the Bible. The utterance helps to bridge the gap between realms. This is also what helped the Apostle Paul be effective as He made known the mystery of the Gospel. This utterance is available for you too.

You and all Christians need every advantage possible during spiritual warfare. The utterance given via the Holy Spirit is another advantage. The utterance that will be given will greatly assist you in spiritual warfare too. Your spirit has a say in the spiritual warfare coming up against you, and the utterance helps your spirit's role against the spiritual enemies. It will unlock the mystery of the Gospel as you speak it boldly as you ought to. If you are without the utterance, ask and you shall receive. Ask in Jesus's name. Speak according to the faith and Word deposited with you. Ask and receive the Holy Spirit today. Amen.

June 20

> For which I am an ambassador in chains; that
> in it I may speak boldly, as I ought to speak.
> (Ephesians 6:20)

We've seen or heard of children fighting when they get off of the school bus. Many times we heard the children not being afraid to fight because they believed their daddies would support them in their fights. This is how we must be in our spiritual fights against our spiritual enemies. We must speak boldly, knowing our Father supports us and will win all of our battles.

Jesus Christ spoke boldly everywhere He went because He was walking in His Father's image. He didn't waver in His efforts nor did He compromise for any reason. He talked the talk and walked the walk because of His Father's power, holiness, righteousness, obedience, faith, and love. He walked as an Ambassador for His Father, and we must do the same.

You are an ambassador of Christ, and He wants you to speak boldly as you ought to according to the purposes of His kingdom. He has empowered all His ambassadors with His Holy Spirit. His ambassadors speak boldly because they believe in His Gospel and the power of His Father. Thanks for your efforts for Him, and speak boldly as you ought to when the time comes. Please Him with your faith and works when you speak. Speak in Jesus's name. Amen.

June 21

> For where your treasure is, there your heart will
> be also. (Matthew 6:21)

One of the capabilities of smartphones is location services. Some people use it to track other people, and it works if it is turned on. Your spiritual location service is always on, and the signal from your heart lets the spirit realm know where you are. This also means that whatever your heart is locked into, that is where you will be found.

Jesus Christ is the greatest treasure, and within Him is love, which is the treasure of the kingdom. Love sent Him to be a living sacrifice for us, and we have to treasure His act of love. Let your treasure be Jesus Christ.

You are drawn to the things that are illuminated within your heart. Your heart should be a repository of good things so you can make a greater impact for the kingdom. Let your treasure be of that which travels with you to paradise. Let it be love! The Lord is attracted to your heart if it is filled with love. Let love be the treasure of your heart as it can also be utilized to help others within the kingdom. Amen.

June 22

> But now having been set free from sin, and having
> become slaves of God, you have your fruit to holi-
> ness, and the end, everlasting life. (Romans 6:22)

Being in a congested tunnel can be frustrating. There are various reasons to why the tunnel is congested, and the only thing you
can do is deal with it with patience. Once you are out of the tunnel,
you never want to go back in it. Just like you don't want to be in a
congested tunnel is the same way you should feel about living a sinful
life.

Jesus Christ died on the cross for our sins. He presented Himself
to be a living sacrifice for the kingdom and pleased His Father in the
process. He is available for all seeking to be free of sin. He can transform a sinful life into a fruitful life in a moment.

Many individuals have experienced a sinful life that created
setbacks that drastically slowed their progress to godly peace. Some
individuals are having that experience right now. The only way out
of such an experience is to allow Jesus Christ to set them free. The
faster they are set free, the faster they can stop living a congested life.
Confessing Jesus Christ as Lord and Savior brings an end to the congested tunnel with the ultimate light at the end of it. Help someone
be free of sin. Ensure you are set free from sin too! Repent and forgive
if need be so you can be set free too. Thanks in advance for helping
someone else be set free from sin through Jesus Christ. Amen.

June 23

> For the wages of sin is death, but the gift of God is
> eternal life in Christ Jesus our Lord. (Romans 6:23)

Many doctors recommend diets to their patients because of
health concerns. There are so many diets. You have to choose what
diet works best for you. All that takes a diet from the world and

accepts Jesus Christ as Lord and Savior will live a healthier spiritual life now and forevermore.

The power of the Lord provides an abundance of supernatural calories that powers eternal life. Eternal life is the gift after the gift called Jesus Christ. You can't have one without the other.

Being a child of God, you have the gift. That gift has freed you from the clamp of death. You must use that gift to bring the Almighty Father more glory. Use that gift to help someone else receive the gift too. That gift is precious, and the enemy doesn't want humans to have it. Please help spread the Gospel of Jesus Christ so as to help others receive this awesome gift from God. Amen.

June 24

No one can serve two masters; for either he will hate the one and love the other, or else he will be loyal to the one and despise the other. You cannot serve God and mammon. (Matthew 6:24)

Some driving schools have cars with two steering wheels. One steering wheel is for the student driver, and the other steering wheel is for the instructor to intervene if need be. In life, only one Master can intervene for you, and His name is Jesus. Let Jesus take the wheel!

The Almighty Father gave His only begotten Son all power and authority in heaven and earth; thus, He is the Master. Satan and others want to be the Master, but they can't be because they are as ants compared to a lion.

The prince of the power of the air feeds off of disobedience to the Almighty Father, so let's starve him. Our Master loves obedience to His commandments, and He loves glory. The only Master we serve is the one that created the heavens and the earth. Let Satan and his children know that you serve the one Master that is power, love, holiness, grace, and righteousness that no other master can compare. He is Master all by Himself. He is Jesus Christ! He and the Father are one! Amen.

June 25

> Therefore I say to you, do not worry about your life, what you will eat or what you will drink; nor about your body, what you will put on. Is not life more than food and the body more than clothing? (Matthew 6:25)

In a computing environment that services thousands of people, the administrators and engineers always have competing priorities. They have to prioritize the ones that have the greatest impact over the ones that have the least impact. This is what God wants us to do too regarding our lives and our bodies.

God used the earth to form our bodies, and He gave us life, then He also gave us His Son so that we can have eternal life with Him. He will help us take care of what He has blessed us with, which is why we are not to worry about how they are to be sustained and covered. Let God!

The Lord can do exceedingly and abundantly above all that we ask for, and He can easily sustain and cover us. He wants us to know that just as He ensures the birds don't starve and don't stress over their coverings, then neither should we. Our spiritual bodies are more important than our natural bodies since our spirits return to Father and live eternal. Our spiritual bodies have eternal food and garments that do not fade away. Switch your focus to that which follows you to paradise. Please allow the Holy Spirit to help you not worry about the things the Lord our God will provide for you and your family. Amen.

June 26

> The Lord lift up His countenance upon you, and give you peace. (Numbers 6:26)

Wearing expensive clothing can help you look better in public and attract attention but can't help you overcome adversity and other hurdles in life. Expensive clothing is effective in the earth realm but doesn't have value in the spirit realm. If we seek and have the best spiritual covering (the Almighty Father), we can overcome anything and receive so much more from Him.

The Almighty Father's countenance provides you the supernatural support that is eternal. His countenance is a supernatural repository of resources for His obedient children. Tap in so you won't have to tap out!

Align yourself within Him, and allow His countenance to provide you the peace you need today. That peace will help your mind focus and calm your spirit while also preparing you to receive supernatural support. No matter what happened yesterday, please ask for and receive peace today. Walk in love and peace today in Jesus's name. Amen.

June 27

> But I say to you who hear: Love your enemies, do
> good to those who hate you. (Luke 6:27)

Gravity is a force that you can't see, but you know it exists. One of the glaring facts about gravity is that it keeps us grounded to the earth. We won't float away because of the power within it. Love is like gravity, and it empowers us to forgive those that are not expecting us to forgive them.

When Jesus Christ was on the cross, He made one of the most profound statements ever. He said, "Father, forgive them for they know not what they do." He said that in love and forgiveness during a moment when He could've used His power to overpower everyone. Love kept Him grounded.

You can't allow your heart to be changed because of other people's actions. Keep doing good even when they are striking against you. It's hard to do, but there is a greater reward for you if you endure for a moment. Show your enemies love, and it will paralyze some of them because they are expecting an eye for an eye. Imitate Jesus Christ and please the Father with awesome gestures of love and forgiveness. Amen.

June 28

> Then they said to Him, "What shall we do, that
> we may work the works of God?" (John 6:28)

When you get new tires on your car, you also need an alignment. The alignments are normally free with the new tires. The alignment greatly improves the wear and tear of your tires. The alignment also ensures your tires will work according to their specifications and the money spent for them. Your alignment with God ensures you are walking in your purpose according to your calling and the ransom Jesus Christ paid for you.

The only way you can do the works of God is to be within Him. We have to go through Jesus Christ to be within the Father. Jesus Christ told us that we will do greater works, and those greater works are possible if we are aligned within the Father.

You have to reflect the image of God to complete His works. There is much to do for the kingdom, and He will employ you if you are willing. Think about completing the works to please Him, not yourself. Your works that you complete for Him today will help another soul and bring you to the kingdom. Complete the works in Jesus's name! Amen.

June 29

> Jesus answered and said to them, "This is the
> work of God, that you believe in Him whom He
> sent." (John 6:29)

Once a text message is received, you can see who sent it to you. The evidence is the sender's number or name and the message itself. God sent His Messenger (His only begotten Son), and everyone that receives the Messenger receives eternal life.

Those that have received His Messenger have received many benefits, and He wants to help others receive those benefits too. This is why adhering to the Great Commission is critical. He loves to see His children adhering to the Great Commission, and He can count on you to adhere to it too.

Receiving everlasting life is a treasure that is attainable through believing in Jesus Christ. He wants you to help spread the Gospel so others can receive everlasting life too. Please ensure that you introduce Him to everyone that you know. Everyone hasn't heard the Gospel of Jesus Christ, and there are so many individuals that need to hear it from you. You may be the missing link to helping many souls receive the Messiah. Thanks in advance for helping fellow Christians spread the Gospel of Jesus Christ. You are appreciated! Amen.

June 30

> Give to everyone who asks of you. And from him who takes away your goods do not ask them back. (Luke 6:30)

While at work, everyone uses the same refrigerator. Sometimes people bring similar items for lunch and mistakenly take the wrong lunch. This has happened to many of us, and many of us have let the person keep the lunch. Situations like that help you to see who you are.

The Lord loves a cheerful giver, and He avenges His givers too. Lose no sleep if someone steals from you as the Lord will repay you. Let the thieves continue to highlight themselves so you will know why the Lord is removing them from you.

We work hard for our goods, and we don't focus on anyone trying to steal our goods, but it happens. Sometimes it's people that are close to us that steal our goods, and please know that God saw them steal it too. Let your humbleness and cheerful giving stabilize your heart and ease you out of asking for the goods back. If you are to receive it back, then let it flow back to you double-fold. Let God help you recover it all! Amen.

JULY

Physical and spiritual perfection is always the aim, and only Jesus Christ attained it. Stay in Him, and He will keep perfecting you physically and spiritually. Ensure you keep pressing on, keeping God first in all that you do. Seek His face more. Ask the Holy Spirit for additional guidance that will help you stay on track in your purpose for the Lord.

July 1

> O LORD my God, in You I put my trust; Save me
> from all those who persecute me; And deliver me.
> (Psalm 7:1)

Professional wrestling matches includes tag team matches. You can tag your partner to come and wrestle while you take a break. The Lord can come in for you if your obedience tags His commandments. Trust in Him to deal with those enemies for you.

God's love is unconditional but comes with conditions. One of those conditions is Him protecting those that trust Him. He will crush a star or planet for His children. Those that go after His children are like fuel to a fire. They are igniting a wrath they can't put out!

When you decide to reflect the image of God and walk like Jesus, you will not compromise your obedience. Your obedience invites the hand of God to avenge and protect you. He already knows who your enemies are, but He needs your permission to deal with them. Ask Him to deliver you from them so you can do more work for Him. Amen.

July 2

> For with what judgment you judge, you will be
> judged; and with the measure you use, it will be
> measured back to you. (Matthew 7:2)

There was this well-known doctor that recently got into a terrible car accident. When he arrived in the emergency room, they gave him the best care possible because they remembered how he took great care of them and the patients that he helped while he was on duty.

There is going to come a time when you are going to see the Judge of our lives. That same Judge has provided us an advocate named Jesus. The Advocate will use your heart for others and your actions to help others as evidence that you are worthy to reside in one of the Father's many mansions.

At some point your intent will return to you like a boomerang. It will return as you send it, and you shouldn't be surprised how it impacts you. If your heart and mind are aligned with the Lord, then you will imitate Him while not worrying about the measure you use. Thanks in advance for watching your measuring. You will help more people if you judge and measure them with good intentions. Amen.

July 3

> And said to him, "Get out of your country and
> from your relatives, and come to a land that I will
> show you." (Acts 7:3)

Would you knowingly give your child money knowing they are going to waste it on disobedient children? You already know your answer. You already know what your children are going to do with whatever you bless them with, which is why you have to protect what you give them. God wants to bless us too, but sometimes He wants us to leave particular places so that others will not receive what He is releasing to us.

The Lord has already set us up for success. His will can't be denied. He is always available to release blessings to His children if they are obedient to Him. Trust your Creator since He has declared the end from the beginning.

A reward from the Father comes through obedience. The fight is already fixed for us to receive an abundance of rewards. If He has placed in your spirit to go to a specific place, please trust and believe that there is a reward that accompanies your obedience. There will be individuals that will not understand the plan, but in due time, they will see why you had to go. God has plans for you to do greater works, but you must be willing to leave the familiar to conquer the unfamiliar. Trust in the Lord our God! The Holy Spirit will help you walk in the revelation from the Lord. Amen.

July 4

> Say to wisdom, "You are my sister," And call understanding your nearest kin. (Proverbs 7:4)

There are methods we can utilize to help us find out who our ancestors are and to connect us to relatives that we have never met. Once the connection is made, we are overjoyed because we have increased more joy in a special area of our lives. Once we connect with other supernatural members within the kingdom, it helps us to increase in other areas too.

Wisdom gives birth to godly knowledge via the Holy Spirit. She will help you unlock the mysteries that have kept you away from progressing in your gifts for the kingdom. She is always willing to assist you in being a greater asset for our Lord.

Our Lord has equipped us with everything we need, to include wisdom and understanding if we ask for them. We can't maneuver through the earth and spirit realm without them. They are in the supernatural family as we are too. Lean on the supernatural family to assist you in your walk today. You don't have it all figured out by yourself, and if you believe you do, then you are figure skating on thin ice. Let the kingdom relatives enlighten a path of knowledge, for that will help you be more effective for the Lord. Amen.

July 5

> Hypocrite! First remove the plank from your own eye, and then you will see clearly to remove the speck from your brother's eye. (Matthew 7:5)

Before you drive your car, please ensure that you clean your windshield. Debris and other things can build up in a moment and prevent you from seeing clearly. Please clean your windshield before you tell another driver to clean their windshield so both of you won't get into a wreck.

Jesus Christ is the only perfect one that walked upon this earth. He did it to the glory of the Father. He simultaneously walked in holiness and righteousness too, which allowed Him to stay in His Father's presence and please Him along the way. Jesus is perfect now and forevermore.

As for us, we are not perfect. We may not do evil, but we are still far from perfect. Ask the Lord to cleanse you so you can help others be cleansed too. He will perfect your imperfections so you can be more effective for the kingdom. As you notice someone's flaws, that doesn't mean you are supposed to expose them. Even if you feel led to speak to them about their flaws, please remember that it must be done in a respectful manner, or else it will do more harm than good. Please let humbleness and the Holy Spirit help you remove your plank first. Amen.

July 6

> For you are a holy people to the LORD your God; the LORD your God has chosen you to be a people for Himself, a special treasure above all the peoples on the face of the earth. (Deuteronomy 7:6)

We have seen in many movies how royal families live much better than others in their lands. They are set apart because of bloodlines, power, money, and their forces. We are of the royalty because of the blood of Jesus, His power, abundance, and the Holy Spirit. We are a special treasure.

Jesus paved the way for imperfect people to be transformed into children worthy to be in the Holy Family. He already knows who will be respectful to His sacrifice and strive better to represent in holy ways.

You are representation of your Lord. He is holy, so you must be holy. There are times when you may not feel like you are holy, but you are within the Holy Family. Repent and forgive with the intent to have clean hands and a pure heart. Others outside the Holy Family will not understand that you are special in the eyes of the Lord, so please don't stress if they are oblivious to your position in the Lord. Keep pleasing the Lord our God by reflecting His image and being holy as He is holy. Being holy as He is holy highlights you being a special treasure! Enjoy your day being a special treasure. Amen.

July 7

> Thus says the Lord GOD: "It shall not stand, Nor shall it come to pass." (Isaiah 7:7)

Kids love to blow bubbles. The bubbles are cool to watch, but eventually they burst without harming anyone. That's how the works of your enemies are as they are launched out but will eventually burst with no effect on you.

The all-seeing Lord of ours is aware of all works of the wicked. Even when it seems like the enemies are winning against you, they are actually losing.

Their plots will help you prosper. They that plot against you actually help add to your testimony and God getting more glory. Some will look you in the eye daily as they are plotting, but the Almighty Father knows their thoughts and will shut them down or use them for His glory. Don't be surprised if the Lord allows you to see someone plotting against you. This is also why you must ensure you inform everyone that you are a child of God to help them avoid the wrath of our Creator. Please lean on the Holy Spirit to help you see everything that is being formed against you. You will overcome it all in the Name that's above all names. Amen.

July 8

For everyone who asks receives, and he who seeks finds, and to him who knocks it will be opened. (Matthew 7:8)

If you make deposits into your account, you believe you will be able to withdraw money from your account. This is why we must check our balances before we try to use ATMs. Similarly, those that complete deposits into the kingdom shall benefit from the kingdom.

Reflecting the image of the Almighty Father will allow you to ask Jesus to let those things come forth that you are in need of. If you invest in Him as He has invested in you, He will deliver the things that you need.

Walk in this day like you own it! Walk in faith the size of a watermelon, remembering that Jesus gave the minimum standard of a mustard seed since the disciples had little faith. However you attain the things you desire, know that it's the love of Jesus that allows you to receive those things. He will only deliver to His obedient children. Stay clean and be obedient to the Word of God, and receive the more abundantly that He has promised to His children. Claim it, frame it, and hang it in your heart! Amen.

July 9

Do not hasten in your spirit to be angry, for anger
rests in the bosom of fools. (Ecclesiastes 7:9)

If a country doesn't have border patrol, then anyone can come into their country. Most countries have checkpoints to screen individuals that desire to enter their country. The Word of God is the first screening of individuals desiring to enter the kingdom. One of the roadblocks that prevent individuals from entering into the kingdom is anger. Anger blocks blessings and creates unnecessary lessons!

There is no place in paradise for anger. An angry person is unstable and not fit for duty for the Lord. Anger adds fuel where it is not needed, and in the process it burns bridges, shuts down communications, and builds wedges where love is supposed to be.

If your spirit is full of anger, then it is impossible for you to effectively do the works of the Lord. You must be an asset, not a liability for the kingdom. You are held to a higher standard and are expected to manage yourself better than normal people. You are a next-level human because you are a child of God. Please don't allow anger to take you down a notch in the eyes of the Lord. Conquer anger instead of allowing it to conquer you. Amen.

July 10

> My defense is of God, who saves the upright in heart. (Psalm 7:10)

In sports, teams play defense to prevent other teams from scoring. They put their bodies on the line to prevent the opposing team from scoring too. This is what Jesus did for us, and it is our reasonable service to present our bodies as living sacrifices too. Sacrifices manifest because of relationships and love. The upright in heart enjoy being living sacrifices.

God loves His children that truly keep Him first. It takes self-examinations to know if you are truly keeping Him first. Adhering to the greatest commandment and seeking Him first are keys to a relationship with God. Love and defend Him, and He will do the same for you.

Love will propel you to protect that which you treasure the most. God knows who loves Him and will show them how He knows. If you love Him, then you already know that He appreciates you loving Him. Let your actions be of Him as they will help others see what reflecting His image really looks like. The more you reflect His image, the more He will use you since you are already in His saving grace. Being upright in heart helps you to reflect His image and in doing so you please Him. Thanks for pleasing the Father. Amen.

July 11

> God is a just judge, and God is angry with the
> wicked every day. (Psalm 7:11)

A family was enjoying a day at the beach. The children told their father that they wanted to build castles. He approved of them building the castles. The father drew a line in the sand explaining to them that they must not go past that line to build their castles. He stepped away and watched them from a distance as they built their castles. The disobedient children went past the line in their building. When they were finished building their castle, they bragged to the obedient children who had just finished building their castle. Shortly afterward, a wave of water came and wiped the disobedient children's castle away, and when the father returned, he rewarded the children that had a castle still standing while the disobedient children received nothing.

God has proven to use the wicked against themselves. He has come down to deal with them, and He has sent others to deal with them. He even allows them to build things, not knowing that they are being used to help His children.

It looks like the wicked ones are always winning but not so. They will have temporary gains that will eventually benefit the children of the Lord. Please don't be amazed nor dismayed at the gains of the wicked as the ends of those gains may be for you. Amen.

July 12

> Therefore, whatever you want men to do to you, do also to them, for this is the Law and the Prophets. (Matthew 7:12)

The purpose of a mirror is amazing. It reflects images, and it can also redirect light. It is an awesome tool. It helps you make necessary adjustments if need be. One of the best features of a mirror is your own reflection. Your reflection helps to define a part of you as well as how you treat other people.

Jesus laid down His life for us because of love, and it is our reasonable service to also present our bodies as living sacrifices to and for Him. We must reflect Him. Even as we interact with others, we must reflect how He would interact with them. What would Jesus do?

Most people will treat you how you treat them. Whether they believe in God or not, their reaction is most likely based upon your action. In many instances, you do not think about the boomerang effect, but it happens daily. Please treat people how you want to be treated, even those that you know do not deserve good treatment. That is what is termed grace! The grace you give influences the way you live! If you are a Christian, then you have no choice but to give grace since you know the Father and Son provide us daily grace. Amen.

July 13

> Consider the work of God; for who can make straight what He has made crooked? (Ecclesiastes 7:13)

Please consider gazing at the stars tonight. Look at the constellations if the sky is clear enough. They are the same every day and have been utilized to help teach and guide individuals. They are similar to the work of God. The work of God is affixed and a joy to watch if you have a relationship with Him.

The work of God will confuse those that are not within Him. His work cannot be altered as it is most powerful and it is eternal. His obedient children benefit from His work as they keep Him first. Are you within the work of God?

Just like no one can stop the will nor the wrath of God, no one can alter the work that He is completing in your life. This is why where they see His work is crooked, they can't make it straight, and where it is straight, they can't make it crooked. He is a one-way God. Please stay in His presence and enjoy His works. His works provide the exceeding abundance that you will receive soon. Amen.

July 14

> If My people who are called by My name will humble themselves, and pray and seek My face, and turn from their wicked ways, then I will hear from heaven, and will forgive their sin and heal their land. (2 Chronicles 7:14)

One of the best moments of being a parent is putting together Christmas gifts for kids. If we follow the instructions while assembling the product, it should be much easier to construct. As Christians, if we follow the instructions that God has provided for us, we are continuously constructing reasons for Him to bless us.

If God said it, then He will see it through. Collectively, the people of God have not always seen things through for Him but He still provided mercy and grace. At some point, the people have to want more, and to receive more requires obedience to His Word. It seems like many Christians have grown comfortable in receiving mercy and grace. It is not good to fall short of the glory of God and live as if it is okay to do so. The narrative has to change if you want the story of your life to get better!

There has to be a sense of urgency in being obedient to the Word of God, and we must reflect that urgency so others can follow our lead. We do not know when He is going to pierce the sky, so let's forge greater efforts in obedience. The more individuals we help with obedience, the more sins will be forgiven, the more lands will be healed, and so much more. Let's do these things in Jesus's name. Amen.

July 15

> But if the unbeliever departs, let him depart; a brother or a sister is not under bondage in such cases. But God has called us to peace. (1 Corinthians 7:15)

When preparing meat for cooking, many chefs trim the fat off of the meat. There are different types of fat, and they are trimmed off for medical, flavoring, or cooking reasons. Just like there are different types of fat that need to be trimmed from meat, there are different people that we must trim away from us because they could be blocking blessings.

If His children will allow Him, God will trim the fat from His children because He knows what is needed for them to prosper for the kingdom. He knows the plans that He has for us, so let's allow His plan to flow. In Jesus's name!

Peace is more important than maintaining a problem. If the source of the problem is an unbeliever, please don't lose any sleep if that problem walks away. When an unbeliever doesn't want to be in your presence, they may be helping you out more than you know. If there is a loss of any kind because the unbeliever departs, the Lord will help you recover it all. Please remember that all your help comes from the Lord! Amen.

July 16

> Do not be overly righteous, nor be overly wise: Why
> should you destroy yourself? (Ecclesiastes 7:16)

The reason why some people don't like humble pie is because its main ingredients are humbleness and selflessness. This is also why we've heard that we shouldn't be so spiritually minded that we are no earthly good. To be overly righteous and overly wise is also to think too highly of yourself, which is forbidden in the Bible.

When you read the first four books in the New Testament, you will see that Jesus was with the people. One of the reasons why He was with them is because how He presented Himself. He was approachable and didn't look down on the people. The people were not made to think less of themselves when He was in their presence.

Humbling yourself and walking like Jesus will allow you to be more effective for the kingdom. Many people present themselves as a higher tier than others, which is similar to putting up a wall similar to how the Pharisees presented themselves. No matter the gifts that you have from the Holy Spirit, please humble yourself and know that although you are gifted, you are still not a finished product. The Almighty Father, Christ Jesus, and the Holy Spirit are the only finished product. Let humbleness be like a muzzle to also keep you from biting yourself. Amen.

July 17

> I will praise the LORD according to His righteous-
> ness, and will sing praise to the name of the LORD
> Most High. (Psalm 7:17)

Leisure is a time when you are free from work and other activities. It is a time to relax and do fun things that are joyful to your heart and mind. In our leisure, let's consider praising God more.

Occupying our souls in this manner can also be therapeutic to us while uplifting our Almighty Father.

God loves to receive praises. He created the heavens and the earth; thus, He should receive praises from all life within it. Giving Him praises is also giving Him respect. He is more than worthy of more praises.

Watching television and playing video games are the leading activities in what people do in their leisure. Children of the Most High God should pause and examine themselves and see how much of their leisure is praising God. Please remember that He is a jealous God. No person, place, thing, or activity should get more praise than God. None of them can do nor have done anything close to what God has done for us. We must sing Him praise more and more without expecting to receive anything for praising Him. This is another reasonable service that we should render to our Creator. Let your praising flow for Him, and believe that He is pleased with your praising. Amen.

July 18

> He who speaks from himself seeks his own glory;
> but He who seeks the glory of the One who sent
> Him is true, and no unrighteousness is in Him.
> (John 7:18)

If a hero leaves the scene of a heroic event, it is the responsibility of the one who witnessed the heroic event to give credit where it is due. Unfortunately, there have been many individuals that have taken responsibility for others' work and have no sympathy for doing it. We can't take credit for the work that God does, and we must make sure that He gets all His glory.

God loves His glory. When we accept Christ as Lord and Savior and He comes in us, we have glory in us. We are glory-carriers that have to give God more glory. Satan wants God's glory, and he can't get it! He also hates God's glory-carriers because we will ensure glory goes where it is supposed to go.

Please go about your day giving God glory. He will love it. He may use you to do something amazing, but please make sure all the glory goes to Him. Most will uplift your name, but please govern yourself and usher in praise and glory to God for using you to bring Him glory. God already knows who is going to lift Him up, so please be that one today. Glory has a home, and we must ensure it is sent home to its Father. In Jesus's name! Amen.

July 19

> He will again have compassion on us, and will subdue our iniquities. You will cast all our sins into the depths of the sea. (Micah 7:19)

A parent's love is powerful. A parent's love is forgiving. A parent's love is endless. A parent's love wipes away pain. A parent's love can hold a country together and rip a city to shreds for their children. A parent's amazing love is seen in their compassion toward their children. God's compassion for His children is unmatched.

God has shown us mercy and grace since the beginning of time. No one will have more mercy upon us than our God. His love endures forever, and so does His mercy and grace. He wants us to stay clean so He can stay in our presence.

Most Christians will agree that God's compassion is amazing as they know that they have done things that they are not proud of, and through it all He still loves us. He has shown you mercy and grace too. You are an amazing work in progress like all other children of God. The enemy will continue to remind you of your past, but let him remind himself as you press on knowing that the Lord has forgiven you and wiped your yesterday away. If you have repented and asked Jesus to cleanse you, please be a greater new creature in Christ reflecting the image of God. Let Him use you! Amen.

July 20

> Therefore by their fruits you will know them.
> (Matthew 7:20)

We know the difference between apple and orange trees because of the fruit they bear. There is no denying what they are as they bear the fruit of their own kind. Jesus Christ is the Tree of Life that walked the earth completing the work of His Father. He bore fruit of His Father, and those that had eyes to see recognized Him as the Son of God.

It is the Promised Seed that bears the fruit that pleased the Almighty Father. His fruit helped others recognize Him as the Son of the Almighty Father. In our reflecting of the image of God, we must imitate Jesus Christ in bearing good fruit so others will know that we are children of the Almighty Father.

We are to be trees that bear good fruit of the Lord. Just like in Psalm 1, we are to be like trees planted by the rivers of water (living water of Jesus Christ) that bring forth fruit in our season for the Lord. Bearing the fruits of the Lord will signify to others who our Father is. Let your fruit be your evidence to help others get closer to the Lord while bringing the Almighty Father more glory too. Let your breadcrumbs (fruits) help lead others to the Loaf (Jesus Christ). Amen.

July 21

> Not everyone who says to Me, "Lord, Lord," shall
> enter the kingdom of heaven, but he who does
> the will of My Father in heaven. (Matthew 7:21)

One of the reasons hospitals exist is to provide care to the community. Their doctors play key roles in the quality of care provided to the community. Sadly, there have been individuals that have been arrested for impersonating doctors. I'm so glad that the human community has the Almighty Father who is the Great Physician, and Jesus Christ is our Great Physician since He and the Almighty Father are one. In the Bible, Jesus Christ told us of others that would present themselves as the Christ but are not. Those ones will influence many to do their will or influence others to disobey the Father.

God has an awesome vetting process before anyone can enter paradise. One of the requirements is obedience to His will. If one can't be obedient to Him, then they can reside in the same house as Him. There are other requirements that are utilized in the vetting process, but obedience is the key.

You have seen so many individuals that claim to be children of God, but their actions say otherwise. Their actions do not show obedience to the will of the Father, and He is not pleased with them, which is why you must consider keeping your distance from them. Please don't stop trying to help them overcome whatever it is that's influencing their disobedience. It is the disobedient ones that when converted to obedience will bring more glory to the Father. Let your "Lord, Lord" be authentic, and He will bless you accordingly. Amen.

July 22

> Therefore You are great, O Lord GOD. For there is none like You, nor is there any God besides You, according to all that we have heard with our ears. (2 Samuel 7:22)

We have heard the saying, "The proof is in the pudding." This is a term to signify the establishment of the truth. All that have confessed Jesus Christ as Lord and Savior have also acknowledged His Almighty Father as the only true God. Jesus Christ and His Father are the truth.

God created the heavens and the earth; no one can deny nor disprove this fact. He is undeniable. He will always be undefeated. He will always be most powerful. He will never waver in His love for His children. He has silenced all so called other gods and put them to shame. No one can create a universe like He did. He is most powerful, most amazing, and most awesome. Another great fact about God is, "Greater is He that's in you than he that's in the world."

You are living proof of God. You are a creation of His, and no other god can stand up to refute this fact. God wants you to reflect His image continuously, showing others facts about Him. The enemy doesn't want us to exist; hence, he uses tricks and other methods to influence depression, suicide, anxiety, and other things to try to rid the earth of God's proof. Let your light shine bright upon others so as to reflect the image of God and to help others be living proofs of Him. Do this in Jesus's name so He can help you bring more glory to God in being living proof that there is none like Him. Amen.

July 23

> You were bought at a price; do not become slaves
> of men. (1 Corinthians 7:23)

If you buy a pet from a pet store, it is yours. When you take the pet home, it is like a slave to you because you control if it can go outside, how long it stays inside, what it eats, and if it receives any treats. That's how Satan wants us to be in the world, which is why he wants to manipulate us to enslave ourselves to men.

The only begotten Son paid the supernatural ransom for us to be free spiritually, and we must do our part in not allowing ourselves to be enslaved in other ways. For far too long, we allowed ourselves to fall into many traps of this world that enslaved our families. Let's be greater stewards of our finances and make better decisions. Leaning on the Lord our God will keep us out of all types of slavery.

Knowing that Jesus paid the price for us, we have to be respectful and not enslave ourselves to anyone else. Are you debt-free? Are you free from soul ties? Are you free from addiction? Those things and other things can make you slaves of men. Please seek the Lord to help you out of or stay away from all things that could enslave you to men. If you are enslaved to men, then you can't be as effective for the kingdom as the Lord needs you to be. Do your part in not being enslaved as the Lord has already did His part. Amen.

July 24

> Therefore whoever hears these sayings of Mine,
> and does them, I will liken him to a wise man
> who built his house on the rock: (Matthew 7:24)

It makes no sense to invest heavily in properties (for long term wealth) on the coast of California since it has been confirmed that it is sinking. Even though it will not occur in our lifetime, it makes better sense to build a home on land that is not sinking. As a Christian, our foundation is Jesus Christ, and He will not allow us to sink.

Jesus is the Chief Cornerstone. He is the strength and power to hold the earth together, which translates to Him easily holding His children together. We are to be His walking temples, which are our reasonable service.

Ensure your obedience to Jesus Christ is the priority. Your obedience is part of your foundation in Christ. Your faith and obedience create the foundation needed to be effective for the kingdom. The Lord is pleased with obedience, so please allow your obedience to strengthen your foundation. Your foundation will allow you to stand in the days of tribulations. How you are grounded influences how you are surrounded! If you are grounded in Jesus Christ, He will surround you with favor and protection. Stay grounded in Jesus Christ, and your temple will never sink. Trust and believe. Amen.

July 25

> Therefore He is also able to save to the uttermost
> those who come to God through Him, since
> He always lives to make intercession for them.
> (Hebrews 7:25)

Whenever the traffic lights are not working at a busy intersection, a police officer has to intercede and direct traffic. Without the interceding of the police officer, there would be more accidents and deaths. For the same reasons, we must be thankful that we have Jesus Christ as our Intercessor.

Jesus Christ is the greatest Intercessor. He has been interceding for us before we were conceived in our mother's womb. There is nothing He can't do for us, especially in the spirit realm. He is available to win more battles for us if we invite Him in to them. We also have to use the Holy Spirit to help us win too.

The stress of life can be overwhelming, and if we try to tackle it on our own, we will be consumed by it. We have to give our obstacles to our Lord and Savior, especially since we know He can do exceedingly abundantly above all we ask for. In helping you get through and over obstacles, please ensure you give Him all the glory. Please highlight Him on every platform you have access to. Please let the world know where your help came from. Trust and believe in Jesus Christ to help you overcome, recover, and sustain you now and forevermore. Amen.

July 26

> But look! He speaks boldly, and they say nothing
> to Him. Do the rulers know indeed that this is
> truly the Christ? (John 7:26)

Military snipers are set apart from ordinary marksmen. They complete training and have the experience to justify who they are; hence, no one questions their skillset. They complete amazing missions because of their confidence in their skills. In delivering the Word of God, we must be snipers too. We must hit the intended target every time God uses us.

Jesus's demeanor spoke for Him. He was simultaneously approachable and nonapproachable. When He spoke, He always enriched the minds of believers. The Pharisees and scribes were not known to speak boldly, and that's because they didn't have Him within them.

When you speak boldly the Word of God with no holes in your speech, no one will question you. Confidence fuels the ability to speak boldly. If you are lacking confidence, then you will not be as effective as you must be for the kingdom. Many individuals will feed off of your confidence as it fuels them too. Please speak as if the listeners' lives depend on it. Speaking boldly will also help to push darkness out of an individual or situation. The Lord is watching you, so imitate Him in your speaking so that He can be well pleased with you too. Amen.

July 27

> But he who did his neighbor wrong pushed him
> away, saying, "Who made you a ruler and a judge
> over us?" (Acts 7:27)

Referees are needed to enforce rules of the game, and sometimes they are not respected if a team believes the referee is working against them. Most of the time, the team that is losing the game believes the referee is working against them. Moses was trying to help someone that was not spiritually winning, and that individual's spiritual state is preventing him from receiving help.

The mind-set and the condition of that individual's heart influenced Him in misunderstanding Moses. The heart and mind have to be stable in order for someone to balance what they receive. As we have renewed minds, we must understand that not everyone we help will have renewed minds.

Everyone is not going to understand your help. Some will believe that you are against them, some will believe that you are seeking personal gain, and few will believe that you are actually helping them. Some of the ones that know about your past will make it harder on themselves receiving your help. Please continue in doing your part to help them though. Jesus laid down His life knowing that not everyone would understand His sacrifice, and as we present our bodies as living sacrifices, many individuals will not understand us either. Let us press on helping as many individuals as we can in Jesus's name.

July 28

> Then Jesus cried out, as He taught in the temple, saying, "You both know Me, and you know where I am from; and I have not come of Myself, but He who sent Me is true, whom you do not know." (John 7:28)

When we take medicine, they come with warning labels. The labels let you know about adverse effects and others impacts from taking the medicine. Some individuals' bodies reject particular medicines, and they have to resort to other medicines. In the same manner, Jesus was giving those individuals exactly what they needed, but their spiritual bodies rejected Him.

When Jesus cried out, it was also a warning to the listeners. This notification was not to puff Himself up but to bring clarity. The notification was delivered in truth even though they did not receive it as being good.

You have to inform others that you are a child of God. Making them aware is not to gain any favor from them but to help them avoid the wrath of God. You cannot become a hidden figure in this world that has souls within it that need to be saved. Highlight to them that you are a highlight for the Lord. Hallelujah! Let your light shine bright before them to bring God more glory. Amen.

July 29

> For He taught them as one having authority, and not as the scribes. (Matthew 7:29)

Gardeners know where they planted all their seeds. After applying the proper gardening processes, the seeds will produce according to its kind. The Lord's seeds are the same. They will produce according where they come from, which is Him.

Jesus taught them with authority because He is the authority. He is always doing His Father's will since He is rooted in His principles and authority. All of the Father's children must be rooted as Christ is rooted.

As we help to make disciples, we must ensure that they understand how important it is to teach with the authority of Jesus Christ. Teaching with the authority of Jesus Christ drives the message home and parks nuggets in the areas that will strengthen believers when they need it. Teaching with the authority of Christ will help drive away darkness and build confidence in others too. Let your teaching of the Word reflect the authority of the Word in Jesus's name. Amen.

July 30

> Therefore they sought to take Him; but no one laid a hand on Him, because His hour had not yet come. (John 7:30)

We set our alarm clocks for various reasons. We set them to wake us up, to remind us and for other reasons. Just as we know the times we have set, the Almighty Father knows all the times that are set for the moments in our lives.

The Word says that only the Father knows the hour when the Son shall pierce the sky, and He knows your hour too. His children must press on as Jesus did, and no matter the earthly power others may have, they can't lay hands on you unless it's within the Almighty Father's will.

You have to keep pressing on with the work for the Lord no matter the situation. There will be resistance, and some may come after you because of the truth, but fear not. Even when it looks like others are about to overtake you, please have faith in your Creator.

Until your time comes, the Lord will protect you from all enemies, foreign and domestic. Amen.

July 31

> And many of the people believed in Him, and said, "When the Christ comes, will He do more signs than these which this Man has done?" (John 7:31)

We've heard that if it sounds like a duck and quacks like a duck, then it is a duck. Sometimes people need more convincing to agree that something is authentic. Jesus did enough, and those believed received, and those that denied cried.

There is no doubt He is the only begotten Son of the Almighty Father. He completed miracles that couldn't be duplicated. He is the only one that the Almighty Father praised before man. He is the Christ.

It is easy for anyone today to say they would've known Jesus was the Christ if they were one of the disciples. Ironically, the majority of them haven't recognized the angels that He has placed in their lives. Most importantly, Jesus Christ came and demonstrated to all that He is the Son of the Almighty Father. He did signs then, and He still does miracles, signs, and wonders today. Call on Him today in faith with clean hands and a pure heart. He will bless you according to the will of the Father. Claim it, frame it, and hang it in your heart! Amen.

AUGUST

New beginnings occur every day, and they are needed to help restore and strengthen our purposes for the kingdom and our relationships. Don't be afraid of new beginnings as directed from the Lord. He will sustain you!

August 1

> O Lord, our Lord, How excellent is Your name
> in all the earth, Who have set Your glory above
> the heavens! (Psalm 8:1)

When you look at the sun, you know it is excellent and powerful. You know that its sunlight can power the earth and beyond. Just like the sun is excellent and powerful, so is the Son. It's His name that's excellent and powerful!

Before the earth was created, His name was powerful, and it is through the His name that the earth and the heavens were created. The Father has given Him all power and authority over heaven and earth. His name is Jesus! Jesus Christ!

To call on His name is an honor, knowing that He hears His children. His name towers over the universe. Keep His name in your heart and on your mind as much as possible. Why? His name is amazing, awesome, and powerful, and it will help you hurdle your obstacles and overcome attacks against you. Let His name help you to do greater works today. His name is your daily guide. His name has already prepared you for today and tomorrow. Ask in His holy

Name to be utilized more to bring the Father more glory. Claim it, frame it, and hang it in your heart! Amen.

August 2

> And if anyone thinks that he knows anything,
> he knows nothing yet as he ought to know.
> (1 Corinthians 8:2)

Education is key to unlocking doors. Once we finished high school, we found out that most people need more education and training to make more money or to work in a passion. As Christians, we could read the Bible a thousand times or more and will never know everything. Let's use what we know to help us know more with an understanding that we will never know it all.

God is the only one that is all-knowing. He is the one that made it possible for us to know anything. We know nothing without Him, and with Him we will know what is needed according to our calling for the kingdom. Remember, someone that thinks they know everything is in more jeopardy than someone that knows nothing.

Educational accolades elevate you and help position you, but they don't provide you with all knowledge. Seek and govern them, but don't let your possessing of them govern you. Jesus Christ informed us that only His Father knows everything, so let's remain humble with the knowledge we do have and use it to help others. We have just enough knowledge to maximize our purpose for God, and He will provide more if we need it to accomplish more work for Him. Stay humble in what you know, and use it in your adhering to the greatest commandments. Amen.

August 3

> So He humbled you, allowed you to hunger, and
> fed you with manna which you did not know nor

> did your fathers know, that He might make you
> know that man shall not live by bread alone; but
> man lives by every word that proceeds from the
> mouth of the LORD. (Deuteronomy 8:3)

Your body needs food to survive, but it also needs water. Water makes up over 50 percent of our bodies, which means we can't neglect the responsibility to keep water in it. Jesus Christ is the living water that we need for our spiritual bodies, and we can't neglect that fact.

Jesus Christ is manna of today and tomorrow. He is the bread from heaven, the living water, and the Word that sustain our spiritual bodies now and forevermore. He wants all to come taste and see that He is good. Call on Him today and let Him help you through this day.

When the Lord interacts with you, it's because you have something special to do for Him. He will get your attention however He chooses to do so. His Word should already have your attention, and if this is so, then please live by His Word. His Word will keep you fed so you can be led! Led by Him to accomplish things you didn't believe you could accomplish. Keep His Word first, and feed off of it as it guides you through your walk of life. The Holy Spirit will help you as you live by the Word. Let Him lead you, believing that He needs you. Amen.

August 4

> Therefore those who were scattered went every-
> where preaching the word. (Acts 8:4)

The awesomeness of the branches of the United States military makes it powerful. Its military power has been displayed throughout the earth, demonstrating its overall awesomeness. Children of the Lord are part of His awesome army that's dispatched throughout the earth too. We have to keep conveying His love through our preaching of His Word.

Our Lord gave us the Great Commission, and we must adhere to it. It is nonnegotiable! We have to forge greater efforts in adhering to the Great Commission. The more souls we reach, the more soldiers for Christ we will have to develop into warriors of His Word. Every child of God must spread the Word.

You may have an awesome church home, but God may be sending you somewhere else to preach the Gospel. You are not confined to a location. Jesus Christ gave us the Great Commission with the intent of all of His children adhering to it. If you are a leader of a church, you have to ensure your church is adhering to the Great Commission too. There are many missions that need to be completed through spreading the Word of God. Spreading the Word will lead to preaching the Word. Let's preach the Word everywhere, believing that we are going to help save souls. Let's please the Almighty Father. Let's be diligent with confidence and boldness in our preaching and the teaching of His Word. Preach it today if you are led to do so, and do it in love. Amen.

August 5

> For You have made him a little lower than the angels, and You have crowned him with glory and honor. (Psalm 8:5)

You don't always need the most powerful weapon or the biggest force to win a battle. Snipers and Special Forces are essential to battles, but everyone doesn't see them when they complete some the most important tasks for the kingdom. Likewise, everyone didn't see the sacrifice, but enough witnesses and continued testimonies through the showing of our Lord's power through His children have proved He has been crowned.

We should always be thankful that the Lord came! He fulfilled what His Father spoke through the prophets. He is the ultimate fulfillment. With evidence then and evidence now, He has proven that He is the Messiah!

God decreased His Son to increase Him for the kingdom. Messiah prophecies had to be fulfilled, but a decrease had to be made first. He will do the same for you if you are willing to make a sacrifice. Children of Christ are to be living sacrifices unto Him. You must ensure you are prepared to do the work of a crown recipient. Trust and believe in your crown, and do the work that you have been purposed to do. Jesus Christ showed us how to talk and walk the Word, so let's please Him with reflections of Him. Remember, wars are won through obedience and sacrifices! Amen.

August 6

> This they said, testing Him, that they might have something of which to accuse Him. But Jesus stooped down and wrote on the ground with His finger, as though He did not hear. (John 8:6)

One of the reasons why some people don't want to have a house by the golf course is because there is a risk of golf balls shattering their windows. No matter if your house is near a golf course or not, your home is always at risk of something shattering its windows. In a similar way, Christians are at risk of things trying to shatter their peace, but we must press on knowing that our Lord will deal with those things.

Satan and his children are always looking for ways to bring accusations against God's children. Let not your heart be troubled by those spiritual distractions. Don't let the distractions pull you away from your assignment.

You have to be a greater example of God every day. You have to stomp temptations and keep evil thoughts silenced. No matter what people say about you, keep pushing. The Lord knows who you are. If you have asked for forgiveness and have repented of all things, then press on with your day. Satan wants to remind you of your yesterday, but those things were washed away, so please respect the washing away and enjoy the newness that Jesus Christ has prepared for you. Enjoy this clean hands and pure heart day in Jesus's name! Amen.

August 7

> So when they continued asking Him, He raised
> Himself up and said to them, "He who is with-
> out sin among you, let him throw a stone at her
> first." (John 8:7)

It is extremely rare for anyone to fly on a plane without bag-gage of some sort. They are either going to have checked baggage or carry-ons. As we take flight in our daily walk in life, all of us have baggage (sinned and fallen short of the glory of God).

Please repent, ask for forgiveness, and forgive to get that bag-gage off of you. Just like Jesus, let them know that they had baggage on their flight too. He knows of everyone else's baggage. Breaking news, checked-in baggage and carry-ons are not allowed in paradise.

We must repent, ask for forgiveness, and forgive daily! Even after doing those things, we still can't highlight other people's sins because we have been cleansed. Our words are powerful, and there are many individuals in need of a soft word and not a wrecking ball of their sins launched at them in the presence of others. Let's stay as clean as possible and help others stay clean too. As we work together to build one another up, Satan and his children become frustrated in their works. Let's keep frustrating them! Lastly, Jesus never exploited a believer's sins with the intent to humiliate and harm them. Let's follow His lead to build up, not tear down. Amen.

August 8

> The centurion answered and said, "Lord, I am
> not worthy that You should come under my roof.
> But only speak a word, and my servant will be
> healed." (Matthew 8:8)

In baseball, the manager sends in a closer to finish the game because the current pitcher can't get it done or the odds are against him winning the game are not favorable. Jesus Christ is our Closer! No matter the odds, we will win through Him.

Many individuals in high positions do not humble themselves, thus keeping them from progression and production that they are in need of. The lack of humbleness is like a wall. That wall can prevent the supernatural from flowing to a needed destination. Eat your humble pie to help your faith be maximized.

It is by faith that we can accomplish greater works. Your faith in Jesus Christ to do exceedingly abundantly above all you ask for is more powerful than you can imagine. An ounce of His healing power trumps all medicines and remedies on earth. If you are in need of it, or if you know someone that's in need of it, please have faith that it will work. In some situations, you may need to pray and fast too. Let faith pave the way to the healing that's needed. Your faith is the key! Amen.

August 9

> But the dove found no resting place for the sole of her foot, and she returned into the ark to him, for the waters were on the face of the whole earth. So he put out his hand and took her, and drew her into the ark to himself. (Genesis 8:9)

When traveling, it is best that you plan ahead instead of running the risk of there being no vacancies in the hotel of your desires. Please plan ahead to ensure you and your family have the best resting place. The Holy Spirit is hovering over the faces of waters, seeking more resting places for new beginnings. Are you seeking a new beginning?

Just as Noah sent the dove out, God has sent the Holy Spirit out too. We have a Helper that will only dwell in good ground. His indwelling is critical to our daily walk, so please try to maximize His help.

The Holy Spirit is always looking for another vessel to rest in. If you have clean hands and a pure heart, then you are a prime candidate to receive Him. He will only dwell in those that reflect the image of God. If you want to receive Him, then please ask the Lord for Him right now. Everyone may not have the same experience of how and when they receive Him, but it is an awesome experience. There is no better time than right now. It is right now that the Holy Spirit can use you. There are others that will benefit from you being filled with the Holy Spirit. Enjoy your indwelling of the Holy Spirit, and allow Him to open the doors that are currently closed. Amen.

August 10

> When Jesus heard it, He marveled, and said to those who followed, "Assuredly, I say to you, I have not found such great faith, not even in Israel!" (Matthew 8:10)

For years electricity has been provided by electric companies. When solar power was introduced to consumers, it provided another option to power homes, businesses, and other things. Sometimes the source can come from somewhere else and provide the same and sometimes greater results.

Faith is another supernatural element that we can't touch nor see, but it is powerful. There is neither a single church nor land that has the greatest faith, but one individual can have more faith than many others and a whole land.

Our faith has to be above-normal faith if our aim is to please the Almighty Father. Your measure of faith is the same as other Christians, but your level of faith is different. Your faith will unlock the doors that are in your path and unlock doors for others too. Ask the Lord to increase your faith if need be to help you with unbelief and other areas. He wants us to have everything that is promised to His children, and faith will greatly help us receive those things. Have faith in whatever it is that you are leaning on the Lord for. Have faith and have what you are in need of in Jesus's name. Amen.

August 11

> But if the Spirit of Him who raised Jesus from the dead dwells in you, He who raised Christ from the dead will also give life to your mortal bodies through His Spirit who dwells in you. (Romans 8:11)

We went to school to further our education because we weren't born with all knowledge. We are hampered in life without it, so we forge efforts to attain it as it opens many doors for us. Just like we need knowledge to open particular doors, we need the Holy Spirit to open supernatural doors.

Many will say they already have life, but this life that's provided via the Holy Spirit includes supernatural benefits for our bodies. He will empower believers in an instant according to His will. If you do not have Him indwelling in you, please ask for Him in Jesus's name, and you shall receive Him.

The Almighty Father is the only one that has it already figured out. He knows what we need, but we have to ask for it. Trust and believe in the Holy Spirit to be the supernatural force within you to elevate you over internal and external humps that you have encountered and the ones that may arise today or tomorrow. The Holy Spirit can do more than give gifts, and we have to lean on the Helper that was promised and sent for us. He is real and available to assist our mortal and spiritual bodies. Please don't neglect His power, but seek His assistance in all that you do. He is limitless, so please don't limit Him in assisting you today! Amen.

August 12

> Then Jesus spoke to them again, saying, "I am the light of the world. He who follows Me shall not walk in darkness, but have the light of life." (John 8:12)

In some churches, stores, gyms, and other locations where many people meet, they have a "lost and found" desk or designated area for the things that are lost and found. Are you searching for a lost item today? Ask Christ Jesus to help you find it.

Jesus is the Light that came to show His lights to light up life. He wants us to stay lit for the kingdom. He wants us to help others walk in His light and not in darkness.

Your light has to shine brighter every day because you never know who is watching you other than God. There are many Christians and others that are in battles that they can't win by themselves, but your light can push away some of the darkness that has a negative impact on them. Your light can also help guide others walk away from darkness while helping to light a path to the Light. Satan doesn't like the light that you bring, so please keep lighting the world up for King Jesus. Your light is more powerful than you know as many are silent toward your presence but enjoying your light. Be the light for Christ, and please the Father simultaneously. Amen.

August 13

> For if you live according to the flesh you will die;
> but if by the Spirit you put to death the deeds of
> the body, you will live. (Romans 8:13)

In Virginia, when taking the driving test, you can't get one question wrong referencing the signs. If you can't pass the portion of the test about the signs, then you can't proceed to the rest of the test. Knowing the signs will lead you in the right directions and help keep you alive when driving on roadways. Similarly, the Holy Spirit will lead you in the right directions and keep you alive for eternity.

You determine the winner of the tug of war between flesh and spirit. You feed the winner, and winner has to be the spirit. Since you are a child of Christ, your spirit is eternal and will never die, so feed it more. Feed it the Word daily.

When was the last time that you prayed and fasted? Your flesh doesn't want you to fast. The flesh is greedy and selfish. The flesh doesn't want your spirit to benefit as much as it does, so please ensure you allow your spirit to benefit more than your flesh. Your spirit returns back to the Almighty Father, not your flesh. Your spirit connects to the Holy Spirit to form a divine unity that elevates you to conquer more than you know you can conquer. You must live according to how the Lord has called you. You have to live to please Him, and the only way to please Him is in spirit and truth. Amen.

August 14

> For as many as are led by the Spirit of God, these
> are sons of God. (Romans 8:14)

Our mortal bodies are different; thus, all diets do not have the same impact. Our mortal and spiritual bodies can't survive from the same diet. The Spirit of God is the heavenly diet. How you are fed impacts how you are led!

The Spirit of God is your Commander in Chief that will lead you in spiritual warfare and other battles. He is undefeated in battle and can't be flanked by the opposition. Salute your Leader, and enjoy His leadership.

Since spiritual warfare doesn't take a day off, the sons of God are always on duty. The Spirit of God leads to daily victories. The Spirit of God connects with the faith of the sons, and victories are made like instant grits when Living Water is added to the battles. You are of the brethren destined to keep winning. You are destined to overcome those obstacles that have appeared to slow your winning momentum. No matter the obstacle, please trust and believe the Spirit of God to help you plow through it or over it. Nothing can stop Him, which means they can't stop you. Amen.

August 15

> But the ones that fell on the good ground are
> those who, having heard the word with a noble
> and good heart, keep it and bear fruit with
> patience. (Luke 8:15)

Planes are amazing. Sometimes when watching them, they don't look real when they take off, maneuver in the air and land, but we know they are real. They can take off, maneuver in the air and land properly because they are properly equipped. Likewise, the Almighty Father has ensured His children are capable of being properly equipped to take flight for and do great things for Him.

Some of the great things that He loves for us to do is bear good fruit. Since we accepted His only begotten Son as Lord and Savior and have the indwelling of the Holy Spirit, we are equipped to bear good fruit for Him.

Let your good heart lead you to bear greater fruit for the Lord. You are a tree that prospers on the good ground of the Lord to bear the fruit that pleases Him. People and other distractions pull on your heart, but don't let them pull you away from bearing good fruit for the Lord. Continue to be like a tree planted by the rivers of waters, bringing forth the fruit in the seasons that the Lord has ordained you too. Enjoy your in Jesus's name day. Amen.

August 16

> For as yet He had fallen upon none of them.
> They had only been baptized in the name of the
> Lord Jesus. (Acts 8:16)

If you are investigating a fight, it is best to hear both sides of the story. If you only have one side of the story, it is hard to determine the truth. This is similar to having both sides (the Messiah and the

Holy Spirit) of what the Almighty Father promised. You need both of them to be most effective for the Almighty Father.

Accepting Jesus Christ as Lord and Savior is step one, and receiving the indwelling of the Holy Spirit is step two of the divine equation. He is the ultimate tool bag. He has endless ways to help and comfort you. Let Him in so you can continue to win.

Do you have the indwelling of the Holy Spirit? He is a must-have, especially for spiritual warfare. He is not in hiding, but He is hidden from those that do not have clean hands and clean hearts. Let Him reveal secrets and unlock mysteries for you to be more effective for the kingdom. He will improve your studying of the Word, and He will show you ways to penetrate the internal issues within man. He is the surgical mastermind that will cut through layers of curses and resurrect the hidden gems within the children of Christ. He is able to do those things and more for you and others in the Name that's above all names. Ask and you shall receive! Amen.

August 17

> And if children, then heirs heirs of God and joint heirs with Christ, if indeed we suffer with Him, that we may also be glorified together. (Romans 8:17)

In US Army basic training, if one soldier couldn't make it through the confidence course, then the team failed. The team had to demonstrate that they are a unit on one accord overcoming obstacles together in the process. That's what we must do as children of Christ.

It is an honor to be a child of Christ. We have to imitate the image of God like Jesus did, be obedient to Him, and present our bodies as living sacrifices like He did. Let's also enjoy our inheritance here on earth and in paradise.

Our efforts are to be to the glory of God since we are His children. To be glorified with Him means we will not be received by everyone too. Our Lord endured suffering as part of the ransom He paid for us to be free and to be glorified together. It is an honor to be an heir, so let's ensure we conduct ourselves respectfully as we ought to. We are daily reflectors of His image and walking royalty to His glory. Claim it, frame it, and hang it in your heart! Amen.

August 18

> And you shall remember the LORD your God, for it is He who gives you power to get wealth, that He may establish His covenant which He swore to your fathers, as it is this day. (Deuteronomy 8:18)

Many wealthy families leave inheritances to their children. They can do this because they have an abundance of wealth stored up for their children and grandchildren. The Almighty Father has stored up enough wealth for His children that will never run dry.

Jesus Christ has all power and authority in heaven and earth, and He is more than capable of releasing wealth to His obedient children. Wealth is part of the reward that has to be utilized to help other children of Christ. Use your Christ-given wealth for the kingdom.

Since you are a child of God, you are entitled to His exceeding abundance. In His house, He has many mansions, and His children shall have mansions on earth since His will be done on earth as it is in heaven. In His will is an overflow of blessings for you. When you became a child of Christ, you became a magnet for wealth. Stay obedient, and portions of your wealth will be released to you according to His will in His time. Trust and believe in Him to provide the overflow that has your name on it in Jesus's name. Amen.

August 19

> Then they said to Him, "Where is Your Father?" Jesus answered, "You know neither Me nor My

> Father. If you had known Me, you would have
> known My Father also." (John 8:19)

You can't judge a book by its cover if you haven't examined the contents of it. The name of some books attracts readers, but it's the content within the book that will influence a reader to encourage another reader to buy the book. When you accept Jesus Christ as Lord and Savior, you are covered in His blood, and now you have to get to know Him and the Father.

We must strengthen our relationship with the Father. He is our strong tower, fortress, shield, the source of our strength and more. He has given us His only begotten Son. He has given us the Holy Spirit. He is our God.

When you accepted Jesus Christ as Lord and Savior, you are joined to the Father. They are the ultimate and most powerful tag team. To know one is to know the other, and to see one is to see the other. To better know the Father, you have to relate Sonship within your relationship with Him. This is why the Son informed His children that no one comes to the Father except through Him. Just like you can't have ice without water, you can't have the Father without having the Son. Please spend more time with Him and enjoy His presence. Amen.

August 20

> But Peter said to him, "Your money perish with
> you, because you thought that the gift of God
> could be purchased with money!" (Acts 8:20)

One of the most important things about love is that it is priceless. It can do so many things for you. One of greatest facts about it is that you can't purchase it. It can't be made nor can it be contained. God is love. Money is not love. Money can't follow us to paradise, but many have made it their paradise.

Money is needed for practically everything, but Jesus showed us that we don't have to chase it. There is no account of Him ever touching it, but He did direct the use of it. Let's make it, direct it, and use it for the greater good.

Don't let money make you. It has become a god to a lot of people, and many others treat it like it's their oxygen. We need it, but we can't worship it. We can't use it to buy anything of the supernatural. It is a tool that we have dominion over, and we can't let it rule over us. It can be a root to evil for you if you water it with love. Let's be great stewards over it and use it wisely to help others. Amen.

August 21

> But He answered and said to them, "My mother and My brothers are these who hear the word of God and do it." (Luke 8:21)

If you were new on the job, one of the ways to identify your coworkers is that you complete work for the same supervisor. That supervisor is pleased with his subordinates as long as they are respectful, follow the rules, and do their job. We have to do the same things to please the Father.

Obedience creates a bond with Him. Obedience is a key to pleasing the Father. He created us, and it is part of our reasonable service to obey Him.

This is one of the hardest verses for some individuals to grasp. This is because it's not easy for everyone to understand that our maternal and paternal family is not more important than the family that does the will of the Father. Our spiritual family through and with Jesus Christ is eternal, and our human family is not eternal. That's two main factors that highlight the difference between the two families. Being obedient to the Father's will is priceless, which brings forth endless blessings from Him. Those that do His will shall reside with Him now and forever more! Amen.

August 22

> Those who hate you will be clothed with shame,
> And the dwelling place of the wicked will come
> to nothing. (Job 8:22)

Two ways to recognize clowns is by the clothes they wear and because of the tricks they perform. If you see a clown performing their normal tricks, you won't get mad at them because that's what they do. Just as you won't get mad at a clown performing their tricks, you shouldn't get mad at a hater when they start hating you.

Jesus conducted His Father's business not concerned about haters nor the wicked ones. Haters are angry doubters that need prayer and deliverance.

Sometimes you don't know why particular people hate you. You just know that through their actions, they hate you. If they don't know, please let them know that you are a child of God. You may have to remind others too. The warnings are needed to help them, not you. Them hating you places them in danger of receiving the wrath of God since He said vengeance is His. Don't place a personal pronoun (*my*) on those that hate you, but place a prayer on them. Give them to the Lord, and let Him sort them out so they won't waste any more of your time. Enjoy your day not worried about haters. Amen.

August 23

> And He said to them, "You are from beneath; I
> am from above. You are of this world; I am not of
> this world." (John 8:23)

It's fascinating to see a bald eagle swim. While a bald eagle can swim in the same water as catfish, catfish can't fly in the air like a bald eagle. They are of two different worlds, but one of them can reach both worlds, and the other can't. Just like the bald eagle can soar and swim, Jesus can maneuver in the spirit and earth realm because He is Lord.

We serve a mighty God that simultaneously sits high, looks low, and is in the presence of His obedient children. When our Lord walked the earth and performed miracles never seen before, most didn't receive Him as the Christ. Their curved understanding prevented them from grabbing hold of the supernatural in their presence.

Although we are on earth, our spirits are not from earth. Our spirits came from the Almighty Father and will return to Him. Jesus was not of this world, and they misunderstood Him, and as you follow Him closely doing supernatural things too, many will misunderstand you too. Keep pressing on with the work you have to do for the Lord. Smile at the haters today and hope they have a great day. There's no need to stoop to a hater level. Amen.

August 24

> And they came to Him and awoke Him, saying, "Master, Master, we are perishing!" Then He arose and rebuked the wind and the raging of the water. And they ceased, and there was a calm. (Luke 8:24)

After natural disasters in particular areas, levies are reinforced or created to stop water from ruining living areas. The people can't construct these levies, so the state has to intervene to build them. Jesus can intervene for you if you need Him too. He can calm any natural disaster if it's in the Father's will to do so.

One of the reasons why Jesus is able to rebuke the wind and water is because He made them. No god can do what our God does. Just like He rebuked the wind and water, He can rebuke anything for you.

You may be going through a serious storm right now, but know that the Lord is with you. The walls may have fallen on you, and the light may seem far away, but the Lord is closer than you know. Trust and believe in Him to rebuke your storms. Your faith might not be as great as it needs to be, so please don't hesitate to call on the Captain of our salvation. He will save you from all types of danger and rebuke all things trying to impede your purpose for Him. Let Him calm the storms in your path so you can be most effective for the Father. Amen.

August 25

> Then He put His hands on his eyes again and made him look up. And he was restored and saw everyone clearly. (Mark 8:25)

Many people are in denial that they need to wear glasses. The glasses will help them see better, but pride prevents them from attaining the glasses. Pride blurred the vision of Lucifer, but don't let it do the same to you.

The power within Jesus can unlock many things as seen in the blind man. The power enhanced the vision of the blind man, and His power can enhance our vision to another level if need be.

Your human eyes may allow you to see the things of the earth realm, but you need your spiritual eye to see things of the spirit realm. Many Christians do not focus on their spiritual eye, but it is a necessary element that the enemy doesn't want us to use. He wants it to be made evil, so the Holy Spirit can't dwell within us. Our Lord can restore our natural eyes and our spiritual eyes if we are having issues with either vision. He wants us to be in position to do greater works, and having the proper vision is critical to completing our works for Him. Let Him clear your sight so you can be most effective when you fight. Fight with and for the King of kings! Amen.

August 26

> Likewise the Spirit also helps in our weaknesses. For we do not know what we should pray for as we ought, but the Spirit Himself makes intercession for us with groanings which cannot be uttered. (Romans 8:26)

As children are growing up, parents have to take them where they need to go and sometimes speak on their behalf. Parents have to get their passports and other important documentation since their children are not capable of doing those things. The Holy Spirit is one of our parents that will ensure we receive the supernatural help that we need to get us to places of need.

The Holy Spirit is the promised Comforter that will help us supernaturally through many situations. When He intercedes, it is instant victory. Let's do better at allowing Him according to why He was sent.

When people ask you to pray for them, you want the prayer to be answered, so it is best that you allow the Holy Spirit to pray for that person. He will pray through you in an utterance. He can see what is needed via the supernatural, so please let Him examine the situation and send the appropriate prayer upward for you. It is collectively not the norm, but we must lean on Him to help us as He was sent to do. He is the ultimate Helper. Amen.

August 27

> Now Jesus and His disciples went out to the towns of Caesarea Philippi; and on the road He asked His disciples, saying to them, "Who do men say that I am?" (Mark 8:27)

When we see a man dressed in a business suit and he is conducting business, it is safe to say that he is a businessman. If we see someone in military uniform and they are doing military duties, it is safe to say they are in the military. As we put on Christ and imitate Him, others should know who we are too.

Jesus fulfilled the prophecies of the coming Messiah. He is the Christ. He is the Anointed One. He is Yahushua Ha'Mashiach. He is the only begotten Son. He is the King of kings. He is Lord of Lords. He is Captain of our salvation. He is our Savior. He is the First Apostle. He is our Shepherd. He is the Word. He is the Beginning and the End. He is Alpha and Omega. He is Lord.

Who do they say you are? Even though they don't say anything to you, they have associated you to something or someone. They should be associating you to Jesus Christ if you are reflecting the image of God. This is significant to your efforts for the kingdom. Just like Jesus wasn't seeking their approval, we are not seeking man's approval, but we are somewhat interested in who they say we are. If you are obedient to God and walking in your purpose, then you know what most of them say you are. All Christians should want others to say we are children of God over associating us to something neither of God nor of our purpose. Your Savior knows who you are, and that's what matters most. Amen.

August 28

> When he saw Jesus, he cried out, fell down before Him, and with a loud voice said, "What have I to do with You, Jesus, Son of the Most High God? I beg You, do not torment me!" (Luke 8:28)

When a white towel is a hanging from a car window on the highway or road, it signifies that the car is disabled and needs towing. That's how we need to have demons throughout the earth. We need to torment them and have them waving a white towel to their father to come tow them away.

In the Bible, demons feared being sent to the deep (bottomless pit). When we encounter them, we must send them to the pit too.

When Jesus walked on the earth, He was the only one that they feared because they knew He was serious about sending them to the pit. They should fear you for the same reason.

When the demons see you, they will respect you too if they know you are reflecting the image of God, are confident, and know where to send them. We have to be on the offensive versus them instead of the defensive. For far too long, we have collectively talked about the demons being active, but we must let them see us be active against them. When they saw Jesus, they knew He was in the offensive position, which prompted them to react like they did. Do they fear you tormenting them? As you reflect the image of God, you keep them on notice. Reflect what they respect and fear! Amen.

August 29

> And He who sent Me is with Me. The Father has
> not left Me alone, for I always do those things
> that please Him. (John 8:29)

Magnet attracts its kind. If you have two magnets and flip one over, it will push the other magnet away. Likewise, as long as we don't flip to the other side (disobedient), the Lord will always be with us.

When the Almighty Father spoke in the beginning, He spoke to His Son to "let" things be as they are. If we want things to manifest, then we have to reflect the image of God. In reflecting His image, we are also pleasing Him. Reflecting His image is the key to supernaturally opening doors. If we don't reflect His image, the Son will not "let" our requests manifest through Him.

In pleasing God, let it be like breathing oxygen. We haven't always pleased God, but we must. We need Him in every nanosecond of our lives, leaving no time for the enemy. Pleasing Him has to be your priority. He loves His obedient, faithful, and obedient children. Please Him through love too. He needs all His children that are called by His name to do better at pleasing Him. We owe Him so much for creating us and sending His only begotten Son and His

Holy Spirit. Please Him throughout your day. Pleasing Him will also keep darkness away for a moment. Let pleasing Him be the joy in your heart, and He will show you how pleased He is with you.

August 30

> So Philip ran to him, and heard him reading the prophet Isaiah, and said, "Do you understand what you are reading?" (Acts 8:30)

Children need help with their homework, and we can't allow them to struggle through their learning. We must know the material too. Just like our children need help with homework, children trying to get to know the Lord and children of the Lord need help with their learning of the Word too.

The indwelling of the Holy Spirit is critical to the equipping of saints. He will guide you to guide others. He is a heavenly instrument given to help the children of the Lord. Let Him work through you to help others.

Everyday someone is in need of interpreting the Word of God. Not everyone is equipped with the Holy Spirit, and there are many that continuously toggle through Bible commentaries which cause more confusion than help in some efforts. Please allow the Holy Spirit to lead you in helping yourself and others understand the Word. Pray and fast for understanding too. Just like our predecessors received help in their research of scripture, we can receive the same help from the Holy Spirit. Hopefully, you can help someone today. Help them in Jesus's name. Amen.

August 31

> What then shall we say to these things? If God is for us, who can be against us? (Romans 8:31)

American football is an exciting sport. The professional teams are composed of great athletes. If an NFL team plays a peewee team, it will not be a contest. That's similar to our enemies going up against God. It is no contest, and I'm sure He would warn them before He destroys them.

The power of God stands alone. There is no other power that rivals it. No other power has stood up to challenge it. He is most powerful. He is undefeated for eternity. He is God.

Our greatness is predestined by God. He has laid the plan for us through Jesus Christ, and all we have to do is obey His Word. If you have aligned yourself in God's plan for you through obedience, nothing can stop you. He will clear jungles, dry up oceans, make highways into portals, create doors out from floors, provide smooth flights through storms, turn iron into noodles, and do other amazing supernatural works for His children. We are in His Hands now and forevermore. Enjoy your day knowing that He is with you. Trust and believe His power protects you and empowers you. Let the enemies speak to highlight themselves, then watch God silence them for you. Trust and believe in Him to fight and win for you. There is no other God than He. He has no opposite nor any rival. He has no competition. He is our God! Amen.

SEPTEMBER

Hopefully, you have already completed some praying and fasting days. If not, please make it a lifestyle. It is an awesome tool that helps you physically and spiritually.

September 1

> I will praise You, O LORD, with my whole heart; I
> will tell of all Your marvelous works. (Psalm 9:1)

Your résumé opens doors. The more work experience you have, the better your résumé will be. Some individuals inflate their résumé, and during interview sessions, they are exposed. The Almighty Father has an awesome résumé that has no comparison while containing all His works but He isn't looking for a new job.

The Bible provides a great résumé of the Almighty Father. His résumé contains His marvelous works, and we must glorify Him accordingly.

The Lord our God's marvelous works consisted of Him creating the heavens and the earth, the creation of humans and other life, miracles, signs, wonders, and other acts of love that confirmed Him as most powerful and most awesome. To top it off, He gave us His only begotten Son who fulfilled prophecies while imitating His Father. Additionally, He sent His Holy Spirit to ensure we have additional assistance on earth and to help us master our purpose for Him. No one can compare to the legacy that He has built. Let today be another day that you elevate His name. Tell more people about His marvelous works. The more you tell others about Him, you build more favor for you and your household. Enjoy your day knowing that you serve a God that enjoys seeing others like you uplift Him and tell about His marvelous works. Amen.

September 2

> Then behold, they brought to Him a paralytic lying on a bed. When Jesus saw their faith, He said to the paralytic, "Son, be of good cheer; your sins are forgiven you." (Matthew 9:2)

Some people keep jumper cables in their vehicles for themselves and to help others. They come in handy especially when you see someone in your neighborhood that needs your assistance with jump-starting their vehicle. Your faith can help jump-start others too.

Faith is a supernatural element that humans cannot completely define, but we know it is powerful. It can be maximized with the help of the Lord even to help others.

Your faith can also be like a battery to help jump-start someone else. All of us have been given the same measure of faith, but your faith might be greater than those closest to you. It is actually quite amazing how we can supernaturally help another child of God be healed or overcome a situation. Hallelujah to the Almighty Father for equipping us with the ability to help each other. There is a child of God that can benefit from your faith today. Ask the Lord to use you to help someone else today, and lean on your faith to accomplish the mission. Thanks in advance for using your faith to help another child of God. Amen.

September 3

> Jesus answered, "Neither this man nor his parents sinned, but that the works of God should be revealed in him." (John 9:3)

In the court of law, a person is innocent until proven guilty. If guilt is established, the person can be convicted of the offense against them. If God was on trial for working miracles for His children, He would easily be found guilty.

God wants to display His power too. We must let everyone know that if they are willing to give Him glory for the miracle that they are in need of, He will perform it for them. He has instituted an awesome quid pro quo system that we must maximize.

The Almighty Father loves glory. He wants the world to see His works, and when the glory hounds try to steal His glory, they will receive their rewards. He will complete more work for and with His obedient children because they will ensure He gets all His glory. If you will ensure He will get His glory, He will complete works through you too. There are many individuals that He can complete miracles for, and we have to make sure that He receives glory for those works too. The Lord works miracles every day, and if you know someone that's in need of a miracle, please ensure they know that if they will give the Lord all the glory, He can work a miracle for them today. Amen.

September 4

> But Jesus, knowing their thoughts, said, "Why
> do you think evil in your hearts?" (Matthew 9:4)

If we are taking baggage on an airplane, the baggage has to pass through a security screening process. Security personnel view the baggage via scanning devices. The scanning devices allow them to view the items on the inside of the baggage. This process is an awesome addition to security process. Our Lord can view our hearts in the same manner.

The Lord can see the hearts of man. He can see our intentions, which makes it impossible to hide the intentions of our heart from Him.

Not everyone wants to give God all His glory. Most of them do not have a relationship with Him, and the others are caught up in receiving some glory too. When you woke up this morning, He knew the intentions of your heart. Your intentions influenced or are influencing your initial response today toward people. Please ensure you remain as clean as possible today and beyond because Satan can use your intentions against you. Check your baggage and ensure it won't prevent you from taking flight. Amen.

September 5

As long as I am in the world, I am the light of the world. (John 9:5)

If the light goes out in your house, after you check the breaker box you have to check with the power company. Sometimes the power companies have issues providing power due to weather and unexpected outages. The Lord will never lose power, which translates to His children always being the lights of the world too.

The Lord's light drives out darkness! The enemy couldn't stop the light of the Lord, so today he forges great efforts to stop our lights. He can't pull the plug on lights that are eternal.

One of the reasons why we must let our lights shine bright is because we are a continuation of His light. We are like the continuous lights on a Christmas tree. We are to help illuminate dark areas and enhance other lights if need be. As long as the Lord has us in the world, there is always going to be light here. Satan doesn't like to see reflections of Christ, which is why we must be greater lights every day. Christ loves when you shine, so please Him today, allowing your light to help someone else today. Shine bright, child of God! Amen.

September 6

When He had said these things, He spat on the ground and made clay with the saliva; and He anointed the eyes of the blind man with the clay. (John 9:6)

When washing clothes, you will need bleach or Clorox to help you keep your white clothes white. Bleach and Clorox work like the Lord as they do what other elements can't do. It's like they produce miracles when they remove particular stains.

In the beginning, God used the earth to create us. We are miracles. Surely, His only begotten Son could use it to complete more miracles too.

There are still numerous miracles the Lord can complete for His children. He can work a miracle for you or through you if you are willing. He is always in the miracle-working business. Working miracles provide more opportunities to bring the Father more glory. Are you in need of a miracle, or do you know someone that is in need of one? Call on Christ to work the needed miracle, and call on Him with the intent of the Father getting more glory. Be prepared to shout glory and give Him your highest hallelujah. No one else can complete miracles like our Lord can. He is always willing, and you should always be willing to give Him more glory for another supernatural moment in love. He might use the earth to heal you too. Trust and believe. Amen.

September 7

> So let each one give as he purposes in his heart,
> not grudgingly or of necessity; for God loves a
> cheerful giver. (2 Corinthians 9:7)

Cubic zirconia stones and diamonds are both stones which humans determine the value of. They have glaring similarities, but it's their internal properties that help to determine their value. In the same manner, the internal properties of our giving determine its value.

God was the first cheerful giver. He gave His only begotten Son cheerfully to the kingdom. He gave the most precious Stone alive in existence. Our Chosen Stone radiates love, joy, peace, longsuffering, gentleness, goodness, faith, power, righteousness, mercy, grace, wisdom, kindness, and more to which no other stone can do. God gave His best.

In all that you do, please do it in the way that the Lord would do it. Imitate Him in your giving. He gave and gives in love. He gives knowing that you and other thankful children of His will give Him more glory. He has set the standard in giving when He gave us life and gave His only begotten Son to be a sacrifice for humanity. He is the King of giving. Please ensure your giving is power packed with love and joy. That ensures it will be receive in love and joy too. Amen.

September 8

> And God is able to make all grace abound toward you, that you, always having all sufficiency in all things, may have an abundance for every good work. (2 Corinthians 9:8)

Ants love sugary things. If an ant had a football field long of sugary food, it would be an overflow. They gather food to sustain them during seasonal work and for the winter. Likewise, as long as we seek Him first, God will ensure we have an abundance of grace to sustain us until the day of the Lord.

Grace is like oxygen. We wouldn't be here without it, and we can't live without it. It is an awesome gift to receive, and God has an abundance of it to release to His children.

The Lord provides the grace we need to sustain us, no matter the season. He equips His obedient ones reflecting His image for His glory. He provides an overflow of grace to ensure His children can proceed another day to bring Him glory. It's not about us more than it is about Him. His grace is actually a way of highlighting Him getting glory from those that receive His grace. Please let Him know how thankful you are from receiving His grace. Giving Him thanks for His grace may release more grace to you. Ensure you maximize the benefit of receiving His grace too, and let Him know that you don't take Him for granted. Amen.

September 9

> The LORD also will be a refuge for the oppressed,
> a refuge in times of trouble. (Psalm 9:9)

When watching movies that we've seen before, we know when people in trouble will be protected or rescued. In real life, we should know that God is coming for us, just like we know how the movie is going to end. We must use our faith in God.

Children of Christ are never alone and are protected against the works of the enemies that work against them. If you are His, then expect His promising hand. Help is on the way when you ask for it.

There is no one that can provide you the shelter like the Lord can. You need shelter from physical and spiritual trouble. Times of trouble normally don't come upon us lightly, which is why we must ensure we have the shelter of the Lord at all times. This is possible if you are in alignment with Him reflecting His image. There are situations that sprout up and try to overcome us, but our Lord has promised to be a fortress and shield to us. Seek Him, reside in Him, and enjoy His shelter. He is immeasurable and nothing can penetrate Him thus He is the best shelter in existence. He is our God. Amen.

September 10

> And those who know Your name will put their
> trust in You; For You, LORD, have not forsaken
> those who seek You. (Psalm 9:10)

There is no doubt that if you dial 911, you will receive the assistance you need from either the police, medics, or firefighters. You should have no doubt when you call on the Lord too. He promises to be there for those that keep Him first and only worship Him.

The Lord has not and will never lie. He has always and will always be there for His obedient ones. He allowed you to wake up today to witness His trust. Let God!

Just as easy as you can inhale and exhale oxygen, the Lord can inhale and exhale your situation. The Lord our God already knows the outcome of our situations, and He needs us to do our part in releasing them to Him. Once He has them, please trust Him to usher in a supernatural response that will bring Him more glory. There is no situation that He can't help you win. He specializes in what man calls the impossible. When it looks like He is not present, He provides evidence of His presence through miracles, signs, wonders, and favor. Trust and believe in Him today for more victories. Amen.

September 11

> And when the Pharisees saw it, they said to His disciples, "Why does your Teacher eat with tax collectors and sinners?" (Matthew 9:11)

In football, the best way for a coach to develop players is through spending time with them on the practice field. He has to meet them on the practice field then engage them accordingly. Similarly, the Lord gave us the Great Commission to help bring nonbelievers to the playing field through introducing them to our Coach we call Jesus Christ.

We have to adhere to the Great Commission and meet nonbelievers where they are. They are in need of the Lord too. We have to help them fill the void that Satan wants open.

Just like our Savior was with the people, so shall His children be. The best way to reach them is to be among them. There are many nonbelievers that we can reach, and we must forge greater efforts to reach them. Many of them believe Christians won't come to their locations, but we must meet them where they are. We must meet them with confidence and love. Many of them are in situations similar to our formers selves, and we must do our part in helping them become overcomers too. Let's imitate Christ and go where we are not expected to go to help others. Amen.

September 12

> Not with the blood of goats and calves, but with His own blood He entered the Most Holy Place once for all, having obtained eternal redemption. (Hebrews 9:12)

An FL diamond has no imperfections, making it a perfect diamond. A perfect diamond is expensive, which translates to everyone not being able to have one. Unlike a perfect diamond, Christ is the Chosen Stone that is perfect but available for all that seek Him.

The blood of Jesus Christ is most precious. There is no other god that can duplicate nor make a sacrifice with an impact like He did. His blood is supernatural and empowered like no other existing element.

His precious blood covers you if you are His. There is no way anyone should be walking this earth without being covered in the blood of the unblemished Lamb. His blood cleanses, covers, protects, qualifies, defeats, heals, elevates, empowers, and more. Please allow His blood to flow in the supernatural that sustains and perfects your natural. He wants others to come taste and see that He is good too, so please tell others about His blood that has helped you and sustains you. He would love for you to introduce His blood to someone today. His blood could help someone you know overcome depression, anxiety, addictions, and other obstacles today. Please help someone get covered in His blood today. Amen.

September 13

> Have mercy on me, O LORD! Consider my trouble from those who hate me, You who lift me up from the gates of death. (Psalm 9:13)

Cruise ships are equipped with emergency boats, rafts, life preservers, and other things that can be utilized in moments of trouble.

If there is a disaster, the focus is always on how the passengers were saved or rescued, and rarely is the cruise line given any credit for preparing for disasters.

The Lord our God can rescue us from any situation. Call on Him to help you, but in Him helping you, please ensure your intent is for Him to get glory.

There is no way we would be living today if He hadn't rendered His mercy upon us. He has always helped us. He doesn't help us for us to ride off in the sunset and rejoice for personal reasons alone, but His help is to bring Him glory to highlight His power. Let your motive be to highlight His power, love, mercy, and grace to include Him receiving more glory in helping you. Think quid pro quo, and when asking Him for help, praise Him in advance, knowing that His help benefits Him too. If you are in need of His help right now, please ensure your heart is prepared to give Him more glory before, during, and after you receive His help. All of your help comes from Him. Amen.

September 14

> How much more shall the blood of Christ, who through the eternal Spirit offered Himself without spot to God, cleanse your conscience from dead works to serve the living God? (Hebrews 9:14)

One of the usages of a microwave is to cook popcorn. Without the extreme heat hitting the kernels, the kernels can't be maximized for pleasing. Allow the blood of Christ to ignite you and prepare you for victory.

Our Lord's work was not in vain on any level, and we have to ensure we present ourselves as living sacrifices holy acceptable to Him. His cleansing of our conscience helps us prepare better for the battles that occur in our minds.

It is the blood of Christ that cleansed you when you accepted the only begotten Son of God as your personal Lord and Savior. That cleansing included your mind too. Your mind is the top target during spiritual warfare, and the workers of darkness look for dead works to exploit, but being cleansed of those things keep you in better position to win spiritual battles. The blood of Christ will also shield you from the spiritual darts of the wicked ones too. Enjoy your covered-in-the-blood-of-Christ day. Amen.

September 15

> And for this reason He is the Mediator of the new covenant, by means of death, for the redemption of the transgressions under the first covenant, that those who are called may receive the promise of the eternal inheritance. (Hebrews 9:15)

The cell phone was an awesome invention. It is a form of communication that connects people over short and long distances in an instance. Initially, unlimited plans were very expensive, but now they are reasonable, allowing you to talk as long as you want to. The Lord has provided an unlimited plan for you too through His only begotten Son. That plan is a never-ending inheritance.

He has paved the way for us to walk like Him now and forever. He told us of the mansions in His Father's house, and we are now eligible to reside in them without being concerned about vacancies.

The new covenant allows Christ to win through us. The promise of the eternal inheritance is priceless and most valuable to those that seek the love of God. You are called to receive the promise if you are reflecting the image of God. Let nothing tamper with your inheritance. You are chosen and more than a commodity for the kingdom. You are a resource for Christ equipped to bring value to every place He sends you. The attained promise is your heavenly eternal passport that never expires. Until you take off on the Day of the Lord, allow your gifts to help others attain the heavenly eternal passport too. Amen.

September 16

> But indeed for this purpose I have raised you up,
> that I may show My power in you, and that My
> name may be declared in all the earth. (Exodus 9:16)

Automobile companies utilize various types of media to push their brand out to the public. The media platforms push the name of the company, its products, and its emblem with hope that memories of the company's name influence you to purchase one of their products. In a similar manner, God uses His children.

He loves to show His power, and He needs volunteers to do so. He can easily show the world His power on His own, but there is more glory and joy in it when His children are utilized in the process.

The Almighty Father has purposed us in His will to do greater works for the kingdom. He knows the plans that He has for us. We must align ourselves within His plan and advance in it with confidence. As you reflect His image, you are helping His name be declared in the earth. Let Him win through you today too. This is another day to let Him use you to help others in need of prayer and more. He has raised you up today to be greater than you were yesterday, so enjoy your day in His name. Amen.

September 17

> Nor do they put new wine into old wineskins,
> or else the wineskins break, the wine is spilled,
> and the wineskins are ruined. But they put new
> wine into new wineskins, and both are preserved.
> (Matthew 9:17)

Old ways and new ways don't mix just like you shouldn't put regular gas in a premium gas designed engine. Putting the wrong fuel in the gas tank could cause engine issues. This is why you must read your owner's manual to ensure you are putting the correct fuel in your car. The proper fuel will allow your engine to flow properly.

The Gospel of Jesus Christ flows through His children. The Gospel can't flow through another gospel nor through nonbelievers. Even fasting according to the Lord has more impact than the fasting according to the rituals of the Pharisees. The authenticity of how the Lord does things can't mix with the rituals and traditions of man. The Gospel of Jesus Christ can't be contained within a nonbeliever because believers are glory-carriers and nonbelievers can't carry glory. This is similar to only Christians having the indwelling of the Holy Spirit.

The Holy Spirit won't reside in unclean vessels, which is why you can't receive His indwelling until you first be cleansed by Jesus Christ. When you are born again, the blood of Jesus flows through you, allowing your spiritual body to become eligible for His indwelling. This is another reason to be thankful for the awesome Almighty Father we have that instituted a standard that prepared us to receive the new wine in our new wineskin. Amen.

September 18

> Therefore He has mercy on whom He wills, and
> whom He wills He hardens. (Romans 9:18)

Car dealerships are not supposed to allow buyers to drive financed cars off of the lot without car insurance. Financial institutions are not willing to risk their assets being driven around without the proper coverage either. In the same manner, the Almighty Father doesn't want His children walking the earth without His coverage either.

Our Lord provides the best coverage. He is a resource of benefits that provide spiritual resources which equip His children to attain victories and favor.

As long as you are doing His will, you are within His will. He provides supernatural coverage to His obedient ones, unlike how you were before you were baptized in the name of the Father, Son, and the Holy Spirit with only liability coverage. Stay supernaturally covered while making a difference for the kingdom. His will allows His mercy too, which is like having additional coverage. Enjoy His coverage, and let others know how they can benefit from His coverage too. Amen.

September 19

> For though I am free from all men, I have made
> myself a servant to all, that I might win the more.
> (1 Corinthians 9:19)

Collectively, we don't rejoice in making bills, but we must rejoice when we pay them off. When you pay one off, you will be able to allocate the freed money to paying other bills off. Becoming debt-free will propel you to more freedom.

Our Lord was never in debt to man, but man is in debt to Him. He became a holy sacrifice for us to set us free from death, hell, and the grave.

Are you debt-free? When will you be debt-free? Freedom from debt will help you win more. It will free up more of your time for the Lord and allow you to help more people. The Lord has set us free to stay free from many things, and it is our responsibility to remain lenders and not borrowers. It is our reasonable service to help others, and we can be more effective in helping if we are debt-free. Look at freedom from debt as a prize. You are of a chosen generation of free children of the Lord and not of the in-debt generation. If you have clean hands and a pure heart with obedience to Him, please call on Him to guide you out of debt. Let your intent to be first for the kingdom so you can be more effective for the kingdom, and He will help you with your debt. Amen.

September 20

> He said to them, "But who do you say that I am?" Peter answered and said, "The Christ of God." (Luke 9:20)

If it looks like a duck, quacks like a duck, and walks like a duck, then it is not a bear. The visual and audio help to formulate an opinion of someone, but it is the internal being that defines the person. Our Lord walked the walk of who He is purposed to be, which helped to yield and continue to yield fruit for His Father.

The walk of the Lord was highlighted with Him keeping His Father first, remaining obedient to His Father, fulfilling His Father's prophecies, adhering to all His Father's commandments, and more. He pleased His Father in becoming the Christ as His Father promised.

You already know what the majority says about you too. You know your actions, intent, and love to others. Everyone is not going to have the same view of you, but as long as God loves your works, then you need not be concerned. Our Lord pressed on, pleasing His Father no matter the commentary of His works. We have to press on like Him. Our purpose for the kingdom will not bring all likes, but as long as it brings one love from God, we are doing fine. Know who you are for our Lord, and that's who you are to be to others. Amen.

September 21

> For she said to herself, "If only I may touch His garment, I shall be made well." (Matthew 9:21)

Before you plant a tree, you must dig deep into the soil to ensure the roots will be able to grow. Without deep roots, the tree will not grow to its potential. Your faith requires you to dig deep in your belief of something to manifest in the natural.

Believing is the first step in activating your faith. Believe first, and your faith follows on another level to connect the supernatural to a natural situation.

If you first believe within yourself that it is possible, then it is. Your faith is the engine that starts the vehicle of manifestation of the possible. Just like the lady's faith convinced her that she would be healed if she touched His garment, your faith has to be similar to her faith or greater. Your faith, whether big or small, can ignite a supernatural result when there seems to be no hope. Please allow your faith to allow the supernatural to flow to your lingering situation or to a friend's lingering situation. Love faith, have faith, use faith, and benefit from faith. Amen.

September 22

> But Jesus turned around, and when He saw her He said, "Be of good cheer, daughter; your faith has made you well." And the woman was made well from that hour. (Matthew 9:22)

Instant grits are easy to make. All you have to do is add heated water to the grits. Your faith is the grits, and the Lord is the heated living water that completes the process. Your faith is the meat and potatoes of the situation of need.

The Lord can complete the work without us, but He has equipped us with a measure of faith to help ourselves and others. He wants us to willing participants too. Let your faith help you win. Increase it so you can release it!

Your faith can make you well in areas of need too. You have to ignite your circumstance with your faith. Think about your current circumstances, and allow your faith to conquer them for you. Your faith is that supernatural element that can work in the earth and spiritual realm for your greater good. The more you exercise it, the more it increases. Let your faith connect with the power of the Lord so you can continue to overcome all your circumstances. Trust and believe in your faith to more than mountains. Amen.

September 23

> Then He said to them all, "If anyone desires to come after Me, let him deny himself, and take up his cross daily, and follow Me." (Luke 9:23)

To be a great leader, you must first be a great follower. The great follower learns so much from a great leader, then afterward the great follower transitions to be a great leader too. This is possible if great followers mature away from their former selves into great leaders. Thanks for completing your transition.

The Leader has set the standard in the Old Testament, then He reinforces it in the New Testament. We can be most effective for Him if we follow His lead.

You can be your biggest obstacle to the blessings that await you. You have to forgive and repent right now if need be. Ask Him to cleanse you if that's what's needed too. There is no time to waste. The Lord needs your presence to help someone else. Let Him know that you are willing to follow Him and be maximized for kingdom's purposes. The harvest needs you. The Lord knows that He doesn't have everyone's attention, referencing coming after Him, but He has a few faithful ones. Keep Him pleased with your efforts, not seeking self-satisfaction but seeking to please Him first. No one can follow Him with their former selves as checked baggage. Thanks in advance for denying all of you and following Him. There is so much that He will use you for. Amen.

September 24

> For Christ has not entered the holy places made with hands, which are copies of the true, but into

> heaven itself, now to appear in the presence of
> God for us. (Hebrews 9:24)

We can represent ourselves in the court of law, but having an attorney to represent us is most beneficial. An attorney can approach the judge, and we can't. This is why it is awesome to be a Christian because Christ goes to the Father for us.

The veil being torn highlighted the beginning of our High Priest's position for us. He is the one that can approach the Father for us. He has and will do for those that are obedient to His Father.

Christ is our High Priest. We don't have to go through another priest to speak to the Father. We take our requests to Christ, and He will make them known to the Father. He does this for His children that keep the Father first in their efforts. The Father loves obedience, and He has shown in His Word that rewards obedience. Let obedience be your twin, and Christ will present your twin before His Father and your requests will be met. Claim it, frame it, and hang it in your heart that Christ will do these things. Amen.

September 25

> And everyone who competes for the prize is temperate in all things. Now they do it to obtain a perishable crown, but we for an imperishable crown. (1 Corinthians 9:25)

Many of the runners in the Boston Marathon participate because the event is on their bucket list. They have no real interest in winning the race but will be satisfied with finishing it. That's not how we are to be, referencing running the race to receive our eternal crown. The way to receive it is to win it!

Our Lord provides eternal life, and that eternal victory awaits His faithful ones. He promises an imperishable crown, and you shall wear it if you remain obedient to Him.

One of the reasons we have to reflect the image of God and walk like Christ walked is because our walk leads to an imperishable crown. We can chase earthly crowns and watch them fade away, but the imperishable crown never fades away. The imperishable crown is not seen with natural eyes but will be seen with the spiritual eye when the time is right. The imperishable crown is the ultimate reward for reflecting the image of God and allowing Him to use you while you were running your earthly race. Claim your imperishable crown, and never lose sight of it. Amen.

September 26

> Therefore I run thus: not with uncertainty.
> Thus I fight: not as one who beats the air.
> (1 Corinthians 9:26)

There are some participants in the Olympics that are focused on winning, and there are some that are just excited to be in the Olympics. The ones that are focused on winning expect to win their events. Please ensure you are focused on winning for the kingdom and not just happy to be in it.

The Lord expects His children to be determined to make marks upon this earth providing more signatures of Him. He has mastered winning, and He can command victories for His children too according to the will of His Father.

The Lord blesses you to do many things, such as fight to win the race, within your purpose for Him. You will encounter many obstacles running your race, but the faith in the Lord to help you hurdle or go through them develops that certainty that surpasses normal understanding. That certainty enforces the belief in your victory. You already know that you serve a Winner and that Winner wants you to win too. Today is another leg of the race you are running, so run it knowing the fight is fixed for your victory in Jesus's name. Amen.

September 27

He answered them, "I told you already, and you did not listen. Why do you want to hear it again? Do you also want to become His disciples?" (John 9:27)

As long as you can retrieve the contents within a can of food, you are not overly concerned on how it is opened. If someone doesn't believe you, referencing how you opened the can, then they should've been there when you opened it.

The Lord pressed on doing the work of His Father, no matter the doubters. You must do the same.

Many doubters were proven wrong, referencing their position against Jesus, as many will be proven wrong referencing their position against you. Thirsting for the Lord and desiring to be greater for Him every day will increase you in favor. Many will spread your name abroad as they see you imitating the Lord. You may be the only Christlike one they've ever seen. Just like you will be seen as Christlike, you will also be seen as something else, but that's typical in this generation. Imitate the walk of our Lord while teaching all nations baptizing them in the name of the Father, Son, and Holy Spirit. Adhering to the Great Commission will attract more blessings for you and your household. Trust and believe in Jesus's name. Amen.

September 28

So Christ was offered once to bear the sins of many. To those who eagerly wait for Him He will appear a second time, apart from sin, for salvation. (Hebrews 9:28)

Children love to hear the ice cream truck coming. They are anticipating purchasing or their parents purchasing ice cream and other treats from the truck. It is a sweet anticipation just like it is a sweet anticipation of the return of Christ.

Yearning for the return of the Lord is a beautiful feeling. His obedient children have no worries of His return. He is coming, and every day seems as if it could be that day.

None of us know the hour, but we do know He is coming back for us. He is coming back for His bride, and we are within His bride. While we wait for His appearance, we must remain clean and reflect His Father's image. We have to help others too while we wait because everyone deserves a chance and all the assistance possible to help them benefit from the return of Christ. Make a daily note to yourself to stay clean and help others prepare for His return. Live like the Lord is on His way to pierce the sky. Hallelujah! Amen.

September 29

> So He said to them, "This kind can come out by nothing but prayer and fasting." (Mark 9:29)

When tenants have rodents, they can purchase various products to rid their residence of rodents or call a company. One of the most popular products is the ultrasonic pest repellent. The device's wave frequency is tuned to a level to specifically repel pests. In a similar manner, praying and fasting is specifically tuned to repel demons too.

Praying and fasting is completed for many reasons, but we must maximize its purpose to help others be delivered too. It's a supernatural element to fight in the spirit realm that many don't utilize as they ought to.

We don't know when we will encounter that kind the Lord is referring to in Mark 9:29. Many individuals come to the altar during church service for prayer, deliverance, and other reasons, and we must ensure there are ministers in position already praying and fasting in advance for them. We must be as proactive as possible to continuously combat the works of Satan. Let's be on the offensive instead of always being on the defensive. There are numerous souls that will benefit from your praying and fasting. Please ensure you have a praying and fasting lifestyle instituted within your household too. Praying and fasting is a weapon that you can form against Satan and His children anytime you want to, so please form those weapons more and more in Jesus's name. Amen.

September 30

> The man answered and said to them, "Why, this is
> a marvelous thing, that you do not know where He
> is from; yet He has opened my eyes!" (John 9:30)

One of the benefits of having car insurance is that they can have a locksmith come to unlock your car if you need that service. It's best that a locksmith does the work instead of you breaking a car window. The locksmith will unlock your car with ease, which will assist you with continuing on with your day. The Lord is your daily locksmith!

Many that walked when our Lord walked didn't know He was the Christ. They had seen false teachers that came before Him. They were stuck in their ways and other factors that kept them from receiving Him as the Christ. He didn't let that stop Him from helping His children.

The Lord can use you in the same manner to help unlock a miracle for someone else too. Since you have accepted Jesus Christ as Lord and Savior and have been baptized in the name of the Father, Son, and Holy Spirit while remaining obedient to Him with clean hands and a pure heart, we can use you. Your purpose encompasses helping others too, and the Lord will use the willing. The love and faith within you are a powerful combination that connects to the supernatural of God to perform miracles for others. Let Him use you today! Shout glory, and give Him all the praise and glory after He uses you too. Amen.

OCTOBER

Jesus Christ loves to see the obedient ones reflecting the image of God. He has many blessings to release to you, and the only requirement to receive them is obedience. He obeyed the Father, and we benefitted from it, so let your blessings from being obedient bless others too.

October 1

> Most assuredly, I say to you, he who does not enter the sheepfold by the door, but climbs up some other way, the same is a thief and a robber. (John 10:1)

The Department of Transportation has placed one-way signs on particular roads to inform drivers of the proper direction of traffic. The signs also help to prevent accidents. Similarly, the Almighty Father has given us His only begotten Son as the only way (one way) into the kingdom.

The Almighty Father ensured we knew which way to go; hence, He sent His only begotten Son. This is also why Christ said, "No one comes through the Father except through Me."

As you understand the significance of driving your car in the correct direction to reach your destination, you should also understand the significance of walking in the correct direction to reach paradise. The only way for a Christian to reach paradise is to follow the Way provided from the Father. Thank you for adhering to the

Great Commission as your efforts help others receive the correct way and not the false teaching and manipulation that are leading many astray. Thanks again for helping someone else receive the way. There is only one Way and His name is Jesus. Trust and believe. Amen.

October 2

> Then He said to them, "The harvest truly is great, but the laborers are few; therefore pray the Lord of the harvest to send out laborers into His harvest. (Luke 10:2)

A great man purchased land with the intent of converting the majority of the land into apple trees. Before he purchased the land, he ensured he had enough workers committed to help him complete the continuous work of maintaining and benefiting from the striving apple trees. Similarly, the Lord already knows who will labor for Him and hopefully you are one of His faithful laborers.

The Almighty Father sent His only begotten Son, and the Son labored for Him in love and obedience. Through His laboring, great fruit follows and continues to please the Father.

The Lord needs all His children to adhere to the Great Commission. There are so many souls that need to be saved, and the enemy knows that there are souls maneuvering throughout the earth without the covering of Christ. We can't allow another day go by without doing this critical work that will also bring God more glory. There are saved souls that need mentoring and equipping; our laboring will help in these critical areas. Your laboring has an impact, and the Lord is pleased every time you help save a soul. Thanks in advance for laboring for Christ. Amen.

October 3

> For though we walk in the flesh, we do not war
> according to the flesh. (2 Corinthians 10:3)

We have heard that we shouldn't judge a book by its cover. It is true because you first have to read the contents of it to make a fair assessment of it. In the same manner, people shouldn't judge someone according their flesh but consider their spirits too.

The Almighty Father created us via the earth and a spirit from Him. That same spirit plays a major role in our interaction with other flesh.

With our normal eyes, we see the people we encounter, and most of time we interact with them from a natural aspect. There are other things working within all of us as we interact with others, and we have to ensure that we govern ourselves to this fact. Our flesh came from the earth and our spirit from the Father, and it is what we received from the Father that allows our interactions in the spirit realm. Our flesh can't go where it is not from, but the spirit can work in the spirit realm. Daily battles manifest in the spirit realm, and flesh participates in an avatar manner. Many individuals have a hard time grasping this fact because humans use their natural eyes more than their spiritual eye. The Father has equipped us to win against the opposition of darkness, and our spiritual eye must be clean so we can win those daily spiritual battles. Win yours today in Jesus's name. Amen.

October 4

> For the weapons of our warfare are not carnal but
> mighty in God for pulling down strongholds.
> (2 Corinthians 10:4)

In the *Transformer* movies, the main characters are alien life-forms that can transform into vehicles or aircrafts. They are most powerful when they are in their alien life-form. In a similar manner, we are most powerful when we maximize our spiritual weapons rather than our carnal weapons.

The Apostle Paul mentioned in other scripture that we must have renewed minds. One of the reasons for renewed minds is so that we can be more effective in spiritual warfare.

The mind is a constant battleground, and you can't allow darkness to advance. We can't give darkness a millimeter of advancement. We must shut them down as soon as they show up. You have to stay ready. You have been given authority and power to dominate them, and they are hoping that you are not mindful to what you have been given from Christ. Let the Lord lead you in dominating them. Let today be another day of you dominating the opposition of darkness in Jesus's name. Put a thousand to flight today! Amen.

October 5

> Casting down arguments and every high thing that exalts itself against the knowledge of God, bringing every thought into captivity to the obedience of Christ. (2 Corinthians 10:5)

Most of the weaker animals in the jungle have to worry about trampling into the territory of the stronger and more aggressive animals. They face grave danger because most of them are not strong enough to defend themselves. We must convince the demons that they face grave danger if they cross our paths since we have access to the highest power and know where to send them.

One of the reasons we must have the mind of Christ is because we must be victorious during spiritual warfare. The forces of darkness can easily be defeated during spiritual warfare if you have the mind of Christ and the indwelling of the Holy Spirit.

Collectively, Christians are always in spiritual warfare. Our spiritual enemies don't take a day off, and we must not take days off from keeping them in their place and sending them to the pit. There are few Christians that want to engage them, and hopefully, you are one of them. We are the ones with the upper hand, but they try to trick us into not exercising our authority and power against them. Please do not give them any slack as they are responsible for manipulating many to commit suicide and murder. When they come up against the knowledge of God, we must shut them down daily. Thanks in advance for being on the offensive against them. You have the power! You are a giant in the earth and spirit realms. Claim it, frame it, and hang it in your heart! Amen.

October 6

> Inasmuch as there is none like You, O LORD
> (You are great, and Your name is great in might).
> (Jeremiah 10:6)

Boxers with undefeated records are highlighted as great. Most of them have encountered many challengers but have remained undefeated because they are the best in their weight class. Our Lord has witnessed individuals trying to promote their gods into existence, but their gods never showed up. If they were of any relevance, they still wouldn't stand a chance against our God but we clearly see how that is working out for them.

There is no denying that our God is the greatest. He can't be silenced as He has silenced any and every challenger. He is the undisputed and undefeated Champion of eternity.

Our trust is in the Lord because He is most powerful. There hasn't been anyone that can rival His power. He uses us to destroy those that come up against Him. There is not a surviving god or a god that can stand up today and speak of power like our God does. We are examples of His power, and the other ones have no proof of their power. His name is great for those reasons and more. Please carve out some time today to magnify His name in praise. He is more than worthy of the praise you will give Him. Thanks in advance for acknowledging who the real God is. Amen.

October 7

Then Jesus said to them again, "Most assuredly, I
say to you, I am the door of the sheep." (John 10:7)

In your neighborhood, you only have the key to the front door
of your house. That key most likely opens the back door too. Your
family has to use copies of the main key to enter your home. There
are no other keys that can open your door.

Jesus Christ is the only doorway for His sheep because He is
also the only with the key to the door. That door leads to everlasting
life with the Father, and no one else can provide that gift.

You have experienced or will experience false teachers in your
lifetime. Christ spoke of them to warn us of them. They impede
progress and cause confusion. Most of them want to take advantage
of your faith. They want to use your faith for their benefit which is
why they covertly present themselves as a door. Our Lord is the only
door because He has the keys that were secured during the infamous
three days. Please be watchful and help others flush out those trying
to present another door for the Lord's sheep. Amen.

October 8

All who ever came before Me are thieves and robbers, but the sheep did not hear them. (John 10:8)

Whenever a salesman knocks on your door, you most likely
don't want to hear another sales pitch, so you ignore them and let
them knock. That's how we must be with the thieves and robbers
that still try to steal us away from the truth.

An established relationship with the Lord will keep you
entrenched in Him. Many will come cloaked, but the Holy Spirit
will help you identify them.

The deeper you are rooted, the less you are polluted! The Lord
provided His Holy Spirit for many reasons, and one of the reasons

was so we could test by the Spirit. The Holy Spirit knows all spirits, and He will be able to help you identify the thieves and robbers of today. They come with other gospels and particular knowledge, but their works won't work on those that are entrenched with Christ. Please be aware of them because they will appear on your job, at stores, and even in the church. Help others identify them too. You might have to cast a demon out of them too. Be ready in the Name that's above all names. Amen.

October 9

> That if you confess with your mouth the Lord Jesus and believe in your heart that God has raised Him from the dead, you will be saved. (Romans 10:9)

In court proceedings, many lawyers convince their clients to plead the Fifth Amendment so they won't incriminate themselves. Christians can't plead the Fifth Amendment when asked if they believe in Christ Jesus. Christ loves when we confess of having Him as our Lord and Savior.

The Lord doesn't require us to do anything immoral or unethical to be His child. He requires a confession and belief in the truth of His resurrection.

Your confession and belief in your heart that God raised His only begotten Son from the dead secures your eternal inheritance. His resurrection was sacred, and supernatural blessings are still manifesting through His resurrection for those that believe. Please introduce Christ Jesus to others and help someone be saved. Helping someone convert into Christianity pleases the Father and covers a multitude of sins. You can help save a soul and simultaneously please the Lord if you are willing. Help someone else get in the Ark of the Lord. Please help. Amen.

October 10

> The thief does not come except to steal, and to kill, and to destroy. I have come that they may have life, and that they may have it more abundantly. (John 10:10)

Particular types of competition can influence individuals to do evil things to prevent others from winning. In sports, one player will attempt to seriously hurt another player because of competition for a victory. You should be excited to know that we don't have to compete with the enemy because we are already victorious. He believes that if he can win little battles, he can manipulate us in to believing we are losing the war. We have already won.

The enemy doesn't want us to have eternal life, nor does he want us to live our lives to the full. He knows that life more abundantly translates to us being able to help one another.

Our Lord wants us to prosper with the intent of us helping others prosper. Our prosperity is tied to a quid pro quo system that He has instituted. He has shown us what He has done for us; now we must do something for Him, and then He will do something for us. The enemy doesn't want us to partake in anything that benefits the kingdom; thus, he wages war against us. If he had things his way, all of us would be extremely poor, not able to help one another. Adhering to the two greatest commandments allows us have life more abundantly. Keeping Him first will allow the abundance to flow to you too. Also, please understand that life more abundantly pertains to more than having more money. In Jesus's name, this is so. Amen.

October 11

> I am the good shepherd. The good shepherd gives His life for the sheep. (John 10:11)

Most children don't know about the sacrifices their parents make for them. Most of them are only focused on what their parents can do for them today, and they quickly forgot everything that their parents have already done for them. We are children of the Lord, and we can't forget His sacrifice for us.

Jesus Christ is the only one who laid down His life for humanity. No other god could do or have done anything remotely close to what our Lord did for humanity. There is no other display of love like that!

Knowing that the Lord gave his life for us, we must be as impactful as possible. He said that we would do greater works, so let's please Him with greater works. Our works are able to manifest because He made it possible. Your works today should be to the glory of God and sacrifice of Jesus Christ. Your works must be in spirit and truth to honor our Lord. Be an honorable child of God today, and win on purpose for Him. Enjoy your in Jesus's name day by introducing Him and the Holy Spirit to others. Please the good Shepherd today and forever more. Amen.

October 12

> But a hireling, he who is not the shepherd, one who does not own the sheep, sees the wolf coming and leaves the sheep and flees; and the wolf catches the sheep and scatters them. (John 10:12)

It takes courage to become great. Many individuals that have fought in battles exuded courage on higher levels to help their comrades win battles. The courage of Jesus Christ is unmatched and can never be matched, which allowed Him to breeze through His battles for us.

Many Christians forgot that it took courage to do what Jesus did for us. He knew the enemy was advancing, and He laid down His life while defeating the enemy in the process.

If you have become a shepherd or are considering becoming a shepherd in a ministry, please understand that you must imitate the Greatest Shepherd. You have to be willing to go into spiritual warfare daily for your sheep (which are His). You can't and won't complete a sacrifice like His sacrifice, but you must be willing to fight off demons daily. Spiritual warfare is every second of every day, and you have to be ready to do battle every day. This is why everyone can't be a shepherd. It requires courage and the ability to dominate in the spirit and earth realms. Be strong and of good courage while leading your ministry. You are a giant for the Lord our God if you are one of His. Lead your ministry with unmatched confidence and faith the size of a watermelon. Put demons to flight daily for your ministry. Keep all demons on notice. Amen.

October 13

> No temptation has overtaken you except such as
> is common to man; but God is faithful, who will
> not allow you to be tempted beyond what you
> are able, but with the temptation will also make
> the way of escape, that you may be able to bear it.
> (1 Corinthians 10:13)

As parents, we have to allow our children to experience as much as possible. We know that they can't win their daily battles without us, but we can't be crutches for them either. God will not be a crutch for us, and He will not allow us to fall without helping us.

The Lord knows of the temptations that we face. He will provide a way out, but we must know Him to know it is Him helping us. He knows what's best for us.

You have been tempted to do many things. Some temptations you have succumbed to, and some you overcame. You know it's not always easy dealing with temptation, but consider the reward of not allowing it to win. If you feel that the temptation is too strong, please listen for the Lord and call on Him to help you. This is also why we must stay obedient to Him so He can help us when the evil ones provide next-level temptations. Trust in the Lord to be there during moments like this if you have remained obedient to Him. You will overcome that temptation with the help of the Lord. In Jesus's name, this is so. Amen.

October 14

> If anyone will not welcome you or listen to your words, leave that home or town and shake the dust off your feet. (Matthew 10:14)

There are pros and cons to being on salary as there are for working for commission. Your pay stays the same if you are on salary whereas your pay can change if you are on commission because it is based on performance and production. We have to work for our blessings similar to being on commission, and if we are rejected in our efforts, we keep moving performing and producing for the Lord.

The Word of God will not be forced upon anyone. We bring the Word to various people, and through faith they receive it. The spreading of the Word of God can't be stopped!

One of the responsibilities of a Christian is adhering to the Great Commission. There is a lot of work to be done throughout the earth. In some instances, some individuals have already had the Word brought to them and didn't receive it before, but you may be the water for the seed that was already planted. You may not be received everywhere you go to spread the Gospel, but know that your efforts are not going unnoticed as the Lord is watching your obedience. If you are led to do so, please pray for those that reject your efforts to spread the Gospel. Believe in your prayers to put their demons to flight. Trust and believe. Amen.

October 15

> Assuredly, I say to you, whoever does not receive
> the kingdom of God as a little child will by no
> means enter it. (Mark 10:15)

At approximately three years of age, children began to ask questions. They are learning and want answers. They are intrigued by almost everything, and that intrigue prompts them to ask questions. We must stay humbled and intrigued like little children.

You can be mature in the Word of God, but you are still His child. No human is an adult of God, but we are all children of God. That doesn't bode well with those that think too highly of themselves.

No matter how much knowledge we attain, we must remain children forever learning the ways of the Word. Please don't think too highly of yourself that you have surpassed the need to be a child of God. Many have attained knowledge and believe they don't need the Lord to reveal anything else to them. While this might shock you, please pay attention to this type as they drift into becoming false teachers too. Please steer away from individuals like that and know for yourself that you are forever learning needing the Holy Spirit daily. Be a joyful child of God, and He will reward you accordingly. Amen.

October 16

> The LORD is King forever and ever; the nations
> have perished out of His land. (Psalm 10:16)

A country's military power greatly assists in it being a superpower. No matter the size of their military, a superpower doesn't stand a chance against the might of our Almighty Father and will dispel them from their lands in an instance, reminding them that it is His land.

Any land that belongs to the Lord is supernaturally powerful. He will protect that land and destroy all its foes. Give Him the land that you want to possess or already possess.

Your home security system is a great tool to have, and you might have home protection, but your overall land must belong to God. He will defend your land since you have given it to Him. There are spiritual enemies that need to be defeated while you and your family are sleeping, and since it's His land, He will easily destroy them for you while you sleep. Trust and believe in the Lord to show His power to defend His children and their lands that they have given over to Him. Amen.

October 17

> So then faith comes by hearing, and hearing by
> the word of God. (Romans 10:17)

When we hear a train's horn off in the distance, we know it's coming. The train engineer sounds the horn because of an upcoming crossing or because of an emergency. That's similar to how faith moves, but faith is silent.

Our faith is more powerful than a locomotive. It is relevant in the spirit and earth realms. Faith is similar to love in the aspects of it being powerful, invisible, and impactful in the spirit and earth realms.

The Almighty Father has given us the same measure of faith as He is the Author of faith. Faith can be used as a weapon as we can form it against the power of the enemy. Our faith doesn't exist with doubt and worry. Maximize your faith today to allow the manifestation of those things that currently do not exist. Put your faith to work like you never have before, and it can also be utilized to help other believers in Christ Jesus. Enjoy your faith walk today, and win on purpose. Win in and with the Holy Spirit. Hallelujah! Amen.

October 18

> And He said to them, "I saw Satan fall like light-
> ning from heaven." (Luke 10:18)

It is great to witness your favorite team win a game, and if you missed it, you can play it back. It is a joy to watch a video of your team winning over and over again, but the losing team doesn't want to watch a video of them losing again and again. Satan and his team have to watch us win continuously, and they can't stop it.

Satan fell to the earth, but his power is beneath Christ and those that imitate Christ. He was kicked out of heaven with his infamous third, and they have to dwell with God's precious jewels that have souls and obedience unlike them.

Satan fell to a place where he can't dominate. We have dominion over everything that creeps upon the earth, and we have authority over the powers of enemy, which translates to us being the giants of the earth and spirit realms. This translates to you winning every day. He doesn't like to see you winning, so let Him see you win and dominate today through Christ. Give God more glory and hallelujahs today too. Our existences is to serve God, worship Him, give Him all the glory, lift up His name, give Him our highest praise, dominate in our purpose, reflect His image, and stay obedient to Him. Satan hates when we are consistent in those things because he has to watch us do in the earth and spirit realms. Dominate and win today in Jesus's name. Claim it, frame it, and hang it in your heart! Amen.

October 19

> Behold, I give you the authority to trample on
> serpents and scorpions, and over all the power of
> the enemy, and nothing shall by any means hurt
> you. (Luke 10:19)

Substitute teachers fill in for original teachers and are expected to attain positive results. The school boards have empowered the substitute teachers to be as successful as the original teachers, even if it is only but for a few days. We won't live on this earth forever, but while we are here, the Lord has empowered us to dominate as the first Teacher did when He walked upon the earth!

It is an honor to receive the authority to defeat all enemies of the kingdom. We are the giants in the earth and spirit realms, so let's dominate them!

We are the only children that have power and authority in the spirit and earth realms. This is applicable to those that are in Christ as Christ is in the Father. You must use this power and authority every day if need because the forces of darkness do not take days off. Please be on the offensive against them if you are led by Christ to do so because we have collectively been on the defensive for too long. Use your authority to trample upon them today with joy, and give God more glory in the process. You are a giant for the Lord! Put them to flight! Amen.

October 20

> Nevertheless do not rejoice in this, that the spirits
> are subject to you, but rather rejoice because your
> names are written in heaven. (Luke 10:20)

One of the most stressful moments of a football player's career is when they have to wait to see if they made the final roster. Making the final roster means the foot player is on the team and can focus on contributing more to the team. Our names being written in heaven means we made the Lord's team and need to focus on team goals, not individual accolades.

Our relationship with Christ allows us access to power and authority to do greater works for the kingdom, and we still have to govern ourselves with humbleness.

Your name being written in heaven highlights your rights within the royal priesthood. It's through the grace of God that our names are written in heaven. The wicked spirits names are not written in heaven; thus, they are destined to the pit. Let's rejoice in our next destination, not in the current and things we can do in it. The authority that we have over those spirits is not the greater achievements over receiving the eternal inheritance. Stay focused on the things that bring God glory. Amen.

October 21

> Then Jesus, looking at him, loved him, and said to him, "One thing you lack: Go your way, sell whatever you have and give to the poor, and you will have treasure in heaven; and come, take up the cross, and follow Me." (Mark 10:21)

When traveling, many of us use our GPS (Global Positioning System) to help us avoid traffic jams. The GPS will provide traffic details and possibly different routes to take to get to your destination. We can't allow the treasures on earth to block our true treasure in and through the Lord. Use the Lord's GPS (God's Positioning System) to lead you to the treasures in heaven.

If Christ is your treasure, then there is nothing more important than Him. The earthly treasures have expiration dates, but the treasures of heaven are eternal. Choose this day.

The Lord wants us to have life more abundantly, but He doesn't want the abundance to be the treasure we desire the most. You can attain a plethora of assets, but you should be able to easily walk away from them if you are led to. Please remember that God can replace anything you have attained, and when He replaces it, please know that He will give you more than you had. The treasures that you have here on earth have expiration dates, but your treasure in heaven is eternal. Deny yourself, the world, and the love of the world treasures, then you can effectively follow Christ. Seek first the kingdom of God and all His righteousness. Amen.

October 22

> The blessing of the LORD makes one rich, and He
> adds no sorrow with it. (Proverbs 10:22)

Implementing allowances to our children has its benefits. We must explain to our children that if one of them misses the mark and don't receive an allowance, they shouldn't be upset at their brother and sister for receiving their allowances. In the same manner, fellow Christians shouldn't get upset when God blesses one of their siblings.

The enemy wants us to believe that we don't deserve the riches of the Lord, but we must press on and receive what God is giving. Enjoy the blessings from the Lord.

The Lord our God blesses His obedient children more abundantly as He wills. He wants us to boast of His goodness and power so that others will know that He is God. Another reason He provides riches to His children is so we can help others that are in need. He doesn't want us to store up riches with the intent to inflate ourselves while ignoring others. When you receive your blessings from Him, please ensure you bless the poor and help someone else meet a need. It's one of our reasonable services. Amen.

October 23

> Let us hold fast the confession of our hope with-
> out wavering, for He who promised is faithful.
> (Hebrews 10:23)

The strength of each link within a chain determines its overall strength. Your hope in Christ is a link within the chain of faith in Him. Your hope also connects you to His promises.

Christ imitated His Father as He walked the earth through the fulfilling of promises and prophecies to include the sacrifice on the cross. He has proven that He will not break His promises, and there is nothing that suggests He will.

Your faith in Christ and belief in His sacrifice will help you maneuver through today. Your hope in Him activates His promises for you as it does for all that believe that He rose on the third day. He is faithful to answer your prayers and meet you where you are. Let your hope unlock the blessings you need today. Enjoy another in Jesus's name day, knowing He is going to answer your request. Amen.

October 24

> And let us consider one another in order to stir
> up love and good works. (Hebrews 10:24)

It is an awesome scene watching when people are rescued from being stranded on an island. You might not rescue anyone from an island, but you can help them get stranded off of negative circumstances. You can do this with love and good works.

Adhering to the second greatest commandment is a must. We don't know who will benefit from our love, so let's love them as we love ourselves.

There are many individuals experiencing depression, anxiety, addictions, loneliness, demon possession, and more to which our love can help them overcome those things. There are many individuals that do not have confidence in those closest to them, but they might have confidence in you because of your love and good works. Please maximize the opportunity to help as many neighbors as possible. Your love and good works may help with the stirring up of their love and good works too. You are a vessel for the Lord to complete great works like this for the Lord. Thanks in advance for helping your neighbors. Amen.

October 25

> Jesus answered them, "I told you, and you do not
> believe. The works that I do in My Father's name,
> they bear witness of Me." (John 10:25)

One of the great benefits of having surveillance cameras is that they capture intruders and thieves. The footage can be utilized to bear witness of their actions, and they could eventually get convicted of crimes. Similarly, even as your works bear witness of who you are to the Lord, not everyone will believe in you.

Christ walked in who He is. He walked knowing that His Father's hand was on Him. That helped Him to walk in confidence to complete His purpose. We must walk like Him!

Do the work of God and believe in your gifts. Speak it even if they don't want to believe you. Doubters are hungry spectators! Chickens will always have beef with you, but don't place yourself on Satan's grill. Let your works bear witness of who you are, and don't concern yourself with those that don't believe in your gifts from the Lord. Amen.

October 26

> Therefore do not fear them. For there is nothing
> covered that will not be revealed, and hidden that
> will not be known. (Matthew 10:26)

The game of hide-and-seek is intriguing because you have to seek out the person or persons that are hiding. Sometimes it takes a long time, but eventually, you find who you are looking for. Although He can see them, the Lord needs us to point out the demons that are trying to influence us to fear them.

The Lord our God will expose those that seek to harm His children. His children need not worry about the opposition, but the opposition should worry about He that avenges His children.

In your works for the Lord, you will anger demons and particular nonbelievers. They will mount up with evil wings, but our Lord will clip them in due time. Please don't worry about those that come up against you because of your belief in and your works for Christ. The Gospel has to be spread, and the truth has to saturate the earth. We are preparing the earth for the coming back of the Lord. Be not fearful of those outside the gate but maintain your fear of the Lord. The Lord has a special place for those that are not His and don't want to be His. Accomplish your works for the kingdom, and let the Lord take care of your lightweights.

October 27

> Whatever I tell you in the dark, speak in the light; and what you hear in the ear, preach on the housetops. (Matthew 10:27)

Every day millions of people go to work and expect to be paid for their work. If they are not paid for their work, they will be displeased and not want to work for their employers again. Be thankful that our God provides blessings to those that do His will. When God tells us to do something, He always ensured we are blessed more abundantly.

The Lord already knows who is going to be obedient to Him. He knows who is going to procrastinate and who is going to keep their feet on the gas for Him. It's best that the Lord tell you to pump your breaks than for Him to tell you to give it gas.

You have to be the voice of the Lord if He speaks to you. If He has chosen you, then He knows He can depend on you pleasing Him. It is an honor to have this type of relationship with Him, so please do it as He commands. The work that you have to complete will also bring Him more glory and simultaneously help others too, so complete your purpose in faith and love. Do it to the glory of the Lord! Amen.

October 28

> And I give them eternal life, and they shall never perish; neither shall anyone snatch them out of My hand. (John 10:28)

On Valentine's Day, while many women received dozens of roses, this one lady received a rose dipped in gold. There was a note that read, "This rose lives forever as my love lives for you." The rose dipped in gold is more valuable than ordinary roses. Children of Christ are most valuable as we are dipped in eternal gold.

Since Christ has the keys to death and all power and authority in heaven and earth, He is the one that gives us eternal life. No one else can give eternal life other than our Lord.

Receiving eternal life is a supernatural gift that we must cherish. Christ is the only one offering and providing eternal life. He can do this because He snatched the keys to death. Having life eternal also translate to us doing more work. The work we are doing now is training us for higher work when we are no longer on earth. The Lord has a plan for us in our eternal life. Rejoice today knowing that you have received eternal life and that you shall enjoy it with the Almighty Father too. We are in the hand of God secured for eternity. There is no better place to be. He is our God. Hallelujah! Amen.

October 29

> My Father, who has given them to Me, is greater than all; and no one is able to snatch them out of My Father's hand. (John 10:29)

People get safes in their homes to protect their valuables. The parents are the only ones that have the combination to the safe that protects their valuables against thieves and others. God is our combination that protects us, and He can't be cracked.

One of the reasons why no one can snatch us out of the Father's hand is because He is most powerful. He is an impenetrable fortress that has a royal grip on His valuables.

The workers of darkness will not take days off trying to snatch you out of the Father's hand. They are convinced that they can; thus, they keep trying with no positive results. It seems as if they don't know what insanity is because they keep expecting a different result. They are clever enough to know that in their doing they influence some Christians to become afraid of them, but we must remind all Christians of this verse. We might fall down, but through our asking for forgiveness and repenting, our Lord forgives us, and His forgiveness reminds us that we are still in the Father's hand. Press on child of God. Remind other Christians that we are secured in glory. Amen.

October 30

I and My Father are one. (John 10:30)

Identical twins are an awesome sight to see. It is said that many of them are opposite of the other, so sometimes you can differentiate between them because of their personalities. The Father and Son are the first spiritual identical twins.

The Son pleased the Father and gained more in the process. The Father worked through the Son, and the Son worked through the Father; thus, the Son could make such a powerful statement.

You have greatest within you, and He is most powerful. There is no other tag team like the Father and Son that we love. When we speak to one, we are speaking to the other. In your prayer time today, please tell them about your love for them and how much you appreciate them. They know the works they complete, and they are pleased when we praise their works. Give the Father your highest praise and all the glory throughout your day. Please Him in your praise. Acknowledge Him in every place and shout the name Jesus when you can. Let them be glorified through you in both the earth and spirit realms. Hallelujah! Amen.

October 31

> Therefore, whether you eat or drink, or whatever you do, do all to the glory of God.
> (1 Corinthians 10:31)

You never know who is watching you. There are individuals that feed off of your every move but won't tell you. This is one of the reasons why you must do all things to the glory of God. You are a glory carrier that must reflect glory in all of your ways.

He loves to see His reflections do things to His glory. He knows that the enemy is shamed every time we complete works that are pleasing to the Almighty Father.

Jesus did everything to the glory of the Father, and in doing those things, He pleased the Father. He is the light that we needed to see, and we are the light that some people need to see. As you imitate Jesus, please know that you are simultaneously pleasing the Father. In your doing, do it with love, faith, truth, mercy, and grace just as the Lord would do. That type of doing will also help you receive more favor from the Lord too. So in your doing today, do everything knowing that you are pleasing the Father. Be a Hallelujah for the Lord. Amen.

NOVEMBER

Things can get out of order, but you can call on Jesus Christ to help you stabilize them. As the Lord helps you, please consider asking Him if He needs you to do something for the kingdom. Very seldom do people ask the Lord that question. Try it!

November 1

> Now faith is the substance of things hoped for,
> the evidence of things not seen. (Hebrews 11:1)

When you were a child, if you have always received the gifts you asked for on Christmas, you are confident and certain that you will receive the gifts that you were asking for the next Christmas. Those past experiences of receiving what you asked for helped to build your faith in your parents. In the same manner, the past experiences of the Almighty Father delivering on His promises to us build our faith in Him.

Through witnessing the Almighty Father and Christ Jesus fulfill promises, we have confidence and the certainty of Him completing promising for us. Our faith in Him is developed from those precepts.

You already know the Father and Son will deliver on their promises. Let today be another faithful day in the Lord. Think about the things that you are hoping for, and think back to all that the Lord has done for all of His children. If you keep Him first, then your faith in Him knows that the things you are hoping for will manifest. They will manifest because the Lord never breaks His promises. He will allow manifestation in His time, which requires you to not be anxious. Maintain your faith in Him, and when you receive what you have been hoping for, please give Him all the glory. The Lord will deliver! Claim it, frame it, and hang it in your heart. Amen.

November 2

> For look! The wicked bend their bow, they make
> ready their arrow on the string, that they may
> shoot secretly at the upright in heart. (Psalm 11:2)

Very important people have security personnel that protect them. The security personnel check the homes and other places that the very important people will be visiting to ensure that the locations are clear of individuals seeking to harm the very important people. In the same manner, we must trust the Lord to protect us against those secretly seeking to harm us.

Trusting in the Lord will help you maintain confidence toward those that mount up wickedness against you. The Lord will do His part, and He needs you to do your part in staying clean so as to help keep His hand of coverage on you.

The more great works you complete in the name of the Lord, the more you will irritate the children of darkness. They don't like the light; thus, they war against His lights. They will plot against you day and night, desiring an opening that they can use to exploit against you. Please ensure that you maintain clean hands and a pure heart today, giving no openings for the wicked ones. They are hoping to manifest evil acts in the earth realm that first formulated in the spirit realm. They are of the wicked warriors within the spiritual warfare in process today as it was yesterday and will be tomorrow unless it's the Day of the Lord. So if they are plotting against you, they will not progress if you are clean as the Lord wants you to be. Stay clean, my friends, and enjoy the protection of the Lord. Amen.

November 3

> But I fear, lest somehow, as the serpent deceived
> Eve by his craftiness, so your minds may be cor-
> rupted from the simplicity that is in Christ. (2
> Corinthians 11:3)

Distractions are one of the main causes of driving accidents. This is also why most parents don't want their teenagers driving with a car full of teenagers. Distractions will take your focus off of the road and open the door to unwanted accidents. In the same manner, we can't allow ourselves to be distracted from obedience to God.

Once Satan distracted Eve and grasped her attention, he was able to manipulate her. He has done the same to others today. He uses others to help his works too. Stay in the Word of God to help you stay out of his snares.

There are many smooth talkers, masterful motivational speakers, and false teachers that will bend the simplicity of the Word of God to meet their agendas. You have to ensure that you are not relying on either of them to feed you the Word of God. You have to study to show yourself approved so you can help rightly divide the Word of truth too. The false teachers and particular others thrive off of Christians that won't allow the Holy Spirit to assist them in their learning, and in some situations it's because they don't have the Holy Spirit. The Holy Spirit can equip you better than any gifted man or woman on earth. Let Him help you today and beyond so you can help others defend against false teachers and particular others. It's your reasonable service to study the Word of God. Amen.

November 4

> By faith Abel offered to God a more excellent sac-
> rifice than Cain, through which he obtained wit-
> ness that he was righteous, God testifying of his

gifts; and through it he being dead still speaks.
(Hebrews 11:4)

You must ensure you put the correct fuel in your vehicle, or it will not function properly. Many individuals have placed regular gas in cars that were designed for premium gas, and they received bad results. We must have premium faith in what we offer to God so we can receive premium results.

The intent of your heart adds value or removes value. The intent of Abel's heart ignited the faith in his offering to God. Please know the condition of your heart in your offerings.

The intent of your heart fuels your faith too. Love and faith are a supernatural duo that can be unstoppable. In your offerings to God, ensure your heart is of love because love helps to increase your faith. Increased faith opens more doors! When you give, please give unto the Lord as you want Him to give to you. Let love fuel your release, which will also bring you an increase. Believe it and receive it! Amen.

November 5

Even so then, at this present time there is a remnant according to the election of grace. (Romans 11:5)

Out of the many elements in a kitchen, salt is the least of them, but it is one of the most-needed elements in the kitchen. It can enhance the taste of the food and help preserve food. This is similar to what the remnant is and can do for others within the kingdom.

Christ has a remnant on earth today. His remnant is His faithful ones that have made up minds for Him and are unmovable for kingdom purposes. Hopefully, you are within His remnant.

There are a lot of individuals throughout the earth, but it's the remnant of Christ that He is pleased with. They are visible to others while also being tucked away by the Lord. He keeps His hand on them as they are precious to the kingdom. If you are obedient to Him, keep the Father first, and obey His commandments, then you might be in His remnant. You and the Lord know if you are or not. Please keep clean hands and a pure heart so you can stay in the remnant, which keeps you safe when He pierces the sky on the Day of the Lord. Amen.

November 6

> But without faith it is impossible to please Him,
> for he who comes to God must believe that He is,
> and that He is a rewarder of those who diligently
> seek Him. (Hebrews 11:6)

If you have deposited money within your bank account, you expect to withdraw your money because you have money in your account. It's just that simple reference your faith in God. Deposit your faith, and withdraw accordingly! Your faith is supernatural currency!

Our Creator has always and will always honor His Word. He is never lacking in resources, nor is He lacking in answering prayers. Have faith in Him that has declared the end before the beginning.

You woke this morning because of the Lord's mercy and grace. Just like you expected to wake up this morning and like you expect to wake up tomorrow, you should expect the Lord to wake up a blessing for you. He loves to answer the call of His faithful ones. You can count on Him to ensure your needs are met. He is the ultimate guarantee! Look at your faith in Him as one key that unlocks many doors. Maintain your faith in Him, and He will maintain answered prayers for you. Claim it, frame it, and hang o tom your heart! Amen.

November 7

> Come, let Us go down and there confuse their
> language, that they may not understand one
> another's speech. (Genesis 11:7)

One of the reasons why some people get a two-story house is because the children can play on the first floor while the parents are upstairs. After receiving instruction not to make loud noises and the children keep making too much noise, the parents will come downstairs to discipline them. As seen in the scripture above, God will come down to deal with disobedience.

The Almighty Father can come down today if He chooses to do so. He loves and will not stop the progress of His obedient ones, but He will move swiftly against the disobedient ones according to His will.

It has been proven that if people work together to accomplish a goal, they will most likely accomplish it. Not every group of people works together for good reasons, and God intervenes according to His will to halt their progress. He won't stop the progress of those that are doing His will, which is why Christians can accomplish so much more if we work together to build together too. We need not be overly concerned about other groups if we can't get it together ourselves. God came down to stop major disobedience, and when Christ comes back, He will be coming to get those working together in obedience. Stay in the obedience group, and you will live for eternity with the Lord. Amen.

November 8

> By faith Abraham obeyed when he was called to
> go out to the place which he would receive as
> an inheritance. And he went out, not knowing
> where he was going. (Hebrews 11:8)

Children don't give thought to if they are going to have food to eat. They have faith in their parents to provide food for them. In the same manner, we must trust in God to provide for our needs too.

If God is sending you somewhere, He has already affixed the provision for you. Whatever you have in your bank account and retirement doesn't compare to what He has for you to help you prosper in your new location.

God has spoken to many individuals about leaving particular locations to go to another location, but the individuals won't go. Most haven't gone because they are in familiar places and trust themselves over what they have been told. Then the other reason they haven't gone as He has sent them is because they don't know the voice of the Lord. If you know for a fact that God is sending you to another location, you must press and have faith in Him to assist you in prospering in the new location. God doesn't make mistakes; we do! Please pray and seek His face if you need more clarity that it is Him that is telling you to go. He will ensure you know it's Him. Have faith in your Creator. Amen.

November 9

> So I say to you, ask, and it will be given to you; seek, and you will find; knock, and it will be opened to you. (Luke 11:9)

Most children believe in their parents because their parents don't lie and have always honored their promises. Not every parent fits that description, but our God does. He is the ultimate promise-keeper!

Having a relationship with God is a sacred connection that He takes seriously. When we are obedient to Him and have faith in Him, it is our way of showing Him that we are serious about our relationship with Him too.

Think back on all of the things that you have asked for but haven't received yet. Have you repented? Have you forgiven those that struck against you? Are you living in unforgiveness? Do you have clean hands and a pure heart? Are you keeping God first and remaining obedient to Him? If you have answered yes to those questions, then the only hurdle you must overcome is having faith in God to allow those things to manifest in His time. He is able! Trust and believe in Him, but most importantly, let your faith in Him be the priority today and beyond! Claim it, frame it, and hang o tom your heart! Amen.

November 10

> As the truth of Christ is in me, no one shall stop
> me from this boasting in the regions of Achaia.
> (2 Corinthians 11:10)

Many individuals in position of power boast of the things they have confidence in. Most of them boast in confidence because they can support their boasting. You are in Christ; thus, you are in position of power too, so boast of Christ with no worries but with confidence.

The Apostle Paul was fearless referencing preaching the Gospel of Christ. He knew the Lord was with Him; thus, he pressed on adhering to the Great Commission, pleasing the Lord.

We must be like the Apostle Paul in his fearless mind-set to boast of Christ. He wasn't concerned about offending naysayers. Jesus gave His life for us, and it is our reasonable service to adhere to the Great Commission with confidence similar to the Apostle Paul. We know that there are parameters set to stop us from boasting in particular places (job, library, court, etc.), but in the places we can boast in, let's boast joyfully in the Lord. Let's lift up His holy name in love letting everyone know He is risen and has all power and authority in heaven and earth. Jesus Christ is Lord, so press on boasting of the Gospel! Amen.

November 11

> These things He said, and after that He said to
> them, "Our friend Lazarus sleeps, but I go that I
> may wake him up. (John 11:11)

When you have computer issues and you call the help desk, most of the time they are going to ask you to reboot your computer. The reboot allows you to receive updates, and it restarts processes. The Lord can reboot His children and situations they are in too.

When Jesus conquered death, He ensured us that we can be resurrected too. Before He went to the cross, He demonstrated that death couldn't stop His power when He resurrected Lazarus. No matter the situation, always remember that the Lord can resurrect His children if it's within His will.

There have been testimonies of resurrections throughout the earth, and these types of testimonies will continue because of the love of our Lord, Jesus Christ. He and the Father love to receive praises and glory; thus, their works continue to bless us. Not only can the Lord resurrect a body, He can resurrect a situation too. Yes, He is in the resurrecting business, and He will never go out of business. As you go about your day loving the Lord, please remember that there is no situation He can't resurrect you from. No matter your medical, financial, or your spiritual circumstance, He can resurrect and will resurrect according to His will. Trust and believe, then you will receive. Amen.

November 12

> Then the cities of Judah and the inhabitants of
> Jerusalem will go and cry out to the gods to whom
> they offer incense, but they will not save them at
> all in the time of their trouble. (Jeremiah 11:12)

If you have issues with your car, you do not take it to a dentist, just like if you have issues with your phone, you do not take it doctor. There is only one Creator, and He is the only one that can save His creations out of any type of trouble unlike man that is limited in his assistance.

Our God has been saving His children out of trouble for thousands of years. No other god can confirm saving their children out of trouble because they don't exist!

Our God is the Creator of the earth and spirit realms; thus, He has no competition from other gods. He is most powerful, most awesome, and most amazing! Throughout the earth, we see so many religions speaking of their gods and other entities, but their power is nonexistent when compared to our God. Uplift His holy name today, and give Him all the praise and glory. Let the others see our God rescue you in your time of trouble, and in their time of trouble, they shall strike out waiting for their god to rescue them. Please be available to introduce our God. Please don't try to force our God upon them because in due time, they will see that their god is nonexistent, then they will come to our God. Amen.

November 13

> If you would prepare your heart, and stretch out
> your hands toward Him. (Job 11:13)

Before doctors perform surgery, the area is prepped with everything they will need to perform a successful surgery. The preparation has to be practically flawless because during surgery, the doctor doesn't have time to look for things to complete the surgery. In the same manner, we must ensure we properly prepare ourselves before something amazing can happen.

We must have clean hands and a pure heart before attempting to plea to the Lord for help. If you want to be seen, you have to be clean!

Let your day start with the proper preparation to walk with the Lord. In your preparation, ensure your heart is full of love and joy as it is affixed on the Lord. Ensure your intent is pure with Him getting glory. Then you can take the next step in reaching out to Him. He connects with those that walk in love. Let hate leave you, and let love lead you. Your preparation facilitates future godly manifestations. Lay the proper foundation of love, and use it as a springboard to the Lord. Amen.

November 14

> Where no counsel is, the people fall: but in the multitude of counselors, there is safety. (Proverbs 11:14)

Air traffic controllers help guide planes both in the sky and on the ground. Without the air traffic controllers, there would be chaos throughout the skies and when planes are trying to land. In a similar manner, the Lord has called His chosen ones to provide the proper counsel to help His children avoid chaos.

The Holy Spirit is the Counselor sent by the Almighty Father to lead the counseling of His children. Holy Spirit-led leaders of churches are more effective in counseling than those that have degrees or training in counseling.

If you have the indwelling of the Holy Spirit, then you can use the Master's degree of counseling. He knows our inner man better than we do, and He can use you to help counsel others. Doctors, psychiatrists, particular leaders, and other counselors do well, but the children of Christ deserve the Holy Spirit, who is the best at counseling. We must not forget that our Creator knows us better than anyone or any machine. It would be disrespectful to continue relying on man and counseling sessions when we have the Holy Spirit who is most reliable and free of charge. Trust in the Lord to provide you the best counseling and lead you in counseling others. Amen.

November 15

> And as I began to speak, the Holy Spirit fell upon
> them, as upon us at the beginning. (Acts 11:15)

A bird will nest in an optimum environment. It will not nest where the environment is not favored for peace, growth, and reproduction. This is also true of the Holy Spirit. He will not reside in any environment.

As the Father promised, the Holy Spirit was delivered to assist His children. Receiving Jesus Christ is step one, and receiving the Holy Spirit is step two. You must have clean hands and a pure heart if you want Him to dwell within you.

Even today, many have yet to receive the Holy Spirit. As seen in the book of Acts, many had accepted Jesus Christ as Lord and Savior, but not all had received the Holy Spirit. There are people in your family, church, and job that have not received the Holy Spirit, but you can inform them about Him. You can introduce Him to them. You can explain to them that the Almighty Father promised to send the Holy Spirit, and we have Him with us. You can explain to them that they will receive power when He comes upon them. You can explain to them that He will give them gifts as He wills. You can explain to them that He is the Master Locksmith that unlocks mysteries and guides them through the simplicity of the Word of God. Thanks in advance for telling others about the Holy Spirit with the intent of them receiving Him. Amen.

November 16

> Others, testing Him, sought from Him a sign
> from heaven. (Luke 11:16)

Some college students believed that they were just as smart as the professor, so they devised a plan to challenge him during a class. During class, the student wrote an equation on the board that they thought the professor couldn't solve. The professor solved the equation with ease. That how Christ is, referencing the overconfident ones. He made them look foolish and makes the ones of today look foolish too.

We can't usher in signs, but the Lord can, since He has all power and authority in heaven and earth. We were not called to entertain but to do greater works and fulfill our purpose.

Many will see the hand of the Lord upon you, and others will seek to discredit you. Not that we should fear them, but we must not be naive to the fact of the plots against Christians. Jealousy, envy, strife, hate, and other similar factors drove individuals to come against Jesus, and they will be the same toward those that imitate Him. Fear not them but the Lord. They will test you as they ought to according to their father, but they shall receive no sign lest our Father show them one. We do not boast in signs, but we do boast in the Lord. If you are challenged about providing evidence of the hand of God on you, please inform them that the Lord handles those requests. Christians don't need to put on a show to please man, so let man entertain themselves. Amen.

November 17

> Then I will come down and talk with you there.
> I will take of the Spirit that is upon you and will
> put the same upon them; and they shall bear the
> burden of the people with you, that you may not
> bear it yourself alone. (Numbers 11:17)

When you are always winning, you want to keep on winning. When others come from losing teams to your winning team, their lives change because they are no longer losing. Your winning attitude can be contagious. Likewise, the Holy Spirit is the winning spirit that is contagious and only resides in hosts that have Jesus.

The Lord can use you to help others receive the Holy Spirit. We are glory-carriers that also have the Holy Spirit in us. The Holy Spirit is contagiously good!

In Moses's time, the Spirit was upon them and not in them. If you have the Holy Spirit within you, you can help others receive Him. If you are a leader of a ministry, your leadership team must have the indwelling of the Holy Spirit. Leadership has to be on one accord to ensure there in no confusion to which the Holy Spirit helps to keep all on one accord for that ministry. There is no other option if you want the Lord to maximize your ministry. Be properly fed so you can keep the sheep properly fed. If you are not leading a ministry please know that you are a ministry. You are a ministry that spreads the Gospel of Jesus Christ and keeps the Almighty Father in all that you do. Press on making a difference for the Lord. Trust and believe. Amen.

November 18

> The wicked man does deceptive work, but he
> who sows righteousness will have a sure reward.
> (Proverbs 11:18)

Sometimes it seems like the crooked people are winning more than the good people. The crooked people receive what they work for in due time. Remember, not every tree can bear fruit, and not every bird can fly.

The Lord will bless those that reflect His image as His image is never wicked. His image reaps of righteousness and attracts its likeness.

Your intentions build mountains. Good intentions build mountains of love, and wicked intentions build mountains that block love. The love of God has to reach you, so please seek righteousness, and let your works be of righteousness. This is another echo of God loving to see those that imitate His Son as He walked upon the earth. His only begotten Son sowed righteousness and was rewarded accordingly. You shall receive rewards during your earth walk and your walk in heaven if you imitate the walk of King Jesus. Claim it, frame it, and hang it in your heart. Amen.

November 19

> As righteousness leads to life, so he who pursues
> evil pursues it to his own death. (Proverbs 11:19)

When there is a fork in the road, you have to make a decision. You must know which direction is best for you and take it. The best decision is the one the Lord wants you to take, but it has to be your choice. Chose the righteous road.

Christ is righteousness and everlasting life. He is more than the logical choice as Lord over your life. There is no other suitable candidate. He is divinely equipped to cover you as you live righteously.

What you pursue will eventually describe you! When you follow the guidance of the football coach, he will show you how to score touchdowns and win games. The Lord wants us to follow the righteous plays that He has planned for us so that we can score touchdowns for the kingdom. We are on the eternal winning team. As you pursue righteousness, you benefit from what it is connected to. Today is another day of seeking righteousness. Help someone seek righteousness too. It is your reasonable service, and you will please Christ in the process. Seek first the kingdom of God and all of His righteousness. Amen.

November 20

> Those who are of a perverse heart are an abom-
> ination to the LORD, but the blameless in their
> ways are His delight. (Proverbs 11:20)

Certain individuals have done many negative things that influence you to not want to answer your phone when they call or open your door when they come to your house. They are not a delight to your eyes and ears.

The Almighty Father loves to see those that imitate His Son. His only begotten Son walked the earth with love, was blameless, and pleased Him. That should be every Christian's daily aim.

Spiritual warfare is not easy to identify for everyone. One aspect of spiritual warfare is influencing individuals to become what God doesn't want them to become. Satan is crafty in his efforts; thus, his children imitate him to manipulate lost souls and others too. They don't want you and God's other children to be blameless. They love the blame game but not the blameless game. Staying blameless will keep the Father pleased with you. While you remain blameless, please seek to do more work for the Father because the blameless can be most effective for the kingdom. Amen.

November 21

> Now Martha said to Jesus, "Lord, if You had been
> here, my brother would not have died." (John 11:21)

When people gamble at the casinos, they believe that they are going to win. They generate such belief because of what's in their hearts and minds. If your heart and mind are affixed on the Lord, then trust that you are going to win with Him no matter the outcome.

No one knows everything that God has planned for His obedient ones. Trusting in Him requires us to let His will be done. This also requires faith in Him.

You will encounter individuals that will tell you that they don't believe in God because He didn't save one of their loved ones. This is common within those individuals that don't have a relationship with Him. He is our Creator, and He knows what's best for us. He will do things to glorify Himself and other things to help where most don't see it as help. Even when Christ completed the resurrection of

Lazarus, it still wasn't enough to convince everyone close to Him that He is the Christ. Either way, no human should be lobbying for God to please them, but all of us should be pressing on to please Him. Christ Jesus can resurrect anyone and anything all according to the will of the Father. Trust in Him to do exceedingly abundantly above all we ask for. Trust and believe. Amen.

November 22

> But when a stronger than he comes upon him and overcomes him, he takes from him all his armor in which he trusted, and divides his spoils. (Luke 11:22)

When children tell their parents that they have been bullied at school, the parents become furious and seek answers. Collectively, the parents want to go to the school to see who the bully is. As for today, Satan was the bully, and God sent His only begotten Son to deal with the bully for us.

Jesus Christ has all power and authority in heaven and earth, so it was easy for Him to bully Satan. When He encountered Satan, it was no competition.

We are the giants of the earth and spirit realms because our Strongman called Jesus Christ overcame Satan in the earth and spirit realms. He has given us authority, and those that have the Holy Spirit have power! You are a giant if you are a child of Christ with the indwelling of the Holy Spirit. Our Lord has set us up to be kings and queens of this earth, and no one can stop it, especially not Satan. Satan devises daily snares to keep us from maximizing our gifts, but we can't let him win. You are a giant equipped to leave giant footsteps upon all the land that you walk upon in Jesus's name. Claim it, frame it, and hang it in your heart! Amen.

November 23

> For assuredly, I say to you, whoever says to this
> mountain, "Be removed and be cast into the sea,"
> and does not doubt in his heart, but believes that
> those things he says will be done, he will have
> whatever he says. (Mark 11:23)

When you place you key into your ignition, you have no doubt that it is going to start if you have gas in it and it has no engine issues. That's how you must be when you want mountains to move. Your faith is the key, and your confidence is the ignition.

When Jesus walked the earth, He had no doubt toward anything. He trusted in His Father to see Him through everything, and that's exactly what happened.

Doubt receives energy from fear and uncertainty. You can't feed doubt. You serve an awesome God that is mighty, and He wants you to be mighty too. Having the mind of Christ will help you be most confident and crush doubt. Having no doubt also translates to the need to rely on faith. God loves His faithful ones. Erase doubt so you can witness the manifestation of many blessings while mountains are being moved. Claim it, frame it, and hang it in your heart! Amen.

November 24

> Therefore I say to you, whatever things you ask
> when you pray, believe that you receive them,
> and you will have them. (Mark 11:24)

In baseball, a pitcher is as good as his delivery. When he is on the mound, the team is expecting him deliver strikes and protect the lead. This is how you must approach your prayer life. You must deliver and not strike out when you are trying to connect to the Lord.

Your prayer life has to be consistent. It has to be a lifestyle. Think of praying like the earth and spirit realm are completing a handshake. Your prayer is like the hand reaching out and if the prayer is received by the Lord then He will complete the handshake.

If you are praying correctly, you will be leaving the earth realm and going into the spirit realm. It's kind of like you are merging the realms but you are not. Prayer gives your spirit the opportunity to work. The Bible says that flesh can't be in the presence of the Lord; thus, when you pray, you have to be in your spirit. Many people seek to have prayer closets because they want to cancel out as much distractions as possible. Now that praying is being done correctly with clean hands and a pure heart in obedience, those things that you are asking for will be released. Please don't forget about your angel's role in your praying. See Psalm 91:11 and Acts 10:4 for a better understand your angel's role in the praying process. Your prayers will be heard by the Lord our God. Claim it, frame it, and hang it in your heart. Amen.

November 25

> The generous soul will be made rich, and he who
> waters will also be watered himself. (Proverbs 11:25)

The train makes the same stops every day, and the only way to get on it is to have the right ticket. Look at generosity as a ticket to get on the train of blessings!

The Almighty Father has always been generous to His people. When we are cheerful givers, we activate other blessings for us too.

If you want it to rain blessings upon you, then you have to rain blessings on others. You have to be a continuation of God's quid pro quo system. God will release to those that He knows will keep being blessings to others. He knows the intent of our hearts and will bless us accordingly. You know how generous your heart is or isn't. If it is not generous, then please work on it as it can help others receive more blessings as well as yourself. Amen.

November 26

> For as often as you eat this bread and drink this
> cup, you proclaim the Lord's death till He comes.
> (1 Corinthians 11:26)

While in military uniform, service members are supposed to salute officers as a form of respect. The officers return the salutes to complete the respectful gesture. When we participate in the Holy Communion, we are saluting the Lord.

When we partake in Holy Communion, it is sacred, and one of the most important gestures of love we complete. Ensure you are clean before partaking in it.

You can complete the Holy Communion daily if you choose to do so. You don't have to wait until the church completes Holy Communion. Do what's best for your spirit, and don't get stuck in a tradition of doing it. Participating in it is a love gesture that is received and appreciated. Show your love for Him by participating in the Holy Communion when you can, and please ensure you have already repented and forgiven everyone. Lastly, ensure you have clean hands and a pure heart. Amen.

November 27

> He who earnestly seeks good finds favor, but trouble
> will come to him who seeks evil. (Proverbs 11:27)

One of the best usage of magnets is that they are used to help doors stay closed. The magnets help to secure locations too. We have to be magnets to the Lord so we can keep doors closed too.

One of the easiest things to understand about good and evil is the magnetism of the two. They are attracted to their elements. Let your elements stay good.

The best way to keep the hellhounds off of you is to maintain a heavenly scent. Just because you are an obedient child of Christ doesn't mean they won't try you. The good thing about being a magnet for good is that it can keep you in the presence of God. Keep seeking good, and help others understand the benefits of seeking good. Seeking good will attract the exceedingly abundantly that the Lord promised. Claim it, frame it, and hang it in your heart! Amen.

November 28

> Come to Me, all you who labor and are heavy laden, and I will give you rest. (Matthew 11:28)

Many employees are upset every year because they didn't receive seasonal bonuses. The bonuses are given to those individuals that exceed the standard and are excelling daily. In the same manner, the Lord rewards those that labor for Him.

Many have accepted Jesus Christ as Lord and Savior but haven't started laboring for Him. As soon as the laboring starts, the blessings start flowing. The Lord truly has a quid pro quo system in effect.

Think about what you have done for the Lord. Have you truly labored for Him? Have you put in late hours or made sacrifices for Him? It is our reasonable service to labor for Him. He will take care of His children that sacrifice for Him. He will ensure a reward for the labor. We shouldn't be looking for a reward since our true reward is our salvation. He will take excellent care of His laborers and give rest accordingly. Thanks in advance for helping us labor for Christ. Amen.

November 29

> He who troubles his own house will inherit the wind, and the fool will be servant to the wise of heart. (Proverbs 11:29)

There have been numerous instances when a person shot themselves in the foot with their own gun. Many of them were careless in their own homes, which led to the incidents. Similarly, don't shoot yourself in foot pleasing the world and others while allowing your home to fall apart.

Your home is your ministry too. The harmony in church should be the same in your household, and if not, then please seek counseling from your leadership.

Have you examined your household and your ministry efforts? They should mirror each other. Your actions must reflect the actions of someone imitating Jesus Christ at home and at church. Too many individuals are butterflies at church, but lizards at home. Jesus Christ was consistent everywhere He went. You have to remain consistent too, as some days it's not as easy as the previous day, but it will be done. Children of Christ have to be authentic and maintain a consistency of good as did the King of kings when He walked the earth. Be an awesome servant to He that came to serve in the earth realm that also has all power and authority over. Humbleness at its best! Serving Him helps you to be an awesome servant in your own home too. Set and maintain the example the Lord has set for us to follow. Amen.

November 30

For this reason many are weak and sick among
you, and many sleep. (1 Corinthians 11:30)

Everyone should conduct self-examinations. Self-examinations help to find hidden things that everyone else can't see. Similarly, you have to examine yourself before committing to the Holy Communion. If you find that you have a plank in your eye, please remove it before you proceed with the Holy Communion.

You can't partake in the Holy Communion as an unclean vessel, lest you curse yourself and family. Please take this effort very seriously and respect it as if your life depends on it.

The intent of the participants in the Holy Communion is critical to what they receive from the Lord. Your intent has to be holy since the Lord is holy. This is why we must stress to all participants to thoroughly examine themselves before participating. This is also why you have to assist us in reminding Christians to repent and forgive daily so as to stay clean in preparation for the next Holy Communion. Respect what you love, and if you love the Lord, then you will respect the Holy Communion. Amen.

DECEMBER

———⚬———

Let your faith keep you aligned within God's divine order so you can complete greater works for Him this month too! Let this year end in order! Let it end in peace and love!

December 1

> Get out of your country, from your family and from your father's house, to a land that I will show you. (Genesis 12:1)

Before a military force goes into battle, specific personnel are chosen to accomplish major tasks to help the fight against the opposition. Similarly, the Lord will select specific personnel to accomplish tasks that will be beneficial to many of His other children.

Our God needs faithful laborers, and He will handpick some of them. Those that are handpicked by Him will have a special anointing to accomplish greater works for Him.

When God speaks directly to you, it is an honor. He is letting you know that you have His total support. It is your faith that could be the long pole in the tent. Allow your faith in Him to propel you to accomplishing what He is sending you to do. Wherever He is sending you has more to do with saving souls over you prospering in a new location. Let the Lord use you. You have been chosen to accomplish mission possible. Complete it in faith, love, and confidence, and He will reward you accordingly. Thanks in advance for listening to the Lord. Amen.

December 2

> Behold, God is my salvation, I will trust and not be
> afraid; "For YAH, the LORD, is my strength and song;
> He also has become my salvation." (Isaiah 12:2)

In American football, the quarterback has to trust his offensive linemen to protect him against pass rushers. As long as they protect him, the team greatly benefits. God will protect you against the enemy too so others in the kingdom can benefit.

The Lord our God has proven to deliver on His promises. He has not and will never falter on His promises. Trust and see.

One of the best ways to start your day is to trust and believe in God to protect and strengthen you throughout your day. As you have seen in the past, you don't know what each hour will bring, but as long as you have God on your side, each hour is like a friend. He has been a fortress and promise-keeper for countless individuals that have come before you, and He will remain consistent for you and other obedient children of His. Trust in your Creator to ensure you have the proper coverage to prosper and do greater works for the kingdom. Amen.

December 3

> I will bless those who bless you, and I will curse
> him who curses you; and in you all the families of
> the earth shall be blessed. (Genesis 12:3)

Most of the time when you drive onto a military base, the security officer will verify who you are and allow you to drive through the gate. You have no worries because you know your identification (ID) card is valid. Your level of faith is like an ID card that allows you to get into high-visibility places.

God can see the level of faith in all His children, and the increased level of faith within some of His children helps in determining who sends on high-visibility missions. Hopefully, you have more than the same measure of faith.

Your faith in the Almighty Father is the ticket for your household and ministry. Your faith in Him is like a loving embrace and respectful hand salute. God knows who is going to give Him the highest praise and all the glory. Let today be another faithful day in the Lord. Know that the Lord has blessed you to do something great today and tomorrow. The major component in you fulfilling your purpose is your faith. It is the fuel that will help you drive into your destiny. There are things manifesting for your household and ministry because of your faith, and no child of darkness can stop them. Claim it, frame it, and hang it in your heart. Amen.

December 4

> There are diversities of gifts, but the same Spirit.
> (1 Corinthians 12:4)

In most computing environment, you will have many computers connected to a server. The computers receive their connectivity, updates, notifications, and other actions from the server that governs them. In the same manner, we are connected to the Holy Spirit; our gifts flow from Him.

The Holy Spirit provides the gifts; thus, He governs them. He is the Overseer of gifts, not man. Please beware of those that say they give what the Holy Spirit gives.

What are your gifts? Are you flowing in your gifts? Are you allowing them to make room for you? Are they making you great before man? When you received the Holy Spirit, you received power, and that power fuels your gifts. Holy Spirit power! Ensure you maximize your gifts as they are for the kingdom, and your gifts can help someone today if you are willing. The gifts from the Holy Spirit are not placeholders, nor are they placed on shelves. You received the gifts as a gift because you have presented yourself as a gift. You have to press on imitating the greatest gift Christ Jesus whom ensured we received the promised gift from the Almighty Father, the Holy Spirit. The Holy Spirit is the head coach, offensive and defensive coach, and special teams' coach of the gifts He provides to Christians. Ask Him to bless you with gifts that will bring the Father more glory. Once you receive the gifts, become the gifts and you will be most effective for the kingdom. Amen.

December 5

> Sing to the LORD, For He has done excellent things; This is known in all the earth. (Isaiah 12:5)

Due to improved technology, sports can be seen throughout the earth. Whenever there is a new champion, the information is known throughout the earth, and the proper respect is rendered to the champion of the sport. God is the Champion of the Universe. Please render Him the proper praises daily.

God has countless testimonies of His excellent works and power. No other god can boast of such testimonies. For thousands of years, others have created so called gods in their imaginations then made them into idols but those idols had no power. The other so called gods are silent because there is only one God. He is unmatched and unparalleled in all that He is. He is mighty throughout all the earth and the universe.

Today is another day to sing praises to Him. He is mighty in all that He does, justifying Him as more than worthy of praise. He is the one that ensures we have air to breathe and lips to praise Him with, so please sing to Him the praises that He deserves. You don't have to wait until church service to praise Him. You can praise Him in your house, car, gym, and other places so as not to bring attention to yourself but to the Father. You should praise Him before He blesses you, not only when He blesses you. Thanks in advance for praising Him. Amen.

December 6

> For whom the LORD loves He chastens, and scourges
> every son whom He receives. (Hebrews 12:6)

Many adults have agreed that they are thankful that their parents disciplined them as a means of correction and training when they were children. Not every child can grow up without some form of discipline and be effective as an adult. Our Lord disciplined and corrected us too as a way of molding us into greater Christians.

We are forever learning as we are being molded by the Christ daily. We need His type of molding, whether through punishment or any means He deems necessary for us to stay in alignment with the Almighty Father's will.

Sometimes we are going through things in life as a form of molding. The Lord will not put more on us than we can bear. His molding strengthens our relationship with Him and keeps us on track to greater works for Him. Examine your past circumstances and how they have made you better. The Bible reminds us to count them all joy because as sure as the rain comes, so will the sun. The Lord's molding is something you must embrace because it helps in equipping you to win the race. Embrace the chastening from the Lord as it molds you to be more effective for the kingdom. Trust and believe. Amen.

December 7

> Then shall the dust return to the earth as it was:
> and the spirit shall return unto God who gave it.
> (Ecclesiastes 12:7)

One of the reasons why we must place a return address on our mail is because the mail may have to be sent back to the sender. Our spirits were mailed to earth, and eventually they will be returned to the Sender.

Your spirit will live on past your flesh, especially since you have accepted Jesus Christ as Lord and Savior over your life. The Creator has sent your spirit as a boomerang is thrown, but you must make sure it returns to stay in His presence.

Christians have to spend more time in the Spirit as it prepares us for life after the flesh. Many individuals spend thousands of dollars on the flesh per year and practically nothing to enhance their spirit. The Bible is the first resource for your spirit, and then the Holy Spirit sharpens it. The enemy provides distractions and trickery, attempting to alter the properties of your spirit, so it will be damaged upon returning to the Creator. It must return to the Creator with the Son's signature on it. This way your spirit will be signed, sealed, and delivered! Amen.

December 8

> Also I say unto you, Whosoever shall confess me before men, him shall the Son of man also confess before the angels of God. (Luke 12:8)

Some people never get tired of playing their favorite song. They play it over and over again because it resonates within their soul. Our confession of Christ is one of His favorite songs that we should consider repeating more while bringing the Almighty Father glory.

Your confession will never get scratched like music records do. You know He loves to hear the confessions, so please let others hear it too. Whereas some don't want to hear it, it's music to His ears.

Your works, daily interactions with others, and your heart's intentions toward things show your confession to Him too. It is our verbal confession of Him that pleases Him too. Our confessions are some of His favorite songs He loves to hear. He laid down His life for us, and confessing our belief in Him as the risen King is the least we can do for such an awesome gesture of love from Him. We please Christ with our confession, and we anger Satan every time we utter our beautiful confession of Christ. Sing that song for the Lord as often as you want, knowing that He loves that song. Make a joyful noise in the earth and spirit realms today in Jesus's name. Amen.

December 9

> And He said to me, "My grace is sufficient for you, for My strength is made perfect in weakness." Therefore most gladly I will rather boast in my infirmities, that the power of Christ may rest upon me." (2 Corinthians 12:9)

Fathers love supporting their children, especially in times of need. It's not that fathers want their children to be in bad situations, but to show up and help them strengthens the bond of Father and child. In our times of weakness and sickness, the Lord is always there for us too, which also strengthens our bond with Him while showing His power as the Great Physician.

He has all power and authority in heaven and the earth, so surely He can strengthen His children when they are weak. He is the ultimate power source for those that are plugged into Him.

Many Christians present themselves as indestructible and hide their weakness from everyone because they view it as a negative sign of weakness. Contrary to popular beliefs, it's best that you let people know of your weakness because in due time, they will witness the power of Christ. He wants others to see His bond with His children, so invite His power into your weakness, and others will be encouraged as you are strengthened. Claim it, frame it, and hang it in your heart! Amen.

December 10

> Then I heard a loud voice saying in heaven, "Now salvation, and strength, and the kingdom of our God, and the power of His Christ have come, for

the accuser of our brethren, who accused them before our God day and night, has been cast down." (Revelation 12:10)

When a ship wants to stay stationary in the water, anchors are lowered to keep it from drifting away. When the ship is ready to move on, the anchors are lifted so the ship can proceed with its mission. We can't allow anchors to keep us from fulfilling our purpose for the Lord.

Pride and disobedience are like two anchors. They can keep you from sailing into your purpose. Surely they stopped Satan from fulfilling his purpose. Don't let those anchors stop you from fulfilling your purpose for the kingdom.

Fulfilling your purpose for the kingdom should be at the top of your list of priorities. Satan wants you to be fallen like him; thus, he sends his children against you and implements his wiles to lure you into snares. He was cast down to the earth, and since misery loves company, he is trying to make you his company. He induces things to try to increase your pride and cause disobedience to God, but you won't take the bait. Thanks in advance for staying obedient to Christ and not serving Satan. Amen.

December 11

And they overcame him by the blood of the Lamb and by the word of their testimony, and they did not love their lives to the death. (Revelation 12:11)

In cyber security, two-factor authentications are recommended to help protect information on computers. This method has proven to enhance computer security, but it can't stop all breaches, such as insider threats. Likewise, the Lord has blessed us with all the guidance and methods to deter the enemy, but we have to ensure our inner man is secure from the world too.

Satan was cast down to the earth where we have dominion. The blood of the Lamb and our testimonies are our first lines of defense, but the third layer of defense is as critical too. The third layer of defense is fortifying us against loving our lives on earth more than our eternal inheritance.

As the world turns, we can't get caught up with those that are spinning out of control in it. Many have denied Christ with their actions, and others are being swayed to and fro via other doctrine. Those things are influencing them to love their lives on earth over staying entrenched in the promised eternal inheritance. Staying entrenched in the promise influences Christians to deny themselves and continue to follow Christ. Have you denied yourself? Denying yourself is the release that helps you attain eternal peace. Claim it, frame it, and hang it in your heart. Amen.

December 12

For the Holy Spirit will teach you in that very
hour what you ought to say. (Luke 12:12)

People hire lawyers to help them win cases in court. In most court cases, lawyers advise their clients on what to say to ensure their clients to not say anything that will jeopardize the cases. The Holy Spirit moves in the same manner for us, especially when we are in situations where others are trying to manipulate us into snares.

The Holy Spirit is the Master's degree of guidance for us. He will help us steer clear of the snares of the enemies.

One of the greatest acts of love the Almighty Father did for us was providing the Holy Spirit. He ensured we had the best Teacher on earth so we wouldn't have to rely on man to guide us. Praying and fasting helps to bring you closer to the guidance of the Holy Spirit because it strengths spiritual disciplines and develops a healthy conscience of denying your flesh. The Holy Spirit is hovering right now, and if you need guidance today, please call on Him and allow Him to guide you. Allowing Him to guide you ensures you are not going into battles blind. His guidance ensures your fights stay fixed for your victories. Trust and believe! In Jesus's name! Amen.

December 13

> Then He said to the man, "Stretch out your hand." And he stretched it out, and it was restored as whole as the other." (Matthew 12:13)

A good business that is striving is flipping houses. Individuals buy houses and restore to increase their value, then the individuals resell them for profit. Our Lord is always in the restoration business to help His temples increase their value for the kingdom.

He is the Great Physician that has never lost a patient, and He never loses His patience. Whether it's a medical need or any other need, the Lord will meet you where you are to increase your value, which helps Him receive a return on His investment (the Sacrifice).

Christ is always willing and able to restore anything that we have lost or in need of healing. After Christ has completed the restoration, please give God the glory and use your restoration to bless someone else, which increases your value for the kingdom. You can't let today end without inviting Christ in to complete a restoration matter for you. Have faith that He will answer your plea, and your testimony will usher in more praise and glory to Him. Also, the restoration can happen instantly or in His time, so please maintain your faith in Him completing the restoration effort for you. It will be done in His holy name. Claim it, frame it, and hang it in your heart. Amen.

December 14

> Then the Pharisees went out and plotted against Him, how they might destroy Him. (Matthew 12:14)

In war, the enemy doesn't stop plotting against the opposition until the war is over. New strategies are formulated to counter the progress of the opposition. Satan and his children operate in a similar fashion. They are plotting against you now, but the Lord already has countermoves manifesting for you.

The Pharisees were more concerned with religious positions and their relationship with the military that ruled that land over recognizing Jesus fulfilling prophecies. They love their lives that they had, and they believed that destroying Jesus would protect their positions. We see how that worked out! He is the Risen King!

Keep in mind that the Pharisees were individuals that taught the Old Testament and believed in God. They were the perfect example of those that were so earthly minded that they were not spiritually good. Satan is always trying to enlist those that are religiously led because he can tamper with how they are fed. Press on with your purpose for the Lord, and don't be overly concerned with those that come up against. Once they identify themselves as enemies, please give them over to the Lord because vengeance is His. Let Jesus take care of your lightweights. He will deal with anyone that strikes against His children. Trust and believe. Amen.

December 15

> However, if you do not obey the voice of the LORD, but rebel against the commandment of the LORD, then the hand of the LORD will be against you, as it was against your fathers. (1 Samuel 12:15)

In war or sometimes for personal reasons, there are personnel that defect to another country. Once they defect to the other country, they are viewed as the enemy too. Please don't let Satan entice you to follow his disobedience and have the hand of God removed from you.

God's hand is like a steel curtain, and Satan's hand is like a bubble against it. Please remain obedient to God so you can keep the His holy hand on you.

Common sense never takes a day off! We can't follow disobedience as it leads to pit. Christ is the best example of obedience, and we must remain Christlike in our obedience. Let's mirror the obedience of Christ and please the Father in the process. Obedience to the Lord is within our reasonable service to Him. Let your day start with, flow with, and end with obedience to the Lord. As seen throughout the Bible, He rewards obedience with His presence. It's best to have His hand with you than against you! Amen.

December 16

> Be of the same mind toward one another. Do not set your mind on high things, but associate with the humble. Do not be wise in your own opinion. (Romans 12:16)

When you get four new tires on your vehicle, most companies offer free wheel alignment. There are some things that can cause your vehicle to come out of alignment, and being out of alignment will wear your tires down faster than expected. The enemy is searching for those that are out of alignment with the Lord, so please repent if need be and stay in alignment with the Lord.

Satan's lack of humbleness assisted in him being cast out of heaven. He thought too highly of himself while he was on high with the Father. Humbleness is like a repellent to him because it leads to good things for the Lord, so maintain your humbleness.

Whatever your earthly eyes are enamored with, the enemy will try to tempt you with! Some of his trickery is designed to get you out of alignment with the Lord. If you are out of alignment, then you can't effectively help your neighbor. Your neighbor needs to see godly consistency from you to include humbleness. Some of your neighbors are attracted to humbleness while steering clear of those that think too highly of themselves. Thanks in advance for your humbleness as it will help you connect to others that are in need of a light in their life. Remaining humble helps you stay on track to residing in Paradise forever. Amen.

December 17

Repay no one evil for evil. Have regard for good
things in the sight of all men. (Romans 12:17)

When girls are playing double-dutch, two girls turn two ropes, and another girl jumps inside the turning ropes. Before the girl jumps in, she watches the ropes turn over and over again, then she jumps in. Just like the girl is waiting to jump in, the enemy is lurking, waiting for an opportunity to jump in your presence so he can influence you to act out of character. Don't let him jump in! Don't turn the rope with the other person!

You have an awesome Lord that will avenge you. If evil has come up against you, please invite the Lord into the matter so He can deal with it. He is the Champion of the Universe and specializes in defeating evil ones.

For every action there is a reaction, but we don't have to always react according to the action. Most evil acts are designed to get a rise out of you in some form or fashion. It is not easy to not strike back if you are lacking self-control. Keep in mind that there is always someone watching you to see if you are going to turn the other cheek or give it to the Lord. Even if you try to walk away from some situations, evil will try to follow you with intentions of influencing you to strike back. Please don't give in to it, but pray to Christ, and He will deal with them accordingly. Trust the Lord to help you stay clean in the sight of all men. Amen.

December 18

> If it is possible, as much as depends on you, live
> peaceably with all men. (Romans 12:18)

Not everyone likes getting vaccinations. Vaccinations help to prevent diseases from spreading. If we know that an area is contaminated, most of us will not enter the area, while some individuals choose to put on masks and stay in the area. Similarly, you have to make a decision to stay among those that are not living in harmony or leave the area so they won't contaminate your efforts for the Lord.

Some situations we can deal with, and some situations we can't deal with. We have to make the best decisions to stay or go as it pertains to our relationship with the Lord.

To live in peace is something the enemy doesn't want to see happening on earth. He disrupted peace in heaven, and he wants to keep being disruptive on earth. We can't succumb to his trickery because it will disturb the peace that we need to have with our neighbors and cause us to separate. Sometimes there is too much disturbance and evil that you can't stay in the area with particular individuals. Please remember to seek assistance from the Lord because you may be on assignment and not know it. Trust in the Lord over your emotions. Amen.

December 19

> Beloved, do not avenge yourselves, but rather give
> place to wrath; for it is written, "Vengeance is
> Mine, I will repay," says the Lord. (Romans 12:19)

Some of the greatest boxers never lost a match because they were great in their time. Staying great requires confidence and experience. Jesus Christ is the undefeated and undisputed Champion of the Universe that has not and will not lose a fight. Our Champion will defeat our foes for us if we ask Him to.

The Lord wants us to fulfill our purpose, and anyone that tries to impede our progress will meet His wrath. He can easily defeat our foes, so we must let Him defeat another feeble foe.

You are a valued asset to the kingdom because the Lord has purposed you with dominion, power, and authority on this earth. With all that you have, and even if you can defeat your foe, please allow the Lord to do it. The time you spend fighting a foe can be used to give God glory and help a neighbor. The enemy wants to steal as much of your time as he can; thus, he wants you to waste your time fighting against those that the Lord will defeat for you. Let Christ in it so He can win it! Amen.

December 20

> If your enemy is hungry, feed him; If he is thirsty, give him a drink; For in so doing you will heap coals of fire on his head. (Romans 12:20)

In wars, some military leaders try to use psychological methods to frustrate their foes. The methods are effective in most instances and can provide leverage for victories. When we humble ourselves and usher in peace toward our enemies, it confuses them, and in some instances it makes them angrier. Hopefully, they like the humble pie.

We have to play chess with our enemies, not checkers! They want us to strike with conventional methods, but we have a Lord that will navigate us to victory. What better way to win against them than to show them some humbleness instead of fire?

Humbleness from a foe is like a slap in the face to those that are full of evil. Most enemies are used to receiving fire for fire, but when you give them water instead of fire, it will feel like lava to them. Humbleness helps you to usher in the unexpected peace that the enemies are not ready for. It will confuse them and disrupt their evil. Give them what they are looking for, and hopefully, it will help change their hearts. Amen.

December 21

> Then they came to Philip, who was from Bethsaida of Galilee, and asked him, saying, "Sir, we wish to see Jesus." (John 12:21)

If people want to see the mayor, governor, or leader of a country, they have to be vetted first, and hopefully, they will get a chance to see the leader. Most of those leaders have extremely busy schedules, so the likelihood of seeing them is slim. You should be thankful that your Savior is available at all times. His schedule is never too busy for those seeking His face.

Jesus Christ will appear to whom He chooses, and we have to be great examples of Him too through reflecting His image. Some people are visual learners, and you may be the only Jesus they see with their natural eyes.

There will be some that will ask you about seeing Jesus too. Are you prepared to point them in the right direction? Are you prepared to lead them into accepting Him as Lord and Savior over their lives? It is then that they will be able to see Him, or if they have been specifically chosen for greater works, He will reveal Himself to them. Until then, please remember that many are watching your walk with the Lord too. Sometimes people become part of a movement because of others. This is also why it is critical for us to reflect the image of God in all that we do. Someone's soul depends on it! Thanks in advance for helping others see Jesus. Amen.

December 22

> Then one was brought to Him who was demon-possessed, blind and mute; and He healed him, so that the blind and mute man both spoke and saw. (Matthew 12:22)

The term "all hands on deck" is used to say "Everyone is needed to help in a particular situation." There are many situations that one or a few individuals can't accomplish on their own, for which a leader will call others to assist with an effort. Similarly, the Lord wants everyone to know that He needs all hands on deck to spread the Gospel.

King Jesus heals His children with ease. He can do it today if you are in need of healing or if you know someone in need. Once you or the people you are helping are healed, He expects the healed to do more in spreading His Gospel.

It is within our reasonable service to help the kingdom. There are a lot of blind and mute people of today too, but from a spiritual aspect. They are blind because of false teachings and trickery they have grasped; thus, they are rendered mute, referencing spreading His Gospel. We can help them too because He needs all hands on deck. All hands are needed to prepare the earth for the day of the Lord. He is coming back! Thanks in advance for assisting others to be healed and delivered so they can contribute to the Great Commission. Amen.

December 23

> Life is more than food, and the body is more than clothing. (Luke 12:23)

It is quite amazing to know that birds have no currency to purchase food but always have an abundance of food. It's also amazing that the Lord waters all His plants throughout the earth and they need not worry about water. He takes care of us in the same manner.

The Lord will provide! He has a repository of blessings for His children. He is the best Father, ever ensuring we are always fed and clothed.

You need not stress yourself over the things you need if you are an obedient child of God. He takes excellent care of His obedient ones. Keeping Him first will open more doors for you and your household. Collectively, the fleshly body is the priority, but when your spiritual body is made the priority, you notice your needs met faster than expected. Trust in the Lord with all your heart, knowing that He is the great God of abundance. He releases blessings every second throughout the earth, so surely He can meet your needs today and beyond. No matter what, trust the Lord! Amen.

December 24

> Most assuredly, I say to you, unless a grain of
> wheat falls into the ground and dies, it remains
> alone; but if it dies, it produces much grain.
> (John 12:24)

We must be thankful for the farmers. They plant seeds to grow produce, which eventually feeds millions around the world. In the same manner, the Holy Spirit is like a farmer overseeing the growth of the seeds of Jesus Christ. Let's lean on Him to help us bear fruit for the Lord.

The Almighty Father planted His seed in the earth so that His obedient ones could live for eternity with Him. His seed is available for consumption, and those that partake of the seed will never hunger again.

You are a branch of Christ. His sacrifice had to be completed so the branches could be properly nourished too. He is the tree planted by the rivers of water, and as living water sustains Him, so shall it sustain his branches. Go about your day knowing that you are a branch of the Lord purposed to do greater works bearing the fruit He desires to see. His sacrifice was the greatest love gesture after His Father sending Him to become the sacrifice. In a show of respect, we must please Him daily via reflecting His image in spirit and truth. It is within our reasonable service! Amen.

December 25

> But Jesus knew their thoughts, and said to them:
> "Every kingdom divided against itself is brought
> to desolation, and every city or house divided
> against itself will not stand." (Matthew 12:25)

Superglue is a great addition to have in the home. It can be applied to surfaces to keep things together. It is used in major projects and in small projects with success. The Lord is our supernatural glue. He keeps us together and benefit accordingly.

King Jesus is our supernatural glue that keeps heaven together. We must maintain a relationship with Him so we can keep the earth together until the day of the Lord.

There are numerous movements and relationships that fall apart because they are not on one accord. Sadly, there are numerous disobedient movements that have some success because individuals come together to accomplish goals. As seen in Genesis 11, the disobedient ones made significant progress working together until the Lord shut them down. There will be similar acts involving disobedient ones moving forward in their understandings, and their works will be shut down too. This is the Lord's house, and those that flow with Him will enjoy the supernatural glue He uses to keep us together. The disobedient ones will reside outside the gates of the kingdom. The kingdom of God is on one accord, and those seeking to be in it eternally have to be on one accord too, lest they be cast away. Thanks in advance for your obedience to the Lord because He can use you for kingdom work too. You are an asset to the kingdom. Amen.

December 26

> If anyone serves Me, let him follow Me; and where
> I am, there My servant will be also. If anyone serves
> Me, him My Father will honor. (John 12:26)

Working for a demanding supervisor can be very stressful. If something is out of order, most of them don't have the patience to work with you to correct deficiencies. The only begotten Son knows that we are all works in progress, and He has shown patience in allowing us to develop. Thank you, Lord!

Christ has all power and authority in heaven and earth; thus, we serve Him alone as He and the Father are one. He is the only way to the Father and in the Father. As He embraces you, so does the Father.

We serve the Master and Commander of life for life. He is the greatest leader! He is the only leader that we can follow into eternity. That is one of the reasons why it is an honor to serve Him. You abiding in Him keeps the Father's hand on you too. You have the ultimate life insurance because you serve Him. Your coverage is endless and will not default. This is also why you go about your day with peace knowing that whatever today brings, the Lord will help you deal with it. Trust in Him to the God that He has promised to be. Believe it and receive it in Jesus's name. Amen.

December 27

> He is not the God of the dead, but the God of
> the living. You are therefore greatly mistaken.
> (Mark 12:27)

Sports fans invest in their favorite teams through claiming and representing the teams and purchasing their merchandise. When the team that they are cheering for is eliminated from competing for a championship, the hopes of the fans are dead. The Almighty Father reigns as the Champion of life; thus, we give Him the highest praises. He will never lose the championship! Never!

The Almighty Father is the living God; thus, His existence is for the living. The dead can't boast of Him, but the living can. Some of the dead can't even boast about the dead gods that mislead them to death. Our God reigns to uplift and sustain His obedient children whom are purposed to bring Him more praises and glory.

You are a child of God blessed with the eternal inheritance. Having Jesus Christ's signature on and in you qualifies you to receive the eternal inheritance. Those that do not have a relationship with Him can't produce the truth of Him. They are far from what they need; thus, you have to help those that are setting themselves up for failure due to a lack of understanding. Many of them have fallen victim to false teachings and trickery that blinds them from the manifold wisdom of God. Please stay ready to help the blind before they walk into an accident that they will have trouble recovering from. Amen.

December 28

> "Father, glorify Your name." Then a voice came from heaven, saying, "I have both glorified it and will glorify it again." (John 12:28)

Before you can withdraw money from the inside of a bank, you have to provide identification and your signature. If you don't deposit any money in the bank, then you will not be able to withdraw any money. Jesus Christ's obedience and sacrifice was the deposit made for us, and the Father was pleased with His love gesture.

The Almighty Father loves glory! He is overjoyed when His obedient ones accomplish milestones for the kingdom. He already knows what's going to happen, but to see it manifest brings Him pure joy.

Your efforts for the kingdom create supernatural deposits that please the Father. You are one of His investments that also have to present your body as a living sacrifice holy acceptable to Him. Although you can't repeat Christ's sacrifice, you can complete sacrifices away from the world and your flesh. The best sacrifice is done in obedience to the Father. You are walking in the name of the Father and Son; thus, your efforts are to be to His glory. There's coming a day when He is going to glorify His name through you too. Let today be another day of bringing Him more glory. The greatest sacrifices ushered in God glorifying His name and when He glorifies it again, please ensure you are in it. Amen.

December 29

> Or how can one enter a strong man's house and plunder his goods, unless he first binds the strong man? And then he will plunder his house. (Matthew 12:29)

Many homeowners have security systems and additional home protection to provide safety for their family. In some instances, the security measures don't work against advanced thieves. Similarly, King Jesus bypassed all of Satan's defenses and walked through His house, completing work as He pleased.

Satan is powerless against Christ. It can't be a fight between them because it wouldn't be fair to Satan. This is why he rages war against us, trying to find joy in influencing individuals to feel weak and useless against him. As a reminder, we must be on the offensive against him and his children and not on the defensive as in the past. We are not sitting ducks, but we are the giants of the earth in Jesus's name!

King Jesus came and conquered the earth and spirit realms. He reminded Satan that the earth is still the Lord's and fullness thereof. Jesus could've showed up and dominated without a sacrifice, but the Father's prophecies had to be fulfilled. It was if Jesus walked into and through the house, cleaned the floors, and took the trash out! He has given us dominion, power, and authority to continue plundering Satan's goods. Enjoy your day knowing that the demons can't touch you but you can cast them out to be destroyed. Enjoy being the additional security throughout the earth and spirit realms for the Lord. Amen.

December 30

> And you shall love the LORD your God with all
> your heart, with all your soul, with all your mind,
> and with all your strength.' This is the first com-
> mandment. (Mark 12:30)

You have to ensure that you have invested for your family's future. You can't depend on your current job to do it alone, which is why many individuals have sought investment firms. Your investments will also benefit your grandchildren. Investing in our Creator will yield best returns on your investment. He provides a lifelong benefit that never zeroes out.

The Almighty Father is the top priority. He didn't have to create us and sustain us, but He did it in love. He is most awesome and most amazing. We must adhere to the first commandment and keep it on our hearts and minds daily.

If you include God in it, you will win it! Please love Him above everything and everyone! Our God has shown that there is no other that can rival Him. He is the promise-keeper, shield of life, fortress of protection, a sniper with His blessings, a foundation that never crumbles, a weapon of peace and wrath against disobedience. He is love, righteousness, most powerful, and more. He is our first heart-beat and forever breath! He is Lord! He is our Master! He is God! Amen.

December 31

> And the second, like it, is this: "You shall love
> your neighbor as yourself." There is no other
> commandment greater than these. (Mark 12:31)

Love is one of the most powerful elements in existence. It is invisible to the natural eyes but powerful like gravity, keeping things grounded. It is a force that is everywhere on earth, and everyone uses it at the same time. God is love. Use love to help your neighbor as God would help them.

The Lord loves obedience, and your obedience will help someone else benefit. An act of love can be like having your favorite dessert and is uplifting like helium does to balloons. Use love to empower your neighbor.

You never know who is in need of loving kindness. Many are suffering from depression, anxiety, sickness, betrayal, addictions, and need of deliverance; your act of love can usher in the start of healing and deliverance. Your neighbor may be an angel of the Lord too. Anyone that comes in your presence should know that you love your neighbors as this helps you in being approachable while simultaneously allowing you to spread the Gospel of Jesus Christ to nonbelievers. God sent His only begotten Son to help, us so we must help others too. Helped people help people! Thanks for seeking first the kingdom of God and spreading the love of Christ. Those things help you help and love your neighbor as yourself. Amen.

Nugget for the Reader

SON OF AN ATHEIST: Father, how do I know you are my father?

ATHEIST FATHER: Your mother and I came together to create you.

SON OF AN ATHEIST: Like how the Christians say we come from Mother Earth and God is the Father?

ATHEIST FATHER: No, son, that's impossible! We come from nothing into something!

SON OF AN ATHEIST: That's weird, because it was possible for you and mother to come together and create me. Anyways, how do I know you are my father?

ATHEIST FATHER: Well, you look like me, you walk like me, do things like I do. My blood is in you, and when people see you, they see me.

SON OF AN ATHEIST: Oh, like how the Christians say Jesus is like His Father, He is in His believers, and when people see believers, they see His Father's image?

ATHEIST FATHER: No, son!

SON OF AN ATHEIST: So, Father, since I wasn't there when you and mother came together to create me, why should I believe you?

ATHEIST FATHER: Son, you have to trust and believe me!

Son of an atheist: Oh, trust and believe like how the Christians trust and believe in God?

ATHEIST FATHER: No, son!

SON OF AN ATHEIST: Father, I'm sorry for making you angry. Do you forgive me?

ATHEIST FATHER: Yes, son. I forgive you.

SON OF AN ATHEIST: Oh, like how God forgives His children?

ATHEIST FATHER: No, son!

SON OF AN ATHEIST: Father, this is my last question. Is it true that Mom sacrificed her life for me to be born because she could have died given birth to me?

ATHEIST FATHER: Yes, son.

SON OF AN ATHEIST: Oh, like how Jesus died on the cross for all of us! Thanks, Father! This conversation has helped me become a believer in Jesus Christ!

ATHEIST FATHER: (No comment.)

ABOUT THE AUTHOR

Calvin Brown is a man of God. Since accepting Jesus Christ as Lord and Savior, he has forged greater efforts to help others. He has the indwelling of the Holy Spirit who blessed him with spiritual gifts.

At the age of seven, Calvin was playing in the local swimming pool with friends. An older person lifted him up and dumped him in the water but forgot the depth of the water they were in. Calvin's head hit the bottom of the pool, and he was knocked unconscious. He eventually gained consciousness and went home. As days passed, Calvin became very ill, and his mother called the ambulance. The doctors told his mother, Shirley McDaniel, that he has a blood clot on his brain and he was dying. After further examinations, they concluded that they could not save his life and gave him two weeks to live. His mother took him home after the doctors said they could not do anything to keep him alive. She took him home because she did not want to give up on her son. Many days went by, and Calvin's illness worsened. His mother didn't give up on him. She called the closest local doctor, and the doctor agreed to examine Calvin. She carried Calvin in her arms approximately four miles to the doctor in downtown Portsmouth, Va. He evaluated Calvin and then called another doctor at a nearby hospital (Portsmouth General) and asked him to examine Calvin when he arrived. The ambulance took Calvin to the hospital on a Thursday. The doctor examined Calvin and performed emergency surgery on him, which saved his life. Calvin has a visible scar on the left side of his head from the surgery and views it as a daily reminder of Jesus Christ and his mother not giving up on him.

On December 3, 2009 (Thursday), he shared with friends and family members the dream of Jesus Christ visiting him. The dream changed his life, and he has since been evolving daily into a greater man of God for the Lord. He kept the e-mail that he sent on that day to friends and family members explaining the dream, and he is always willing share it with others. He received that encounter with Lord as a reminder of his purpose. Since the dream, the Lord has shown the world His hand is upon Calvin.

His first book was published in 2012. He currently leads a global praying and fasting effort called 365 Days of Praying and Fasting (365fasting.com). The Lord is also leading him in launching multiple projects in 2020, which will allow him to help more people as he is led by the Lord to do so

He is married to Kenya Brown, and they have four children. He was born in Lemoore, California, and was raised in Portsmouth, Virginia. He retired from the United States Army in 2009. He currently works as a Department of the Navy civilian supporting cyber security efforts at Dahlgren, Virginia. He also supports various ministry efforts throughout the United States and the Mercies of Hope International Ministries in Kampala, Uganda. As blessed by Jesus Christ, he will lead the Remnant of Christ Kingdom (ROCK) ministry church that will be built in northern Virginia. The ROCK ministry will continue partnering with other ministries to spread the Gospel of Jesus Christ, help fellow Christians, and help communities.

Since Calvin was born on a Thursday, had emergency surgery on a Thursday, and was visited Jesus Christ in a dream on a Thursday, he has committed to praying and fasting every Thursday for the remainder of his life on earth.

Calvin loves bringing the Almighty Father more glory, spreading the Gospel of Jesus Christ, and being led by the Holy Spirit.

CPSIA information can be obtained
at www.ICGtesting.com
Printed in the USA
LVHW040751300920
667476LV00003B/136

9 781647 730703